Stephen Chambers

1986

Sports and Games in the Ancient World

SPORTS AND GAMES
in the Ancient World

Věra Olivová

Bloomsbury Books

London

ACKNOWLEDGMENTS

The Publishers would like to express their gratitude to Roger G. Broomfield, Michael Dixon, Paul Jenkins, Douglas Mazonowicz, Professor James Mellaart and Dr Wenig.

The following museums have kindly given permission for their pictures to be reproduced:
Badisches Landesmuseum, Karlsruhe; Bibliothèque Nationale, Paris; Boston Museum of Fine Arts, H. L. Pearce Fund; British Museum, London; Deutsches Archaeologisches Institut, Athens; Egyptian Exploration Society, London; Fitzwilliam Museum, Cambridge; J. Paul Getty Museum, Malibu; Kunsthistorisches Museum, Vienna; Metropolitan Museum, New York; Musée National du Louvre, Paris; Museo Arqueológico de Barcelona; Nationalmuseum, Copenhagen; Oriental Institute, Chicago; Réunion des Musées Nationaux, Paris; Rijksmuseum van Oudheden, Leiden; Staatliche Museen Preussischer Kulturbesitz, Berlin.

Illustrations were provided by the sources listed below: Archivio IGDA, Milan; Bruce Coleman; Ekdotike Athenon; Werner Forman; Sonia Halliday; Hirmer Fotoarchiv, Munich; Michael Holford; Alan Hutchison; Mansell Collection; Photoresources; Scala, Florence; Roger Wood.
Graphic design by Bedřich Forman

Endpaper: The Greek hero Heracles with a tripod. Detail of a painting on a red-figure amphora, Athens, 520-510 B.C.

Half-title page: Men running. Mural painting from the Etruscan "Tomb of the Olympic Games", Tarquinia, 6th century B.C.

Frontispiece: Ruins of Roman amphitheatre in Puteoli (now Pozzuoli).

Page 8: Gem with a picture of an acrobat jumping over a lying bull. Crete, around 1500 B.C.

Translated by D. Orpington

English translation © 1984
Orbis Publishing Limited, London
© 1984 Dr Věra Olivová
First published in Great Britain by
Orbis Publishing Limited, London 1984
© Orbis Publishing Limited, London
This Edition published 1986 by
Bloomsbury Books an imprint of
Godfrey Cave Associates Ltd, 42 Bloomsbury Street,
London WC1B 3QT
by arrangement with
Orbis Publishing Limited

ISBN 0 906223 19 9
Printed and bound in Czechoslovakia
2/99/79/51-02

Contents

Foreword

The title needs definition since the idea of "sport", as we now entertain it and translate it in our different ways, is a fairly modern notion. But the elements that have gone to create it, human need, combative spirit, spectator excitement and others, are not so modern, and in this exciting book Dr Věra Olivová traces the elements to their origin, or rather, begins at the beginning and explains how techniques of survival developed into random practice, organized practice, competition in practice, competition for its own sake, interest in competition by the non-competitor, audience participation and then, almost, audience control.

A sportswoman herself, Dr Olivová is also an historian (she was Professor at Charles University). The combination is perfect. As a non-sportsman, I am delighted to remember that the last time I saw her she had engaged herself in some ridiculous "sporting" enterprise and that I was able to remind her that Pythagoras once remarked on the three types of people at the Olympic Games, those who competed, those who sold candy-floss, and those (the best) who merely watched. They are even better watchers if they understand what they are watching. At my first game of American football, my host remarked that I was making an elementary mistake in trying to follow the ball. "Look," he said, "where the ball isn't." "How," said I, "can I look where it isn't, unless I know where it is?" "You just don't understand," said he. This book brings us nearer to an understanding.

W. G. Forrest,
Professor of Ancient History, Oxford

Introduction

Sport is one of the striking features of twentieth century life, as evidenced by the variety and popularity of sporting events in the most diverse parts of the world. This new phenomenon in society has attracted the interest of researchers in many fields, and ever more urgently calls upon historians to contribute to a deeper understanding of sport through their knowledge of the past.

This is no simple task, indeed, the very word "sport" suggests problems in the way it developed. The word is derived from the Latin *se deportare,* which survived in the Romance languages in the sense of "to amuse oneself". In the early twelfth century it is attested in Spanish as *deportarse,* in French as *déporter* or *se déporter.* In Anglo-French it appears in the same sense in the fourteenth century as "disport". The noun (French *déport* or *désport,* Anglo-French "disport") was formed from the verb, and in the fifteenth century English the shortened form "sport", which meant the free time, relaxation from the more serious claims of life, merry entertainment, games.

The actual forms of amusement also changed. In earliest times hunting took prime place, and equestrianism, while animals were gradually included too, acrobatics, wrestling and other bouts, races and various theatrical performances or shows. By the end of the eighteenth century the term "sport" (which had already superseded the longer word) was more and more frequently used for specifically athletic contests and races; these became the typical form of entertainment of the new English citizen society, and also present the first phase in the development of sport as we know it today. These semantic changes in the word "sport" express in brief the complex process of crystallization of modern sport from its origins in the most varied games and entertainments.

In the nineteenth and especially in the twentieth century, modern sport underwent further fundamental changes determined by the demands and criteria of the industrial society which was changing so rapidly itself. The decisive factor was the increasingly competitive spirit of this society, reflected in sport by the greater emphasis on the agonal (competitive) principle. Some of the modern sporting disciplines developed out of the older athletic contests and races; others were artificially created, while some were the result of adapting to the needs of modern sport kinetic activity and games from all parts of the world and from the most varied periods of history. This meant that besides the contemporary reality which gave modern sport its basic character, the heritage of very diverse cultures and of man's ancient past is also encoded in sport today.

It is history alone that could decipher this fascinating code. To break it, however, it is not enough to seek in the past the elements similar to those of modern sport. We are to attempt the reverse: we must seek the genesis of modern sport in the specific evolution of the history itself. It is this difficult path that the present work has tried to follow. Starting from a study of the societies of the ancient world, it attempts to determine how people spent their leisure time, to explain why and how various physical activities evolved, to trace their formal refinement and clarify their changes. The word "sports" is used for those physical activities in which the agonal principle is evident. Yet this principle itself underwent changes in the course of history, from the simple display of physical skills and vaguely competitive performance, to real contests − although they naturally took a different form from that of modern sporting contests.

This book also traces other criteria which influenced the overall conception of sport, and deals with certain subsidiary aspects. Physical activity has been a constant phenomenon throughout the history of mankind, for it is linked to the biological − and therefore unchangeable − nature of human existence, both physical and spiritual. Specific forms of human activity, however, have always been linked with certain useful human activities, although developed and cultivated by man in his free time. They were influenced by the character and structure of society. They were a significant cultural phenomenon, reflecting contemporary ideas about the world, about moral and aesthetic norms, the degree of social differentiation and the political evolution of society. All these factors determined the many and changing forms of these activities at different moments in history.

Modern sport evolved as part of the culture of Europe, but the foundations of this culture had been crystallizing for thousands of years in the context of the ancient civilizations. These evolved gradually in the foothills of the mountains of the Near East, in the ancient societies of Mesopotamia flourishing between the Euphrates and the Tigris, in ancient Egypt on the continent of Africa, and round the Mediterranean, particularly on the island of Crete. The civilization of Greece absorbed elements from all these sources to form its own culture, while the Roman Empire later became the connecting link between the ancient world and medieval Europe.

Sports and games in the ancient world form a vast chapter of human history which in spite of breaks and gaps, yet reveals a remarkable continuity. Many forms of physical activity died with the ancient civilizations that bore them; others were revived to new vigour after long oblivion. Many of the modern sporting disciplines, in spite of their resemblance to classical sports, evolved in their own specific manner. As a whole, however, the physical culture of the ancient world had a many-sided influence on the genesis of modern sport, and this thousand years' heritage is a living part of it.

Cave painting showing a world shared by prehistoric men and animals. South Africa.

Inset: A prehistoric hunter with a bow and arrow. Cave painting from Tassilia, southern Algeria.

PROLOGUE

In his earliest beginnings man was an integral part of nature and even today his behaviour reveals strong parallels with that of animals. These parallels can be seen in many of his games involving movement, for the animal world, too, has its dances, its contests and its play, including ceremonial forms of challenge, greeting, defence and triumph.[1]

The specific evolution of man and of human society, however, led him to develop his instinctive games and create new forms of them, one of which grew into modern sport. At the first stage of this evolution man improved the movements and features which distinguished him from the animals around him: upright posture, prehensile hands and potential reasoning powers.

During the first stage of his development man spent most of his life wandering in search of food, gathering berries and collecting small creatures, just as the Australian aborigines were still doing not so long ago. Success in hunting larger animals at first depended mainly on fleetfootedness, and achievements in walking and running have been recorded in all parts of the world. Swift feet to flee from danger were also man's simplest form of self-defence.

Man's hands, which were capable of grasping and rapidly acquired skills of their own, were an added advantage. With his hands he gathered food, and caught and chased game. With his hands he gripped things, not only to defend himself and drive off attack, but to move into the attack himself;[2] it took thousands of years, however, before man reached this active stage.

When man developed his thinking powers, his ability to move about and his physical strength acquired a new dimension. Sandals and various kinds of snow-shoes made walking easier; rafts and boats conveyed him across stretches of water. From these he evolved litters, wicker cradles to be dragged along the ground, and later, the ancient civilizations saw the invention of the wheeled cart. Early man sharpened flints, and slivered wood, and made his axe or a bow and arrow, the weapon of an advanced hunter. The dagger and the sword were exclusive weapons of later, mature civilizations.

The evolution of man's physical and mental powers led him on from passive food gathering to new, active ways of acquiring his food, and the creative urge expressed by this active behaviour transformed groups of food gatherers into hunting communities, which later gave way to a settled pastoral and agricultural way of life. Out of these communities were born the civilizations of the ancient world.

As the production and management of tools and weapons became more and more demanding, greater and greater importance was attached to physical readiness. The preparatory period was that of childhood, and the training took the form of children's games with additional useful features. Gradually an artificial element was incorporated into this training, more or less organized and led by the adults; certain groups, mainly boys, were

Left: A group of running hunters with bows and arrows. Cliff painting from Tassilia.

Right: Dancers with ceremonial headdress. Art of nomad shepherds. Cliff painting from Ued Mertutek in the Sahara.

trained for their future role as hunters and warriors. The future chieftains were given special training and later, with the emergence of civilizations, so were aristocrats and royal princes.

At first this preparatory phase of human life was the same length for all, and ended at sexual maturity. After proving his physical courage and skill at initiation ceremonies, the individual was accepted as a fully-fledged member of the community. Organized training led to the emergence of specially trained and therefore more exclusive groups.[3] In the civilizations of the ancient world a longer time was needed for this special training, and a new phase of life was thus established for the privileged − that of youth.

Active behaviour transformed the quality of the human community, and gradually changed man's attitude towards the world around him. The fears which characterized life at the stage of passive gathering were gradually dispelled, and using his own powers of reason, man tried to explain the world and man's existence in it, to formulate his own attitudes, his ideas about man and society. He expressed his thoughts in song, poetry, story-telling, painting pictures and by evolving all sorts of customs and rituals. One of the particularly significant forms of expression was that of physical movement. A special body language was created, which was not only capable of expressing and communicating ideas but of passing them on from one generation to another. This particular function of physical activity, as distinct from utilitarian movement, was developed during man's free time − at festivals.

It is clear from the ethnographic material that so long as man was fully occupied with food gathering, festivals were unheard of.[4] They did not appear until the community was capable of storing up surplus food, thus providing for a period of rest and recreation devoted primarily to eating, sex and movement. Excessive indulgence of these vital human instincts brought relief from, and submerged the other emotions of fear and aggression. Consequently, the sobriety necessary for everyday life was re-established and society could continue to function with all its members feeling content. These three purely instinctive ways of relaxing — eating, sex and movement — were also basic ways of expressing ideas about the world.

When the hunters ceremonially partook together of the flesh and blood of the animals and men they had killed, they were ensuring that the vital forces of the dead passed to the living. The bigger and stronger the animal, the greater the significance of the act. For a hunting society nature, whether endowed with life or not, was a unity, and man and beast were linked almost indistinguishably. Man was always the weaker partner, which is why the gods of the hunters were given animal shape. Ceremonial eating of animal flesh brought man into direct contact with the gods and their exceptional powers were thus passed to him. In later evolutionary stages the magic power of these ceremonial meals was conveyed by sacrifices and symbols.

Sexual activity found its expression in various fertility cults. When man reached the stage of sexual fertility it was as if he were reborn. Blood, the symbol of life, entered into all initiation rituals by means of bloody wounds inflicted on the body and particularly on the sexual organs; this was initiation into sexual life. During festivals sexual activity brought man into direct contact with the gods of fertility and ensured the fruitfulness of his animals and fields, and prosperity for the whole community.[5] The act of procreation was crucial in the stories of the birth of the gods and the creation of the world. As time passed the act itself was replaced with the representation of these ideas in various symbolic activities like swinging, tug-of-war, and so forth. The earliest dramatic texts show how complex the forms of this symbolism were in the civilizations of antiquity.[6]

The third and most variable of these three ceremonial activities — movement — underwent the most striking changes. The basic form was communal dance of an ecstatic kind, which culminated in the catharsis of trance. These dances drew on all the elementary movements of the human body, gestures made in children's spontaneous games, and in useful daily tasks, all mixed together in varying combinations. Movements of plants and animals were introduced into dancing, too, adding new expressiveness to human movements. The other senses were brought into play; different sounds — shouting, imitating animals, banging, clapping, drumming, and so on — marked the rhythm and were an early form of music, which organized the movements of individuals and the whole dancing group. The dance was also made more effective by the use of leaping flames, intoxicating scents, beverages and drugs to induce states of excitement, and also by the appearance among the dancers of animals, dead ancestors, or defeated enemies in symbolic form. They were shown in the form of trophies (animal and human skins, heads, scalps, genitals or horns) and masks, whose creators gave free rein to their fantasies. These dances provided a way of freely expressing human emotions, and at the same time they told the stories of the origins of the world and of man, of the miracle of birth and the mystery of death, of the community and its leading figures. They resulted in complete physical and mental exhaustion, and so brought relief and relaxation to all.[7]

These ecstatic communal dances were the principal form of festivity in the earliest societies, which were only weakly structured and organized internally. They were markedly emotive in character and gave all members of the group the chance to participate. They survive in various popular forms of entertainment at all stages in human history.

In these ecstatic dances all the fundamental elements of the festival are found concentrated; the dance, together with eating and sex, was a way of achieving complete physical and emotional relaxation as well as self-realization. This opened the door to feelings of human happiness and individual creativity. The dance transmitted all kinds of ideas and was a means of communication within a society, a specific kind of language, best described as body language. Although dancing represented a time of rest from useful activities, many kinetic elements were adopted from practical life and the dance was often a form of preparation for it. Because the dance allowed human instincts free play for a certain period of time, it protected society from their possible destructive effects and was therefore a form of social control. As society became more highly organized, however, these instinctive outbursts were more and more strictly restrained and other inhibitory devices were formed.[8] Community dance always resumed its importance, however, in times of crisis, when social structures were weakened and beginning to break down.

In these communal dances movement assumed a wide variety of forms, presenting in embryo the many activities that were later, after specific development, to form separate disciplines, ranging from dance itself, to drama. Each of these specialized activities embraced, to a varying degree, all the basic functions concentrated at first in the communal ecstatic dance.

Privileged individuals began to display their exceptional physical strength and skills, at first as part of the communal dance, and then gradually apart from it; in this way they also demonstrated their social standing. To begin with the leader or chieftain gave a show of prowess, thus submitting his physical powers — on which great demands were made — to frequent regular

Scene from a prehistoric hunters' ceremony. Their heads decorated with feathers, the men dance in ecstasy with spears and bows. The women mark the rhythm by clapping. Cliff painting from South Africa.

testing. The ethnographical material reveals much about ritual races, dances and contests of all kinds, including the chieftain's duty to hunt particularly dangerous wild beasts, and the historical material confirms that these trials were continued in many royal courts. Besides ceremonial occasions, the kings indulged in physical exercise for their own enjoyment, as a way of passing their ample free time. This kept them in good physical condition, and at the same time contributed to the further evolution of these activities.

Groups of privileged individuals also took part in the contests, and gradually other members of society joined in. The group character of their activities encouraged the competitive spirit. It is clear from ethnographical material that simple forms of sporting contest probably emerged during the most highly developed phase of the hunting societies, and during the early stages of the pastoral and agricultural societies that succeeded. For this period there is considerable evidence of wrestling and racing, and also of boxing, shooting contests, fencing with various weapons, jumping, throwing, swimming and rowing contests, sometimes also of riding on animals and of ball games.[9] In the civilizations of the ancient world chariot races were added to the repertoire.

Certain groups favoured specific sports or indeed they were their special privilege. The element of competition encouraged the ambitious and groups chose their representatives to compete for them; the increasing coherence of these social groups, who identified themselves with their representatives, the competitive struggle and uncertainty of the outcome increased the excitement for the onlookers and relieved their tensions. At the same time, strong ties persisted between the dance, the simple demonstration of physical strength and the skills of the competition. In the historical period various types of real and mock contest accompanied by music still abounded, forms of sporting competitions influenced by the dance, and dances ending in real or mock battle, and the reverse.

The evolution of sporting competitions was closely bound up with the order and organization of society. The competing groups corresponded to existing elements in the social structure and were formed by the same criteria, that is according to sex, age, place, practical occupation, position in society, and so forth. While the hierarchy was not too clearly defined it encouraged competitive testing of strength and the agonistic, competitive principle acted as an important inhibitory mechanism, restraining aggressive tendencies within society. As a result of the continual process of arranging society in groups, more natural bases for competition were formed.[10]

Ideas of growing complexity were expressed during the festivals in ever more intricate religious ceremonies. These ritual performances consisted of elements of communal dance, simple displays of strength and skill, and sporting contests which thereby acquired a new function. Sacrificial ritual was extended and supplemented by fighting between animals, fighting between men and animals, duels between men, and symbolical contests expressed in dance, in leaping over animals, in races and in masked contests or mimed dramatic representation of events. Mock fights and races were staged, the results of which were decided in advance and various steps were taken to ensure that one of the contestants was weaker – by giving him less effective weapons, hindering his movements, specially protecting the destined winner, and so on.[11] At first the actors were privileged individuals and groups, and later professionals were used.

Professional performers played a unique role in the festivals, as their only obligation was to provide relaxation for the others. In the earliest forms of society they were not members of the group but animals or captives taken in the hunt who were killed and eaten as part of the ceremonial. Gradually they were given a more active part to play, in various forms of contest that preceded their death. As time went on, members of the community, mainly from the lower ranks, joined the professionals and exhibited their physical strength and skill. It was no longer necessarily their death that was demanded in the interests of the onlookers' enjoyment, indeed the reverse became the case: the successful professional actors won many advantages and their social standing was sometimes improved by their successes. They were organized round the temples as privileged actors for the religious mysteries.

Not only the actors, but the onlookers, too, changed. Although the festivals took place in free time, they were at first perceived as a specialized form of useful activity, to achieve closer contact and reconciliation with the gods, and by entertaining them, to ensure their favour and protection. The gods themselves held an exclusive position. Sacrifices and libations provided them with a sufficient amount of good food and drink, while human beings performed for their entertainment. The gods were the first spectators. In hunting societies they were animal gods, but as pastoral and agricultural societies took a different view of the world, these ancient gods were ousted from their place as privileged spectators, and relegated to the ranks of the professional actors.

Gradually human spectators appeared on the scene. By virtue of their exclusive roles some of the actors not only kept in closer contact with the gods but also gained particular favour because they gave the gods more interesting and specially refined entertainment. Their reward was to be made privileged spectators. As the religious rituals became more complex, however, more and more of those taking part became spectators for the duration of the ceremonies. Awestruck by the all-powerful gods and their allies, the human rulers, they were better prepared to fulfil both divine and human commands.

Outbursts of unrestrained instincts and emotions were all the more dangerous to society as it grew larger and became more complex and highly organized, and as more and more people started to live in urban-type conglomerations. In these conditions aggressive instincts found fewer and fewer outlets in day to day occupations and unless they were chanelled into warlike pursuits, created a threat to the functioning of a united society. Festivals therefore increased in importance, and at the same time their character began to change. The religious and ritual aspects weakened, and human beings — at first only kings and heroes — were now celebrated as well as gods. Historical events, such as war and the conclusion of peace, the building of cities, and other remarkable occurrences, were also commemorated, and the greater the opportunity for individuality to be expressed, the more marked were the secular aspects of the festivals.

This process was reflected in the people's conscious attitude towards their festivals, when they gradually came to regard them not only as a pursuit serving a useful purpose, but as a free-time activity. This change of mind altered their basic reasons for taking part, and the desire for amusement and entertainment now came to the fore. In the ancient world this change was never complete, nor was it straightforward. It developed in accordance with changes in the structure of society, and it was the highest ranks, the kings and the aristocrats, who first found awareness of this aspect of their festivals, as their exclusive position in society allowed them the greatest amount of free time to devote to entertainment.

Exciting secular entertainments, performed by professionals, were introduced at public festivals, to keep the onlookers amused and excited. These spectacles included all forms of public executions, baiting of animals, torturing of human beings, "blood sports" and dangerous contests, dancing and acrobatics, and comedies and tragedies. As the scope of the festivals was enlarged, new opportunities arose for the public to

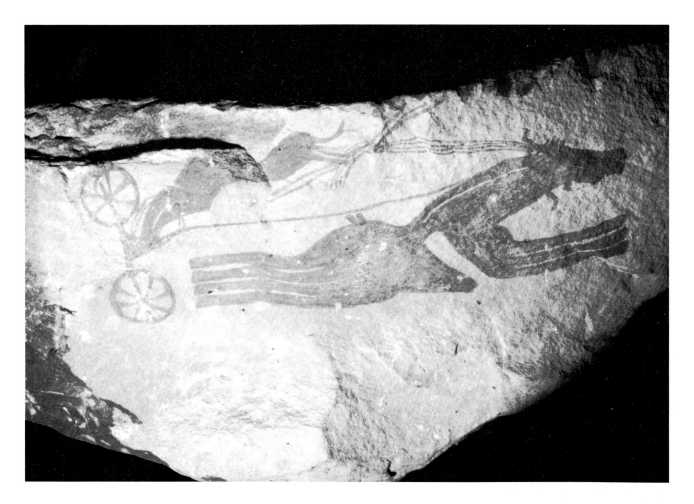

A charioteer with a stick driving a two-in-hand. Cliff painting from North Africa.

take an active part, the most suitable being all kinds of sporting contests.

Originally, man learned to make use of his kinetic ability while engaged in the useful activities of gathering food, hunting, and all forms of physical labour. When society progressed beyond the stage of a hunting economy, hunting and fighting, previously undifferentiated, became distinct activities. Movement was specially developed at festivals, in time of peace, and communal dances, displays of physical skill and competitive tests of strength were specially introduced to provide relaxation and entertainment. The form, course and content of festivals are therefore of fundamental significance, not only for an analysis of the early forms of physical activity but primarily for the assessment of their value and function in society. The basic ways and means of developing man's kinetic ability were already formed at a very early stage and were to be revived over and over again in the course of civilization, old forms giving way to new, to meet the needs of different cultures.

These mechanisms can be seen in a variety of forms in the civilizations of the ancient world, whose slow emergence began during the prolonged Neolithic revolution, first discernible in the tenth and ninth millennia B.C. The latest archaeological evidence has revealed that during this period a vast new cultural region was evolving over an area stretching from the western foothills of the Himalayas to the eastern Mediterranean. A protective ring of mountain ranges, adequate rainfall and the existence of domesticatable animals and wild cereals together created conditions in which man could advance, from food-gathering and hunting, to the settled way of life of farming and animal husbandry.

17

A number of important Neolithic sites of an urban type arose in the Near East in the seventh and sixth millennia B.C., including Tell Halaf, Samarra, Byblos, Jericho, Hacılar, and Ras Shamra (later Ugarit). Neolithic finds outside this region show that the culture gradually spread into south-east Europe, the islands of the Mediterranean, and part of the continent of Africa. Among these finds are figures and fragments of paintings depicting plants (trees and flowers), animals (fishes, birds in flight, butterflies, bees, bulls, stags, sheep, jackals and dogs), and human figures. Remnants of looms and of cloth, buttons, ivory combs and metal mirrors, ivory vessels for cosmetics and gold ornaments all point to an increasing interest in physical culture. Hunting scenes and communal dancing are subjects frequently depicted, while music is attested by drawings of drums and finds of bone pipes.[12]

A round dance with masks. Neolithic Siyalk culture, Samarra pottery. Northern Mesopotamia, 5th millennium B.C.

There was a particularly important centre of Neolithic civilization at Çatal Hüyük at the foot of the Taurus Mountains in Asia Minor. It is calculated that the population of this Neolithic town was several thousand, and its influence was felt far and wide. The labyrinth of dwellings excavated here yielded not only figurines of goddesses, cult objects and bull and stag heads, but painted murals depicting festivals. In one scene, a group of men are dancing before the giant figure of a bull, their costumes indicating an important ceremonial occasion: instead of the simple garments of Neolithic hunters, depicted in hunting scenes, these men are clad in gaily-coloured kilts and caps of leopard skin. Some of them hold bows and arrows, while others are beating drums to set the rhythm of the dance. There are strange headless figures among the dancers, half white, half red, probably representing dead ancestors, while naked figures appear to be leaping and running. The differences in dress seem to indicate social distinctions, leopard skins being superior to nakedness. The giant bull is the divine spectator, in whose honour the festival is being held.[13]

Evidence of similar festivals has been found on fragments of murals and vase paintings on other sites, some of them depicting round and processional dances, ritual dances with bulls' horns or symbols of horns, and in some cases the wearing of animal masks. Such finds have come from Syria, from the lowest levels on Mesopotamian sites, from caves on Crete, and from the earliest sites in Egypt.[14]

In man's next evolutionary phase the focal point moved from the foothills down to the fertile river valleys where the conditions were favourable for agriculture. Knowledge of copper smelting and the manufacture of bronze implements and weapons were among the next advances necessary for the emergence of mature civilizations in the Near East, Egypt and the Aegean.

Right: A dancing hunter with bow and arrow, dressed for the ceremony in a skirt of leopard skin. Painting on plaster from the Neolithic town of Çatal Hüyük, Asia Minor, 6th millennium B.C.

A round dance of naked girls. Painted shard of a vase. Neolithic culture, Iran, 4th millennium B.C.

Dance scene from a ceremony of Neolithic hunters. Men are dressed in skirts and caps of leopard skin and carry bows or boomerangs. One marks the rhythm with a little drum. Two naked figures jump or run. Çatal Hüyük, 6th millennium B.C.

19

THE OLDEST CIVILIZATIONS

The Near East

"When the Kingship descended from Heaven it rested first at Eridu." So begins the story of Mesopotamia, in a king list from Nippur. Although the culture of Eridu was destroyed by Sumerian invaders, in the middle of the fourth millennium, the newcomers developed the heritage they found into a new civilization which was centred particularly on the cities of Ur, Uruk, Lagash, Larsa and Nippur. The legacy of Sumer, in its turn, was expanded by the Akkadians, the Babylonians and the Assyrians, all of whom founded successive powerful empires in the region between the two life-giving rivers, the Tigris and Euphrates. At different times their influence was felt in varying degrees by the states in the neighbourhood, Ebla, the Hittite Empire, Mitanni, Urartu and the region that is now Palestine. Towards the end of the sixth century B.C., however, the neo-Babylonian Empire was overthrown by the Persians and incorporated into their vast empire, which stretched from Asia Minor to the Indus.

The influx of new peoples, mainly from Asia, but also from the Mediterranean, was a stimulating factor in the evolution of civilization during the first few thousand years; only strong, well-armed centres of power were capable of withstanding these onslaughts. Out of the recurring cycles of war and destruction, death and resurrection, were crystallized the features of ancient Mesopotamian civilization, which were to exert their influence throughout the Near East.

It was a civilization founded on the Sumerian belief that the universe had been created and was ruled by almighty, immortal gods − *dingirs* − who made man of clay, only to serve them; man was at the mercy of the gods, his only purpose in life being to obey their commands. This view of the world and man's place in it lay at the root of all the cultures that arose, not only in Mesopotamia, but throughout the Near East. This Sumerian heritage passed into the Jewish, Christian and Islamic faiths.[1]

Gradually, however, the rulers in each city state began to break free from this complete subordination to the gods; as their powers grew, so their

"Stele of Uruk". A nobleman hunting lions on foot, with a bow and arrows and a spear. Sumerian culture, Mesopotamia, around 3400 B.C.

21

role as servants changed to that of representatives of the gods on earth, masters of their own subjects. Ultimately the rulers of the great Mesopotamian kingdoms took their place among the gods themselves, they became "kings of the four regions of the world", "kings of the universe". The annual "sacred marriage" with the goddess Inanna secured them not only a place in the company of the gods, but the right to share in the gods' despotic power over their subjects.[2]

A combination of theocracy and despotism, based on the Mesopotamian model, became the characteristic form of government throughout the Near East, with varying degrees of intensity. Only the gods and the divine kings had a right to individual existence, the lives of ordinary mortals were of no value. Science and art were not yet defined and the questions of free will and

human individuality never troubled the thinkers of ancient Sumer, or their successors.

Yet generations of people lived their lives in the midst of wars and power struggles under the cloud of theocratic despotism. Even today their infinitely melancholy "lamentations" over the fall of flourishing cities and lost lives are moving testimony. New life always sprung up again on the ruins, and the creative spirit of ancient Mesopotamia laid the foundations of the science, literature and art which form part of European civilization to this day. The imposing architecture of the cities, with their temples and palaces, built with attention to hygiene and surrounded by great battlements, testifies to a high level of civilization; complex irrigation systems made the land more fertile, crafts flourished and trade prospered. Under the Persian Empire roads were built, linking all parts of the Near East.

The characteristic features of this way of life were also reflected in physical culture. In the same way that man was a thing of no value in himself, so his physical form, his body, was worthless. In art the human body was of no importance. While animal bodies, at rest and in dynamic movement, were portrayed in excellent detail, a naked human body only rarely appeared and was then treated schematically, with the body reduced in proportion to the face. Nakedness expressed humiliation and subjection, as in a suppliant praying to the gods, a servant, or a prisoner of war led into slavery. A naked woman's body was even less often depicted and the Greek historian

Herodotus tells us that it was typical of the people of the Near East to be ashamed to be seen naked, men as well as women.[3]

Mesopotamians could not, however, be described as ascetics, since their conception of happiness was closely linked with the fundamental enjoyment of the physical side of life. In the epic story of the legendary king of Sumer, Gilgamesh, human happiness is depicted in terms of plenty of food and drink, bodily cleanliness, physical love, delight in children, and festivals complete with games and dancing. Man's mortality had to be offset against enjoyment of life while it lasted. Banquets were the most popular form of entertainment among the gods − frequently attested in the literature − and in particular drinking bouts, which ended in intoxication. The desire for cleanliness of garments, body, and hair by bathing and washing of hands is already evident

Left: Two pairs of wrestling and one pair of boxing men. Fragment of a limestone votive tablet from Khafaje-Nintu. Turn of the 4th and 3rd millennium B.C.

Right: Two men boxing dressed in a loin-cloth. Fragment of a limestone votive tablet from the valley of the river Diyala, turn of the 4th and 3rd millennium B.C.

in the literature of the Sumerian period. Water was not only a means of purification, but a magical "water of life" that could revive the dead.[4]

All pleasures of life could be enjoyed by powerful kings in their luxurious palaces. Clean beds and beautiful garments were theirs for the asking; excellent food and drink were theirs in abundance; and they could satisfy their sexual appetites to the full. Perfumes, music and dancing were added delights, along with pools in which to bathe their bodies in scented oils and unguents. They paid particular attention to their faces, carefully curling their hair and whiskers, and women used coloured powders to enhance the beauty of their eyes. Physical beauty was demanded of all the Near Eastern rulers, as we can see from the Bible, where beauty is the natural asset of Jewish leaders and their families. It was not the naked body which was considered beautiful, however, but one clothed in precious raiment, as depicted in the art of the time. The principal sign of royal majesty was a rich garment, embroidered and bejewelled, and accompanied by other emblems of royal power. A carefully, realistically modelled face crowned the figure, and the imposing effect was enhanced by the virtual lack of movement.

The exceptional physical prowess of the kings was also symbolic of their exclusive positions, and, according to contemporary theocratic thought, it sprang from their divine origins. The most powerful heroes of all were those of divine and royal lineage, whose exploits were the subject of innumerable hymns and epics.[5] In reality, however, their strength came from their access to the most up-to-date weapons, the bow and arrows, and above all the sword and dagger. These weapons became much more effective when horse-drawn chariots were introduced. All these revolutionary inventions were at first the exclusive and most highly prized possessions of the kings alone.

These three factors combined gradually led to the crystallization of the most glamorous sport of the ancient world, chariot racing. Before this sport could reach its final form, however, many centuries passed, during which weapons were developed, the construction of the chariot was perfected, and the breeding and training of horses was established. By tracing this process of evolution we can begin to understand how this exclusive sporting discipline came into being.

In all the cultures of the ancient Near East there is evidence of training in the use of many different weapons — throwing sticks, slings, spears and lances. At first the bow and arrow were used exclusively for hunting and in the early Sumerian period, the middle of the fourth millennium B.C., the Stele of Uruk illustrates a royal lion hunt, the lord, *ensi,* using both bow and spear to get the lion. There are innumerable such scenes to be found all over the Near East. The bow was the symbol of the kings of Persia, and a motif found on the earliest Persian coins. The bow and arrow were adopted as military weapons only after the use of horse-drawn chariots became common.

By using horses to draw his vehicles, man increased his mobility and it was the most important development in the ancient civilizations of the Near East. The chariot, which was derived from the idea of the boat, was first constructed in Sumer, as shown in the earliest pictograms, dating from the end of the fourth millennium B.C. The runners used to draw the vehicle were

Driver sitting on the box of a chariot with disc wheels steering a four-in-hand of onagers. Bronze statuette from Tell Agrab, Iraq, turn of the 4th and 3rd millennium B.C.

*Two men, perhaps acrobats,
wrestling with vases on their heads,
grasping each other's loin-cloth.
A copper vase from Khafaje-Nintu,
4th to 3rd millennium B.C.*

then replaced by four solid wheels. A chariot of this type is depicted on the Stele of the Vultures and the Standard of Ur, both from the third millennium B.C. A copper model of a chariot was found in the temple at Tell Agrab, and similar models in clay come from northern Syria, where the chariot was a common motif on cylinder seals. The oldest finds of two- and four-wheeled chariots in royal tombs date from the middle of the third millennium B.C.

From the end of the third millennium up to the seventeenth century B.C. the chariot spread to wider areas, in particular Asia Minor. Several improvements in construction were made, and the chariot became lighter with the invention of the two-wheeled type, which had spoked, instead of solid, wheels. From the sixteenth to the twelfth century B.C. the chariot found its way all over the Near East.

At first carts, used to carry loads, were drawn by oxen, later by onagers, and replaced still later by horses. These changes, together with the lighter construction, enormously increased the speed of the chariot. It found its place primarily in cult and ritual; the idea of the god riding in a chariot is common in mythology, in art, and even in the mature astrology of ancient Mesopotamia, which gave the name of the Great Chariot to the most clearly defined of the constellations.

In practical life the chariot was at first the exclusive vehicle of the king in

25

battle, as we see from the Stele of the Vultures and the Standard of Ur. Later its use spread, and in the Bible there are references to chariots among the Philistines and the Israelites under the kings; the tradition of war chariots was strong in Syria, Palestine, Assyria, Urartu and Iran, in Egypt and throughout the Mediterranean region. As war chariots became more numerous special types were invented, with room for two or three men, special places for weapons, and so on. An eighteenth-century Hittite inscription tells of king Anitta at the head of 1,400 foot soldiers and 40 war chariots. In the battle of Qadesh, 1286 B.C., the Hittites put 17,000 foot soldiers and 3,500 war chariots into the field against the Egyptians. The men manning the chariots formed the army's élite. In the course of time special carts were evolved to carry shooting towers and battering rams for the assault of well-fortified city walls, as depicted in Neo-Assyrian reliefs.[6]

Along with the chariot, the horse became widely known. It may have been the nomads of Indo-Iranian origin who overran Asia Minor from the northern Black Sea region in the second millennium, and gradually spread throughout south-west Asia, who brought the animal with them. Evidence of horses in eighteenth century Mesopotamia, almost exclusively in combination with chariots, is recurrent in the Mari archives.

As the horse became widely used, breeding and training became important. In the fourteenth and thirteenth centuries B.C. the knowledge of several hundred years was codified in special handbooks, of which the earliest information is one by the groom Kikkuli of Mitanni. The author (or authors) was a Hurri, and the book is written in poor Hittite for the use of the rulers. One striking feature is the use of a number of technical terms in Indo-Iranian, showing that in Kikkuli's native land, Mitanni, the traditions of horse breeding and training had been taken over from the Indo-Iranians.

In the second millennium B.C. an Indo-Iranian language was spoken all over south-east Asia, as can be seen from numerous Hittite and Middle Assyrian texts and from the cults of specific Veda divinities. In the second half of the second millennium B.C., the time of Kikkuli's handbook, the language had already died, however, and survived only in special terms concerned directly or indirectly with horse breeding. There are also about a hundred names which can be assumed to be of Indo-Iranian origin, and these, too, are connected with horses and chariots.[7]

In Kikkuli's handbook the training of a horse is spread over 169 days, and consists primarily of teaching the animal to draw a chariot and to run unharnessed over long distances. The type of ground to be covered, and the horse's gait, are carefully specified, as is the load the horse is to carry and the grooming necessary to keep it in good condition. The other known texts are similar, among them veterinary advice for dealing with sick horses, written in Ugarit and found in Syria, lists of horses from Alalakh and Nuzi, and two thirteenth-century Hittite texts. Basically the information given is derived from Kikkuli's text, but in the latest manuscripts, dating from the end of the Hittite Empire (c. 1200 B.C.), there is new information which not only corrects the original text or makes it more precise, but also suggests a completely new approach to training.[8]

The archaeological evidence of horse breeding includes finds of bones, revealing that Troy was one of the many important centres, before Greek times. In Ugarit, in Syria, stables and a covered riding hall have been excavated, and stables found at Megiddo in Palestine, dating from the second half of the tenth century B.C., would have held about 150 chariots and 450 horses standing in yards where the horses could be trained. All this confirms the Bible record of the care bestowed by Solomon on his horses and chariots.

Model of a two-wheeled chariot with a relief of a seated god. Mesopotamia, around 2000 B.C.

Driver standing on a four-wheeled chariot drawn by a winged beast. Cylinder seal from the Akkadian Empire, around 2400 B.C.

Sumerian war chariot with a crew of two, drawn by two horses. Detail from "Standard of Ur", around 2500 B.C.

Throughout the Near East, however, horse riding seems to have been rare at first. The earliest pictorial representations of horsemen date from the thirteenth century B.C. and a relief of this date showing Ugarit horsemen has been preserved. In the eleventh and tenth centuries B.C. warriors on horseback become more and more frequent on Syrian-Hittite reliefs, including the Tell Halaf relief. All the evidence suggests that during these centuries significant changes in military technique were taking place in the Syrian and Asia Minor regions and cavalry began to take the place of horse-drawn chariots. In Mesopotamia this change does not seem to have been accomplished until the ninth century, when men on horseback are sporadically depicted alongside the chariots.[9]

The few depictions in art show riders bareback suggesting poorly developed equestrian skills. The fact that riding on horseback was considered a dangerous venture is evident in the advice given by his minister to the king of Babylonia, to preserve his royal safety and not mount a horse. It is not until the seventh century B.C. that horsemen are more frequently portrayed in reliefs.

In the Persian Empire the cavalry formed the main body of the army. Horse riding spread throughout the extensive area of Persian communications, particularly along the "Royal Road", which was 2,500 kilometres in length and led from Asia Minor across the upper Euphrates and Tigris, and on towards the East. Strategically important points were equipped with special posting inns, where mounted messengers could hand on their reports. The Persian word *angaros,* a royal courier, is related to the Greek *angelos,* messenger, and passed into Christian literature as "angel", the messenger of God. Even the kings of Persia were proud of their skill as horsemen, as we

Bowl with a hunting scene. The huntsman stands on a light two-wheeled chariot, driving the two horses with the reins fastened round his hips and hunting bulls and goats with a bow and arrows. Ras Shamra (Ugarit), Syria, 14th century B.C.

Jugglers and acrobats. A Hittite relief on the city wall in Alaça Hüyük, Asia Minor.

Two boxers with bound wrists wearing short skirts. Tell Asram, Iraq, around 2000 B.C.

learn from Greek writers such as Herodotus and Xenophon, as well as from the Behistun inscription carved on the tomb of Darius, King of Persia, at the turn of the sixth to fifth centuries: "My hands and feet are well trained; on horseback I am a good rider; with a bow I shoot well, on foot or on horseback; I cast my spear well, on foot or on horseback."[10]

Skill in the use of weapons, while standing in a fast moving chariot, called for special training for princes and young aristrocrats, and from the fragmentary information remaining, it is known that the education of the Assyrian king Asshurbanipal involved cultivation of both the mind and body. A Hittite letter has been preserved, in which a vassal prince recalls his teacher: "…as head manager of the stables he would often climb on to a chariot with me in the days of my youth. Likewise with thy brother and with Tavakalava he frequently entered a chariot." It is clear from this that sons of the nobility gathered in the Hittite capital, either voluntarily or under obligation, to practise chariot riding and the use of arms in the company of the royal princes. Later on, similar training was organized in the Persian Empire, and probably in other countries as well. The need for specially trained riders and charioteers greatly increased when the use of mercenary troops became customary.[11]

The exceptional prowess of the kings and nobles was tested in the field. Warfare was one of the royal duties, a service demanded by the gods, but at the same time was a means of extending their power and acquiring loot and slaves. It also gave the king a unique opportunity for self-fulfilment, and the risks involved were considerably reduced by his special armour, the finest weapons, fast horses, and of course the companions at hand to protect him. For the king warfare was both a pleasure and an entertainment, the danger of which lent a dramatic tension, and victory brought with it booty and the most precious trophy of all, the head of the defeated royal opponent. Such

29

a victory was confirmation of the king's exceptional abilities and the reports of warlike successes carved on rock faces, incised on tablets, and recorded in works of art were meant to ensure the kings of Mesopotamia, of the Hittite and Persian Empires, and other rulers, the immortality of which man has always dreamed.[12]

In the ancient Near East hunting was the special pastime of the kings, in

A barefooted warrior with helmet and shield, riding a horse bareback. Tell Halaf, Syria, 1300–1000 B.C.

Right: Lion hunting from a chariot. A dog runs alongside the horse. A Hittite relief from Malatya, Asia Minor, 850–700 B.C.

search of wild animals, lions, wild asses, bulls, boars and leopards. The primary purpose of the royal hunt was to kill these dangerous creatures which represented their enemies and evil spirits, and it was often seen as a battle against these hostile forces. A cylinder seal of the thirteenth century B.C., of the Middle Assyrian period, shows heroes fighting winged dragons; another, of the New Assyrian period, depicts a god standing on a winged and horned dragon, shooting at an escaping lion with bow and arrows. Scenes such as these are innumerable. By defeating wild beasts the king proved that he possessed the exceptional prowess on which his claim to rule was based, and in the Persian Empire the ancient Mesopotamian theme of a king fighting wild beasts came to symbolize the struggle between good and evil that informed the religious dualism of Persia.

In the literature of ancient Mesopotamia the royal hunt was often linked with, or substituted for, the idea of war, a throw-back to hunting societies in which no clear distinction was made between hunting man or beast. The campaigns of King Tiglath Pileser I, for example, at the turn of the twelfth and eleventh centuries B.C., are celebrated in the manner of a hunting song, in which the king is extolled as the ensnarer of his foes and the latter are symbolized as mountain mules. In the same way, the Stele of the Vultures

portrays Eannatum holding a large net full of the enemies he has gathered up. Hunting terminology is also applied to human combat in the Sumerian hymn to the god Enlil, and the connection appears again in the person of Ninurta worshipped in Uruk, the god of both war and hunting, a figure that survives in our cultural consciousness to this day in the biblical legend of Nimrod of Erech.[13]

In the middle of the second millennium B.C. the hunting motif appears in the kingdom of Mitanni, depicting the king in a two-wheeled chariot hunting in a wooded landscape. The motif gradually spread throughout the Near East and into the Mediterranean region, where it survived for centuries.[14] It was in ancient Mesopotamia, however, that the motif found its most characteristic expression.

The throne-room of the palace of King Asshurnasirpal II of the ninth century B.C. is decorated with cult scenes of warfare and hunting. In the various friezes the king is shown mounted on a two-wheeled chariot, slaying a bull or shooting a lion with bow and arrow. The most remarkable of all is the monumental series of reliefs covering the wall of the Northern Palace at Nineveh which depict a great lion hunt of King Asshurbanipal, in the seventh century B.C. The whole drama of the chase unfolds before our eyes in vivid detail. Grooms bring up the horses for the royal chariot and servants lead the great hounds. Then comes the king himself, grandly arrayed, with a magnificent, neat beard, aiming to shoot an arrow from his chariot. Two servants bearing arrows and a lance are stationed protectively behind him. The charioteer is gathering speed, leaving behind him a field strewn with lions, dead or dying. One of the wounded beasts leaps at the chariot, and to meet the challenge the king has passed his bow to a servant and taken the spear in its stead. Hurling it with mighty strength he kills the attacking lion. The final scene shows the king's attendants approaching on horseback.

Another important feature of the King Asshurbanipal cycle is the appearance of an entirely new element — the human spectator. A number of Assyrian nobles are shown climbing a tree-covered hill to watch their monarch in action, and the excitement of the scene is emphasized by their lively gestures, reminiscent of a sporting crowd today and in marked contrast to the impassive mood of other ancient Mesopotamian art. The presence of these spectators is cogent evidence that the royal hunt was slowly assuming the character of a game. It clearly implies that the animals were first driven into a hunting area which was fenced off, and this accounts for their large numbers. This is confirmed in other scenes of King Asshurbanipal's hunts, where two rows of Assyrian bowmen and spearmen with high shields form a human barrier and in these scenes the lions have been caught beforehand, transported to the "arena" in cages and released there one at a time. Another possibility to consider is that the lions were partly tamed, for the king now approaches his prey on foot, surrounded by servants on horseback, and kills it with a bow and arrow, or an axe. In one relief he is even shown holding the lion by its tail, declaiming, according to the inscription: "I am Asshurbanipal, ruler of the world, king of Assyria. In my dread pleasure I have seized the lion by its tail and on the orders of Ninurta and Nergal, my divine masters, I myself have cloven its skull in twain with my axe."

In the course of time the royal hunt took on new forms; sometimes the stress was on marksmanship, sometimes the duel between man and beast, and in the meantime spontaneity gave way to a greater degree of organization. Both the shooting and the one-to-one struggle were carefully prepared beforehand, and the first hard and fast rule of the game was established: a predetermined outcome, with the king victorious. In ancient Mesopotamia the royal hunt was an entertainment reserved for an exclusive social group, the king as the principal actor and a group of nobles as his spectators.

Following their Mesopotamian models, the kings of Persia surrounded their palaces at Parsagad (Pasargadae) and Parsa (Persepolis) with great parks which were stocked with game. It testifies to the size and magnificence of these parks that the word *paradeisos,* which comes from Persia and described these parks, came to be used for Paradise in the Greek translation of the Bible. In this "paradise" the Persian monarchs indulged their passion for the hunt.[15]

There are innumerable portrayals of royal hunts, throughout the Near East, which affirm that hunting was the favourite sport of royalty. The royal hunting scenes make it quite clear that both the kings and the gods took great delight in the sport and the rare inscriptions accompanying them confirm this. Phrases referring to the king's enjoyment of this leisurely activity occur also

Above: A chariot in battle. The charioteer drives the two-in-hand while the warrior shoots his arrows. A stricken enemy lies beneath the horse's hooves. Hittite relief from the city gateway in Zenjirli, Asia Minor, beginning of the 1st millennium B.C.

Right: An archer on foot in a short decorated skirt. Relief on a stone tablet. Tell Halaf, Syria, 1st millennium B.C.

Far right: Gilgamesh wrestling with Enkidu. Relief on a stone tablet, Tell Halaf, Syria, 1st millennium B.C.

in Hebrew psalms and ancient Egyptian literature. Some scholars use the term "sport" in their translations, reminding us that the modern term originally bore this meaning.[16]

Whether horse-drawn chariots were also used for racing remains an open question. Not the slightest trace of evidence from Mesopotamia exists for such races, and indeed the agonistic principle runs contrary to a theocratic form of government; the idea of the king competing with other mortals was absolutely incompatible with his unlimited personal power and exclusive social standing. War and hunting were the only exceptions, for in these contexts he was vying with equals, whether it was an enemy monarch, the king of beasts, dangerous animals or demons.

On the other hand, the technical conditions necessary for effective racing already existed. Chariots were now light-weight and highly qualified training was available for the horses, which were strong and fast. Asia Minor and Syria had long been centres of experienced horse breeding and seem to have also been the origins of hunting in two-wheeled chariots. The steady influx of new ethnic groups from Asia and Europe repeatedly interrupted social evolution, however, making it more difficult for a despotic centralized form of government to emerge, and favoured the formation of a broad aristocratic stratum, as seen in the Hittite Empire, where the royal princes were educated alongside vassal nobles. Technical, as well as social and political prerequisites therefore existed for this aristocratic form of entertainment to become established in the region. It is from this region that there is most evidence, of the earliest date, of cavalry replacing horse-drawn chariots in war. Chariot driving nevertheless retained a place in the cultural tradition, in religious ceremonies and as an aristocratic sport. A hunting party of aristocrats in their chariots was the forerunner of the chariot race proper. The hypothesis that such races existed in Asia Minor and in Syria is supported by later developments, which will be discussed in due course.

Above: Assyrian soldiers swimming on inflated animal skins towards an enemy stronghold. A relief from the palace of Nimrud, northern Mesopotamia, 9th century B.C.

Left: A nobleman shooting birds, which are picked up by his servant. Relief from the palace of Khorsabad, northern Iraq, around 700 B.C.

Right: Assyrian noblemen watching from a wooded hill as King Assurnasirpal hunts lions. His chariot and an attacking lion can be seen through the arch. Relief from the palace of Nineveh, northern Mesopotamia, 7th century B.C.

Although of a much later date, we have the testimony of the Greek historian Xenophon that the Persian King Cyrus instituted horse races; the winning post was set up at a distance of one kilometre, on a suitable plain, and the competitors divided according to nationality. Persians, Medes, Scythians, Armenians, Hyrcanians, Kadusi and Saqs all took part. Each group competed among themselves, and produced a victor. The credibility of this report is unfortunately diminished by the fact that it refers to the sixth century B.C., while Xenophon was writing in the fourth, and traces of contemporary Greek thought, as well as the author's own enthusiasm for horse-riding, are evident. On the other hand, group activity adds a touch of authenticity to the description, since races of this kind were held in the Persian Empire during Xenophon's lifetime, in the fourth century B.C.[17]

Unlike the leisure pastimes of kings and nobles, which were confined to a narrow circle, public festivals were open for all. The earliest record of festivals in celebration of the renewal of the vegetation cycle comes from the region of Syria and Palestine. The central point was sacrifice, performed on hill-tops, in the open air, to invoke the gods. These festivals culminated in mass sex, symbolic of the fertilization of the earth goddess by the rain god, which was essential for the renewed fertility of the ground. Those taking part therefore had a direct influence on the propitious course of the festival.

In ancient Mesopotamia, after the third millennium this custom was transferred to the "sacred marriage", *hieros gamos,* which was the highlight of the festival. After a solemn banquet the king climbed to the highest point of the temple — the *zikkurat* — for his union with the goddess (represented by the high priestess). This union, like the royal hunt and the waging of war, was one of the fundamental duties of the monarch. It was essential in order to awaken the earth to new life and ensure its fertility. The priest announced

The Assyrian King Asshurnasirpal II
hunting lions from a light chariot
driven by a driver. In the chariot
there is a spear ready, a quiverful of
arrows and an axe. The king shoots
the lion from his bow. Soldiers with
shields restrict the hunting space.
Relief from the palace of Nimrud,
9th century B.C.

Top left: Detail from relief below.

Left: The Assyrian King
Asshurnasirpal hunting: 1/ The king,
protected by a shield-bearer with
a spear, hunting on foot with bow
and arrows a lion that has been let
out of the undergrowth.
2/ According to the inscription the
king caught the lion by the tail and
cut its skull in half with an axe. In
front of the rider with a whip another
lion is about to leap. 3/ After the end
of the hunt the king pergorms
a libation over of the dead lions.
Relief from the palace in Nineveh,
7th century B.C.

the successful climax of the union to all those assembled for the festival.

This "sacred marriage" was part of the Spring festival, the most important in the series of more or less regular festivities held at full moon and new moon, when a temple was consecrated or a new season began. The Spring festival was held in March (Nisan) and the annual investiture of the king by the god Marduk (represented by the High Priest) symbolized the arrival of a new Spring and the start of a new vegetation cycle. There are detailed records of the Spring festivals from Neo-Babylonian times, when they were extended from seven to twelve days, with a programme of corresponding length. An important feature was the recital of an epic of the creation of the world and other myths, most of them centring on a duel between the hero (or a god) and an animal or monster.

The principal actors in these Spring festivals were the king and the priests. It is probable that the story was communicated through various forms of mock contest, perhaps with the actors wearing masks. Not only in Mesopotamia itself, but throughout the ancient Near East, the most frequent motif on relief carvings and cylinder seals was a duel between a hero and an animal. The theme of Gilgamesh fighting the bull is so frequent that it must be considered a possibility that the story was performed to the public as a bull-fight. There is similar evidence of fights between animals, and between men. Special festival games formed part of the programme, acting out legends in which the king and the priests played the parts of the different gods.[18]

The Spring festivals followed a similar pattern throughout the Near East. A Hittite inscription, dating from about 1200 B.C., tells of a mock fight between two teams, which may be reminiscent of the arrival of the Hittites in Asia Minor. The outcome was fixed beforehand, as is indicated by the weapons used, of unequal strength. The inscription reads:

"Then the men divide into two companies and they give them names:

The one company they call the men of the city of Hatti,
The other company they call the men of the city of Masha;
The men of Hatti have bronze weapons, but the men of Masha have
weapons of reeds. Then they fight, and the men of Hatti win..."[19]

In every case the physical activities of the festivals, especially the various duels and contests, were used to transmit a mythological or historical story.

The various stages in the Babylonian New Year festivities were linked together by the journey of the god Marduk, whose image was carried in procession on land and water, from one sacred place to another; he was transported in a boat, or in a cart, whose shape was still derivative of the boat. Everyone who brought gifts for the god, and so became his guest, could take part in the festivities. He could watch the mysterious rites, play an active part in the festival processions and take a share of the sacred meal in the temple precincts in the evening.

The official part of the programme was accompanied by spontaneous popular entertainments. According to Gudea's notes, dating from the end of the third millennium B.C., existing law and order was suspended for the duration of the festival. Feuds were dropped and quarrels made up, parents refrained from punishing their children, work ceased and slaves were the equals of free men. Musicians dressed in animal skins passed through the streets of Babylon, wearing animal heads − bands of musical lions, bears, asses or foxes. A king of the festivities was elected − a condemned prisoner who was set upon the throne and adorned with the attributes of royal power. He could issue orders, and eat and drink to his heart's content, but in the end he was stripped, bound, and publicly executed. The general merriment rose to a climax of music, dancing, drink and sex.

This was the pattern not only in Babylon, but in many other cities such as Uruk, or Assur, and it served as a model for the Neo-Babylonian festivals. The same pattern occurs in many other Near Eastern countries, and through the Jewish feasts of Purim and Rosh Hashanah the tradition passed into the Christian Easter festivities and the Islamic Spring feast. The cart-boat used for the god's progress was given a Latin name in later centuries, *carrus navalis,* and still survives in the word "carnival", meaning masked popular festivities.[20]

The sporadic archaeological material provides information about the other popular activities on these occasions, especially the duels and contests. On a fragment of a limestone votive tablet, dating from the turn of the fourth to third millennium, the lower frieze depicts two men wrestling. Another tablet of the same period shows a duel with spears and there exists a small model of two naked wrestlers holding on to each other's belts. Furthermore a cylinder seal, of the middle of the third millennium B.C., depicts two pairs of naked wrestlers, while a relief carving of the same period shows a boxing match. Apart from all this, there is literary evidence of wrestling; for example the Gilgamesh epic, describing his battle with Enkidu, says: "They caught each other like wrestlers, and sank to their knees..." All these scenes date from the earliest period of Sumerian civilization, and are not found later, when warlike scenes predominate. In the context of military campaigns swimming is also attested, using inflated animal skins. These were also used in the construction of boats. On an Assyrian relief two men are swimming, fully clad; one is using an inflated skin, the other a swimming stroke rather like modern crawl. On another relief there are three naked men, one sitting on the shore blowing up a bladder, one swimming with a bladder, and one doing the crawl.

There are interesting references to running in the extant material. In the Bible running is the simplest form of hunting, in which the hunter ran his quarry down. In a hymn at the time of the transition from the Sumerian to the

The Persian King Darius hunting lions with bow and arrows from a chariot driven by a charioteer. Under the hooves of the horse is a dead lion, above its head a divine being with the body of a bird. Cylinder seal, around 500 B.C.

Akkadian civilization the king boasts of his running exploits: "I, the king, ran like the ass of the steppes... my brave men watched me with amazement." By this performance the king seems to have displayed his physical fitness, the requisite for high office. This ancient custom seems to have changed with time, until the ceremonial races were run by professional couriers, probably those who took care of the system of communications in ancient Mesopotamia.[21]

A cuneiform tablet of Hittite provenance, dated approximately 1200 B.C., describes races run during the New Year festival, which seem to have been of earlier origin. The text is fragmentary and incomplete; in the better preserved section it describes the king's journey during the festival, from the city to his palace. Before he dismounted from his chariot the men of the palace ran a race, and the victor was awarded the privilege of holding the reins of the royal horses. Races also seem to have been included in the New Year festival programme in Babylon, for "the race held in the month of Nisan before Bel (Marduk) and the sacred places" is mentioned. The special term *li-is-mu,* used for the race, proves that it was widely known, and it seems reasonable to assume that running races, like wrestling, were a popular old custom.[22]

It is characteristic of the evolution of the ancient Near East that physical culture should be one of the privileges of the rulers or of a narrow circle of aristocrats, and a sign of social exclusiveness. It was developed for the cultivation of the body as a whole, for physical pleasure, and training for war. Contests were a form of royal entertainment, for which the useful activity of hunting had been specially adapted.

Ordinary people spontaneously developed the physical attitudes necessary for work and fighting. Dancing was a popular relaxation, as were simple sporting contests — wrestling and running.

The fragmentary and sporadic archaeological and literary material of this period points to a sharp contrast between spiritual and physical culture. It reflects the theocratic attitude of the time and the despotic form of government, in which physical culture was not a generally accepted social and cultural value, and therefore given little attention.

39

Egypt

During the Neolithic period several waves of migratory peoples from Asia poured into the area inhabited by the ancient African cultures, and at the end of the fourth millennium B.C. the remarkable civilization of ancient Egypt blossomed in the fertile Nile valley. The history of this culture falls into four principal periods: the Old Kingdom (27th−23rd century B.C.), the Middle Kingdom (21st−18th century), the New Kingdom (16th−11th century) and the Late Period (7th−6th century).

Towering cliffs on one side of the valley, and a vast expanse of desert on the other, formed a natural protective barrier, and for centuries the area developed in peace. Peace and the unification of the country was not achieved without fierce fighting however, and there were innumerable raids by neighbouring nomad peoples, but the Egyptians always quickly established their superiority. It was not until the Hyksos invasions of the eighteenth century B.C. that Egypt experienced a lengthy war; the invaders in their horse-drawn chariots ruled the land for a time, until the Egyptians themselves mastered this new military art, and drove the Hyksos out.

The New Kingdom followed, a period of aggressive campaigns which extended the Egyptian Empire over Palestine and Syria, as far as the Euphrates. In the Late Period all these territories were lost, and after a short period of prosperity in the seventh and sixth centuries B.C., Egypt was ruled by the Persians. From the fourth to the first century B.C. the land was part of the Hellenistic World and later of the Roman Empire. Thus from the middle of the second millennium B.C. onwards, Egypt maintained close contact with the civilizations of the Near East and the Mediterranean.

It was in the earlier period of peaceful security, lasting for nearly two thousand years, that the basic characteristics of Egyptian civilization crystallized, leaving an indelible mark on the spiritual as well as the physical culture. Elements from all stages of prehistoric and historical evolution existed tolerantly side by side, with their marked differences in outlook, a hierarchy of deities had not yet been established, and ancient popular cults

Pharaoh Djoser, wearing a crown and holding other emblems of royal power, engaged in a religious run. Mural relief in the royal tomb in Saqqara, 2650—2630 B.C.

lived on. The social upheavals which shook the Old Kingdom cast doubt on all accepted values, and diverted closer attention to the internal problems of society and of man himself.

According to the "Coffin text" of the Middle Kingdom man was a part of the god, "men were the tears that flowed from the eyes of the gods"; man was the descendant of the gods and therefore had a right to his own individual existence. The world had been created for him, "that every man might breathe freely during his life", and indeed, the gods had "created each man equal to his fellows". It was man himself who had upset this equality.[23] In the course of time the divine origin of the kings was given less emphasis, so detracting from their social exclusiveness and even during the Old Kingdom the king-god was replaced by the son of a god, born of a human mother. In the New Kingdom and the Late Period, he was a mortal, pure and simple. Attempts by officialdom to restore the royal divinity failed; the pharaoh, surrounded though he might be by the trappings of power on a monumental scale, could not deny his humanity, nor the fact that in many cases he was of positively humble origin.

In this humanizing process during the period of the Old Kingdom the pharaohs lost their unique status; the sovereign was now only one, albeit the first, of an ever-widening class of nobles who modelled their life-style on the once exclusive ways of the pharaohs. They, too, now demanded beauty and happiness on earth, and the continuation of that happiness after death. Alongside the monumental pyramids and temple-tombs of the Old Kingdom pharaohs, smaller but equally magnificent tombs were erected for nobles, all of which reveal an interior décor conveying the colour and gaiety of life.

The fundamental attitude to human life was formulated in the middle of the third millennium by the royal official Ptahhotpe, in his "Instructions". Happiness, seen as pleasurable and joyful experience, was the positive goal in life and Ptahhotpe made a conscious distinction between work, which was a disagreeable duty to be reduced to the minimum, and leisure which provided the opportunity for true self-realization. He put it quite plainly:

"...Be merry all your life;
Do no more than you are ordered to,
Nor shorten the time accorded to leisure.
It is hateful to the spirit to be robbed of the time for merriment."
Throughout the history of ancient Egypt men endeavoured to achieve the greatest measure of enjoyment and a tombstone dated in the twentieth century B.C. bears the proud inscription: "I am one who used every day to the full, wasting no part of it. Never did I miss a moment of bliss."[24]

Although this search for "moments of bliss" was indisputably an aristocratic ideal, it had its effects on the lower social orders. "Bliss" was to be found in everthing that brought man pleasure and delight – beautiful objects, flowers, animals, the wonder of nature and the simple comforts of

Naked boys throwing pointed sticks at a target on the ground. Relief from the tomb of Vizier Ptahhotpe in Saqqara, around 2300 B.C.

everyday life, in short everything that "warmed the heart". The high aesthetic standards of everyday life in ancient Egypt bear witness to this. Pleasure could be obtained from good food and drink, especially to excess, as this resulted in a happy mood of relaxation and ecstasy. Another aspect was physical love and the beauty of the human form. For a body to be beautiful it had to be slim, as obesity was not only repugnant, but a sign of stupidity, and foreigners were commonly depicted as flabby and pot-bellied.

Besides lovely clothes and jewellery, beauty was achieved by careful attention to the naked body; baths, scented oils, perfumes and cosmetics all played a part, and eurhythmics were cultivated to a high degree. The naked human body is often seen in Egyptian art, and even the king and the royal family are often depicted without clothes. King Ramesses III himself was portrayed playing chess with one of the ladies of his harem; both are naked, the king wearing only his crown, necklace and sandals.[25]

The "moments of bliss" also embraced all the amusements enjoyed by the kings and nobles. Most of these pursuits were of a peaceful nature and they preferred to take the role of onlooker, but in all of them the demand for joyous entertainment was paramount. Hunting was the most widely practised form of aristocratic amusement, and there are many effectively portrayed hunting scenes in Egyptian art. At first the hunting of dangerous wild animals, particularly the hippopotamus, was one of the royal duties. The founder of the first royal dynasty, Meni, was "carried off by a hippopotamus and perished", after which the pharaohs decided it was safer to have their servants hunt the creatures while they looked on from a distance. The rulers themselves enjoyed fishing and fowling, a privileged sport which was opened to the nobles from the middle of the third millennium.

An equally popular form of entertainment was to watch other people hunt; the pharaoh and his nobles looked on excitedly as his servants hunted hippopotami, fished or caught birds. A tomb from the Old Kingdom shows the dead man, Metjen the chief huntsman, eagerly following the performance of his hounds as they chase gazelles and ibex in the desert. Many such scenes have been preserved. At the beginning of the Middle Kingdom combat, in a closed arena as opposed to the open countryside, is depicted in the form of bull-fighting. Each of the competing bulls was given a name: "Darling" and "Brave Warrior". Men armed with short poles, probably herdsmen, directed the fight and acted as umpires. The scene suggests that this entertainment was already fairly organized, and points to a long tradition.[26]

Boys wrestling. The relief clearly shows different holds at various stages of the fight. From the tomb of Vizier Ptahhotpe in Saqqara, around 2300 B.C.

Boys playing. Relief in the tomb of Vizier Ptahhotpe in Saqqara, around 2300 B.C.

Joyous music and dancing performed by professionals were the indispensable accompaniments to "moments of bliss". Education in music and dancing was part of harem life. The king, the temples and regional nobles employed bands of singers, musicians, and male and female dancers, all of whom had a particular social status; at the royal court the singer, musician or dancer who proved his worth was promoted to the head of his "department", while further up the ladder was the director of festivities, director of court festivities, and ultimately director of royal festivities. Besides this official hierarchy there were of course groups of musicians and dancers who could be hired either for private entertainments, or to perform in hostelries for the amusement of the customers.

As taste became more refined, a higher standard of dancing was expected. Movements became more graceful and flowing, and acrobatic elements were incorporated. Ball games were also combined with dance movements, as can be seen from the literature and the art. The dance showed off the beauty of the human form, especially that of the female, to perfection, and jewels and flowers were used to enhance the charm of the naked or gently veiled body. There were also dances in which the comic element predominated, however, evident in scenes of dwarfs dancing.[27]

Both pharaohs and nobles particularly enjoyed watching performances in which the strength and dexterity of the human body were displayed, the earliest form of this amusement being that of watching children at play. The tombs of the viziers Ptahhopte and Mereruka in Saqqara from the middle of the third millennium, and many others of the period, contain reliefs which vividly depict a large variety of children's games. One child is shown riding pick-a-back on another, a boy is balancing on the shoulders of four others, and another is leaping high in the air, a feat still popular with Egyptian children today. In tombs of the Old Kingdom scenes of this kind are accompanied by inscriptions like "Hold tight!" and "Look out, I'm coming!" A common game was for a file of boys to pass the stiff body of one of their number back over their heads, and another, for several children holding hands to spin round in a circle.

There are also illustrations of a tug-of-war between two teams of three

*Young men in bound up light tunics
boxing with unprotected fists. Relief
from the tomb of Vizier Ptahhotpe in
Saqqara, around 2300 B.C.*

*Young men in light tunics fencing
with papyrus stalks, presumably
re-enacting an actual event. Relief
from around 2300 B.C.*

Left: Men dancing. Relief from the tomb of Vizier Mereruka in Saqqara, around 2250 B.C.

children, of a game with one child in the middle of a ring trying to catch one of the others by the feet, and of boys scrimmaging with their elbows, or sitting back-to-back with arms linked, trying to pull each other over. They are portrayed squatting in the yogi lotus position, or standing on their heads with their arms folded across their chests; throwing pointed darts at a target or pushing along a hoop with a bent stick. In Ptahhotpe's burial chamber six pairs of wrestling children are depicted on a frieze. Among the children's games recorded from the Old Kingdom there are some which tell a story, the most interesting one referred to by some scholars as "leading on a captive" and by others, as "the little war". In the middle of a group of running boys is one who represents the prisoner, with his hands tied behind his back and sometimes with a lion's mask on his head. The other boys carry papyrus leaves, evidently as make-believe weapons. This is valuable evidence of a "war game" or mock combat in the context of children's play.

In the Middle Kingdom portrayals of children's games are superseded by scenes of young men and girls at play. Some of their activities still resemble children's games, like the round game in which the young men and girls hold hands, with their heels dug in at the centre of the ring. But for the most part, the games are new, and girls are more in evidence. Ball-games are very frequent, including one in which a group of girls toss a ball, while the others clap a rhythm. Alternatively, girls are shown juggling with a ball, or playing ball in pairs, with the players carried on their partners' backs.

Young men display and test their strength by wrestling in pairs — a sport whose extraordinary popularity at the time is attested in countless representations. They range from small groups of figurines of wrestling matches in progress to numerous large murals in the burial chambers of viziers and other high officials. On one mural there are fifty-nine wrestling couples, on another 122, and a third presents as many as 219, showing different stages in the match or different styles of wrestling.

The wrestlers are usually naked, except for a broad white loin-cloth, and are drawn in contrasting skin colours, making it easier to identify the intertwined limbs and to distinguish the various holds. It is clear from these mural paintings that no holds were barred. It is equally clear that there must have been intensive training to achieve mastery of the various holds and counter-holds. In some pictures referees are shown, suggesting some form of

military training. All these forms of physical activities were either performed by professionals for the entertainment of the king and his court or else they were spontaneous children's games and popular amusements.

As early as the Old Kingdom there are reports of various forms of exercise included as part of the training for useful employment. Running is among them, and there is also considerable evidence of water sports. Water was second nature to the Egyptians, and from the earliest times swimming was a common accomplishment. There was a special hieroglyph for swimming, and a goddess of swimming, Wadjet, was worshipped in the Old Kingdom. In the Middle Kingdom a reference is made to an aristocrat learning to swim with the royal princes and in later Egyptian art figurines of girls swimming exist. In the literature of the cult of Osiris a contest between the god Horus and Seth is described, which was to be decided by a feat of underwater endurance, and in another case by a rowing race.

Boats were a common means of transport and there were temple and state boat-yards in various parts of the country, where different types were kept. This implies the existence of professional rowers. In the art of the time the boats are often manned by crews armed with long poles with which they try to capsize the enemy's vessels. This may be a form of sport, and the possibility of boat-races cannot be excluded.[28]

During the New Kingdom a marked change came over the forms and nature of physical exercise and sport, as a result of the military campaigns of conquest directed at the countries of the Near East. This situation changed the life-style of the pharaohs, and of the aristocracy too. New tactics, employing horse-drawn chariots, called for a new type of training. The pharaoh was now a military leader, first and foremost, the type idealized by the monarchs of the Near East: "Like a true god who exults when battle begins, the king takes delight when he crosses the frontiers of his land. He is happy to draw blood. He cuts off the heads of his enemies, would rather one hour of battle than a whole day spent in leisure." So reads this inscription of the mid second millennium B.C., and many other similar declarations. War is described as the king's favourite and most exciting entertainment.[29] Monumental battle scenes, immortalized in temples and burial chambers, tell the same story.

The hunting tableaux, which often form part of the battle sequence, are equally grand and fundamentally comply with the Near Eastern stereotype: the king is the only active performer, riding in a chariot and hunting mainly lions and bulls. There are many references to the hunting prowess of the pharaohs in the literary sources, including almost all the rulers of the New Kingdom. This was part of their new image.

Pharaoh Amenophis III of the fourteenth century B.C. made known his liking for the hunt throughout his realm by sending out scarabs which were inscribed with his successes in the chase. One of them reads as follows:

"The total number of lions killed by His Majesty with his own arrows, from the first to the tenth year [of his reign]: 102 wild lions."

In another inscription the pharaoh announces his achievements in hunting wild cattle:

"His Majesty mounted a chariot drawn by a team of horses and the whole army went with him. Both the commander and the rank and file as well as the people of the region had been told to keep watch on the herd of wild cattle [reported from these parts]. His Majesty then ordered that the herd should be enclosed inside a fence with only one free way out. His Majesty then ordered them to count the herd. Their number was one hundred and seventy head of cattle. And on that day His Majesty's bag was fifty-six head."

Dancing men. Relief from the tomb of Vizier Mereruka in Saqqara, around 2250 B.C.

This inscription reveals with remarkable candour the real setting for the great hunting scenes of Egyptian art. Far from taking place in wild open country, the Pharaoh's hunt was held in a restricted area enclosed by a fence. Similar situations are depicted, in which the boundary was formed by several ranks of troops. Like the Mesopotamian rulers, the pharaohs adopted the fashion of having lions captured in foreign lands, transported in cages, and released into an arena for carefully staged hunts.[30] This is how the event became a magnificent and socially exclusive entertainment.

Another equally popular royal sport, derived from hunting in a chariot, was that of shooting at a fixed target; it is attested in both the art and literature. Driving in his chariot, the king took aim at one or more targets, which were apparently made of wood, although the sources more often mention the use of copper. The king's shots were so forceful that they not only shattered the wooden targets, but went through several inches of copper. Of course these reports are highly exaggerated, but they do confirm a characteristic which can be distinguished in the paintings of such scenes: that the targets were shaped like the ingots of copper imported to Egypt from Cyprus and the Near East, similar in appearance to a bull's hide. It was presumably on account of this that the royal targets of wood were described as copper.[31]

It is clear from the extant material that the emphasis placed on battle as a form of noble entertainment was an artificial one, modelled on the Mesopotamian and other Near Eastern courts, and is explained by the aggressive policy of expansion being carried out by Egypt at the time. Fighting never became the pharaohs' favourite sport, unlike the new forms of hunting and shooting at targets, which were much more in keeping with the Egyptian mentality. The traditional activities of fishing and fowling nevertheless retained their popularity.

The pharaohs now fished in artificial ponds laid out in the royal gardens, rather than natural lakes, and although the traditional sport of spearing the fish continued, rod and line were also used. Among the loveliest landscape scenes from the New Kingdom are those which show fowling; the hunter sails on the waters of the Nile, in his light papyrus boat, the river banks hidden by reeds and flowering plants, from which flocks of birds rise. A servant hands the hunter his weapon, and often there are women looking on. The old-fashioned throwing stick, once used in the hunt for food, enhances the playful, sporting character of the pastime.

The most up-to-date military techniques, however, were also adapted in this period for the royal sports; the bow and arrow and the chariot were used for hunting dangerous wild animals. Target shooting was also modified. The

Right: Statuette of a wrestling pair, around 2000 B.C.

pharaoh stood alone in his chariot, no longer part of a team of two or three, as in real fighting. The reins were twisted round his waist, leaving his hands free for shooting, while the strength and dexterity of his body controlled the chariot. The chariot itself was now as light and elegant as possible, as confirmed by representations in painting, and by a fifteenth century find reconstructed and known as the Rosellini chariot.[32]

The pharaohs' delight in these forms of sport was reflected in their love of horses, which were carefully tended and fed in the royal stables, and given regular exercise. The royal princes seem to have taken an active part in training them. It is known that the horses of Amenophis II were so well trained that they did not sweat or tire, even when put to the gallop. Thuthmose IV had horses that were faster than the wind and it is recorded that Ramesses III inspected his horses regularly.

The pharaohs not only hunted and shot for their private pleasure, but performed for their admiring public. A granite relief from Karnak shows Amenophis II shooting at a target from a moving chariot, and the inscription tells us that "His Majesty performed these feats before the eyes of the whole land". The onlookers seem to have been the nobles and the army. There are even reports that this same monarch showed no hesitation in measuring his strength against other men, apparently his soldiers. This is attested in a text found at Luxor, which records that the pharaoh not only challenged his soldiers to a shooting match, but set prizes for the victors.[33] Amenophis even competed in running and rowing races, and he most clearly embodies the characteristic features of the rulers of the New Kingdom. A stele from Giza recalls his outstanding sporting achievements:

"His Majesty ascended the throne as a young man in full command of his body. At eighteen he was peerless in courage and knew all the ways of Mont [the war god], so that he had no equal in war, and he understood horses, so that he had no equal among the many soldiers. Nor was there anyone who could bend a bow like him, and no one excelled him in running against others. His arms were so strong that he was never faint when he grasped the oar and rowed abaft his arrow-swift ship, the best of the crew of two hundred. Many were faint after a course of half a mile, exhausted and weary of limb and out of breath; but His Majesty still rowed powerfully with his twenty-ell oar, laying his oar aside and bringing his ship to shore only after all had seen what he had done.

"He also bent three hundred strong bows and compared the work of the bowmakers, telling the good craftsman from the bad. Then he came and performed what I shall now relate: entering his northern garden he saw that four targets of Asian copper had been set up for him, as thick as a man's palm, and the distance between one target-post and the next was twenty ells. Then His Majesty appeared on his war chariot like Mont in all his might. He bent his bow and seized four arrows at once. Then he started up his chariot and shot at all four targets, like Mont in all his glory. His arrow sped through one target and hit the next post; he let fly his arrow at the copper target so that it came out of it again and fell to the ground — a deed no one else had ever performed and of which no one had ever heard...''[34]

The greater demands made on the pharaohs to maintain their physical fitness meant that the royal princes had to be specially trained. Their teachers were the highest nobles, the top officials of the royal court, who then bore for life the title of "nurse" to a particular prince. In paintings the gods themselves are shown as teachers of the royal princes. The children of the nobility were trained alongside the royal children, and one of the principal skills they were taught was how to shoot with a bow and arrow.[35]

The demand for fitness in a pharaoh was not without effect on the nobles. They seem to have been somewhat unwilling to change their life-style and continued to enjoy its refinements, but inscriptions in many aristocratic tombs indicate that many were also prepared to test their strength in the dangerous hippopotamus hunt.

The policy of expansion adopted by the rulers of the New Kingdom resulted in noticeable changes in the organization and training of the army, which at this time, of course, was almost completely mercenary, made up of men from Libya, Nubia and Asia. The principal form of training was wrestling, with other forms of fighting, for example with special knobbed sticks, in addition. The contestants protected themselves with small shields bound on to the left arm, and sometimes the face, the chin or the ears might be protected by special bandages. There are numerous references to boxing. There seem to have been special units of sporting fighters in the army,

Left: Women dancing with a ball. The two smaller dancers are probably marking the rhythm with their rattles. Part of a burial scene from the tomb in Saqqara, 19th century B.C.

Women performing a religious dance. Relief from the temple of Queen Hatshepsut in Karnak, around 1480 B.C.

Top right: Detail from the scene below.

judging from a tomb painting showing a company of Nubian soldiers, the last of whom is carrying a standard representing two wrestlers.[36]

Various forms of physical activity seem to have been included in the festival programme. The information at our disposal points to a remarkable continuity, not only in the history of ancient Egypt, but much further back into prehistoric times. The greatest festivals were connected with the different phases of the vegetation cycle, and at the start of the summer floods the New Year was celebrated with great pomp. The Spring festival was one of joy for the renewal of nature, and the harvest was yet another occasion for celebration. The full moon and the new moon were feasted, as were the intercalary days. On all these occasions the chief divinities were worshipped, and in addition there were many festivals in honour of local gods and the ancient animal gods. In the New Kingdom and the Late Period the cult of Osiris became the most popular of all, embracing many of the older local gods. There were also strong secular elements in the Egyptian festivals, including the celebration of historical events, such as the unification of the country at the end of the fourth millennium. The funeral of a pharaoh or a member of the aristocracy lasted for several days, and the crowning of a pharaoh was an important occasion for celebration. In the New Kingdom and the Late Period the conclusion of a peace treaty or the visit of a foreign emissary were further excuses for festivities. The "festival of drunkenness" had a special place of its own in the philosophy concerned with "moments of bliss".

The central point of every festival was a sacrifice, symbolizing the destruction of the enemies of the gods and men. The sacrifice was accompanied by a meal for all those present. The general public played an active part in the processions, which linked together the various parts of the programme. At the head of the procession was the statue of the god, to whom the festival was dedicated, drawn in a cart-boat, to the accompaniment of song, music and dancing.[37]

53

The literary evidence has preserved some of the details about the festivals. In Abydos, where the kings of Egypt had been buried since the end of the fourth millennium, a great Osiris festival was held lasting ten days; it is described on a stele, dating from about 1800 B.C. The central theme was the struggle between Osiris and his enemies, his death and solemn burial. In the end, however, his enemies were conquered and Osiris, alive again, returned in glory to his temple in Abydos. The mysteries that were performed reflected the ancient history of Egypt and used dramatic texts rooted in prehistoric times. Other sources describe the ceremonies surrounding the pharaoh's coronation, and the pictorial instructions and stage-directions make it possible to reconstruct the way the ceremonies were presented.[38]

The simplest of these was a running race, in the earliest days of the monarchy, in which the king demonstrated his physical prowess and at the same time gave symbolic expression to a certain action. In a hymn dating from the Old Kingdom appear the words: "Step forward with beauty. Step forward with beauty along the beautiful way where the beloved of the Great God have always walked in peace, in peace."[39]

Dancing provided an alternative means of presenting the story, and here too the king was originally the chief performer; he danced a harvest thanksgiving dance, in honour of the god Min, and he danced before the goddess Hathor of Dendera as he handed her a pitcher of wine, while the chorus sang: "The king has come and is dancing. The king has come and is singing…" At the coronation ceremony the priest, or the master of ceremonies, danced and handed the king a cake. During the festival of the dead, in the early years of the Middle Kingdom, dancing girls enacted the victory of the king over his enemies in exactly the same way as can be seen

Two women dancers performing for nobles during a meal shown in the adjoining part of the scene. The three seated women are singing and clapping in rhythm, the fourth is playing on a double flute. Mural painting from a tomb in Thebes, around 1400 B.C.

A group of Nubian wrestlers marching with the Egyptian mercenary army bearing a standard that shows their profession. Mural painting from a tomb in Thebes, around 1450 B.C.

54

Right: Pharaoh Amenhotep II standing on a light chariot, driving horses with the reins tied round his hips and shooting arrows at a target in the form of a copper ingot. Relief from Karnak, around 1420 B.C.

depicted in the murals of the pre-dynastic period, the Old Kingdom, or the Late Period. The dancers' hair was made to resemble the crown of the kings of Upper Egypt. Dance was also used in the presentation of mythological scenes. Soldiers danced war-dances, to imitate mock combat, beating time with boomerangs while two of them staged a fight with bent throwing-sticks.[40]

Mock combat was also part of the symbolic performance of the mysteries, and the winner was predetermined by the story to be told. The sources refer to combatants who fought with papyrus stems instead of weapons. The combats in the Osiris mysteries were also of a symbolic nature, as recorded by Ichernofret, keeper of the royal treasury, in the Middle Kingdom. A New Kingdom tomb painting shows six priests in combat, and another in which several groups are fighting with fists and sticks; according to the inscription over two of the groups, one is from the town of Pe, the other from Dep, both places which played an important role in the prehistoric development of Egypt. The combat apparently depicts real fighting between them.

Herodotus has left a historical account of the mock combats, which formed part of the mysteries of Osiris in the city of Papremis. On a certain day the statue of the god was taken from its temple in a gilded wooden shrine, and carried to another; the following day it was carried back in procession, but at the door of the temple a struggle broke out between the people carrying the statue and the priests denying them entry. Herodotus feared that there would be many casualties, but the Egyptians assured him nobody would be hurt, for he had witnessed not a real fight, but a mock combat, the outcome of which was decided in advance – the successful return of the god and his followers.[41]

At some festivals, however, there were straightforward displays of skill and strength, in which competitive elements were paramount. We can deduce from the literary allusions that running contests fell into this category. One of the dramatic texts used during the coronation festivities describes with illustrations a contest between teams of craftsmen (butchers and cabinet-makers) who are revealing their skills to the new monarch. Since this manuscript dates from the end of the third millennium B.C., and yet describes a ceremony which was almost a thousand years older, it is safe to

A girl dancer in an acrobatic back-bend. Painting on limestone, around 1300 B.C.

A nobleman on a light papyrus boat using the ancient technique of throwing a curved stick to hunt birds. Mural painting from a tomb in Thebes, around 1400 B.C.

Right: A pair of wrestlers. Painting on limestone, Medinet Habu, around 1200 – 1100 B.C.

Pharaoh Ramesses III hunting wild bulls in the traditional way by hurling a spear. Relief from the temple of Ramesses III in Medinet Habu, around 1160 B.C.

58

Wrestling and fencing with sticks: a wrestler is holding his rival by the hair, trying to hit him with his knee. Another wrestler is about to throw his rival to the ground. Two men fencing with sticks protect their heads with raised arms. One of the contestants greets the spectators with a bow, another has taken up position to start fencing. The scene continues below.

Noble spectators eagerly watch the contests. Two men are fencing with knobbed sticks and protecting their heads with narrow shields fixed to their forearms. A wrestler has caught his rival's head under his arm and is trying to throw him to the ground.
(continued on page 60)

assume that such contests were a traditional part of this, and maybe other festivals.[42]

At Medinet Habu there is a New Kingdom frieze, dated about 1160 B.C., celebrating Ramesses III. It shows the grandstands and ten pairs of wrestlers in the ring, some of them armed with sticks. An inscription reveals that the contest was held to entertain the pharaoh, the Egyptian nobles, and the foreign dignitaries. The onlookers are following the fight with excitement, commenting and gesticulating. Umpires keep a careful watch on the wrestlers and reprimand one of them: "Take care, you are here before your lord, the pharaoh!" The wrestlers are Egyptians, fighting against prisoners of war, Negroes and Asiatics, a fact disclosed by an onlooker's remark to the monarch: "Amon defeated thy enemies, and they have come here to distinguish themselves." The Egyptians challenge their opponents: "Defend yourself, Negro enemy!" and "Defend yourself, Syrian enemy!" and utter threats such as: "Look how I catch you by the feet and throw you over to your side of the ring!" The onlookers also encourage the Egyptian wrestlers: "Forward! Forward! valiant warrior!" The frieze depicts the culmination of two matches, with the defeated man, a foreigner in each cace, lying on the ground while his victorious Egyptian opponent stands with arms raised joyfully to Heaven, thanking the gods for his victory.[43]

Herodotus is our source of knowledge for another festival at Chemmis (now Akhmin in Upper Egypt), which included an athletic display with contests in every discipline, the prizes being cattle, cloaks and skins. He comments, moreover, that in holding this festival the people of Chemmis

were unique among the Egyptians. Competitions were held in honour of the ancient god of Upper Egypt, Min, god of the universe and of fertility, who was later incorporated into the Osiris cult. From the second half of the third millennium onwards, his celebrations included an interesting event; eight men, "armed" with quills, tried to keep their balance on poles fixed round a tall mast, which was repeatedly lifted into the air and dropped to the ground again, by a group of men pulling on ropes. This performance was meant to stimulate the earth's fertility. Since Herodotus makes no reference to this strange custom, which would certainly have drawn his attention had he come across it, it seems likely that these ancient activities had been replaced by races and tests of strength by his time.[44]

Under the New Kingdom a military review seems to have been incorporated into the festivals. Wall paintings in the colonnade of the temple at Luxor depict the celebrations in honour of the god Amon; standard bearers, musicians and soldiers parade in front of the pharaoh. In the final scene a group of Negro warriors are performing an ecstatic dance to the sound of trumpets, which suggests that it was traditional for Egyptian festivals to culminate in "moments of bliss", induced by excessive drinking and frenzied dancing. At the same time various elements from the African hinterland left their mark on Egyptian culture, and it became possible to distinguish African features in the popular festivities, in particular the various ecstatic phallic cults described by Herodotus.[45]

The wealth of art and literature surviving from the civilization of ancient Egypt, and the thousands of years of uninterrupted cultural evolution there, provide an unusually clear view of the complex process, in which a wide variety of physical activities were developed, and frequently altered to accord with social changes and political events.

(continued from page 59)
The gesticulating woman is evidently one of the spectators. One of the wrestlers is trying to break his opponent's arm at the elbow. A defeated man is lying on the ground while the victor raises both hands delightedly. The inscriptions suggest the fighters' shouts and the spectators' comments. Relief from the temple of Ramesses III in Medinet Habu, around 1160 B.C.

Speeding chariots manned by two charioteers, each trying to overtake one another. Detail of the painted chest from the tomb of King Tutankhamun in Thebes, around 1350 B.C.

A Pharaoh seated in a chair shooting fish in an artificial garden lake. Detail of the chest decorated with inlaid ivory, semi-precious stones and glass paste from the tomb of King Tutankhamun in Thebes, around 1350 B.C.

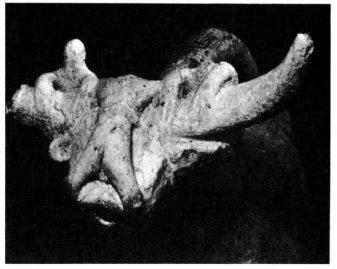

A clay ritual rhyton in the shape of a bull with small figures clinging onto its horns. Koumasa, Crete, around 2000 B.C.
Left: Detail of the bull's head with figures.

The Aegean

The Aegean Sea with its innumerable islands made close contact between settlers possible as early as Neolithic times, when wave after wave of migration spread from the Near East all over the Aegean area. In the seventh and sixth millennia B.C. there were centres of Neolithic culture on Cyprus, on the Greek mainland (in particular Thessaly), and on the neighbouring Cyclades islands. A number of Neolithic sites have been discovered on Crete, the largest at Knossos. All these centres had many features in common with the Near Eastern Neolithic cultures, especially that of Çatal Hüyük, but they continued along their own evolutionary path. In the course of the third millennium B.C. three distinct cultures were formed in the Aegean area.

The Helladic culture developed on the Greek mainland, and unusual elements appearing towards the end of the third millennium B.C. reveal the arrival of new ethnic groups — the Greek tribes who gradually gave form to the individual Mycenaean culture.

At the beginning of the third millennium B.C. it was the Cycladic islands that led the Aegean forward. The many marble statuettes of slender female figures in the nude, the figurines of musicians, and the clay vessels that probably held toilet necessities, all testify to the high level of this Cycladic culture. At the same time they indicate the amount of attention paid to the human body and confirm that dance already existed as a basic form of movement.

Towards the end of the third millennium B.C. the focus of cultural evolution moved to Crete. The great palaces of Knossos, Phaestus, Mallia, Hagia Triada and Zacros were centres of the mature Minoan civilization which left its mark on the culture of the whole of the Aegean for almost a millennium. Although the history of the palaces of Crete was interrupted more than once by natural catastrophes — earthquakes, followed by fires and floods — they were always rebuilt and flourished anew. Around the year 1470 B.C., however, the catastrophe which befell the island of Crete, and many others in the vicinity, was unprecedented. On the island of Thera, one

Gem with a picture of an acrobat jumping over a running bull. Crete, around 1500.

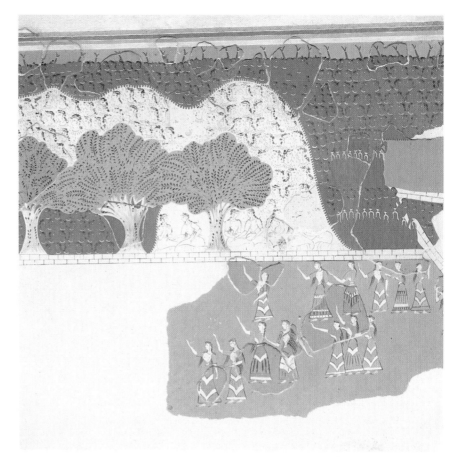

Central court of the palace in Phaestus, the setting of ceremonial performances. On the left a graded stand for the spectators.

of the important centres of Minoan civilization, there was a terrific volcanic eruption and the greater part of the island sank into the sea. The sea swelled and the high waves and violent earth tremors caused the Cretan palaces to be buried in lava and ash, and the Minoan culture was laid waste over a large area.[46] Reports of the catastrophe have been preserved in Egyptian sources and in the Greek legend of the destruction of Atlantis.[47]

After this disaster, Minoan civilization underwent marked changes, principally because the palace of Knossos, the only one to be restored, acquired new rulers − Mycenaean aristocrats who came from the Greek mainland. The decipherment of the Linear B script, among other things, confirmed their presence on Crete.

From the earliest days of the palaces the Cretans knew two scripts, a pictographic one and the simplified linear script, now known as Linear A. Neither of these has been deciphered as yet, and so we do not know the language of the Minoan civilization, nor can we read the few surviving inscriptions. A third Cretan script has been deciphered, however; known as Linear B, it proves that it was adapted for use with the Greek language. Clay tablets thus inscribed have been found in Knossos, and on several sites on the Greek mainland, particularly in Pylos.

The new rulers of Knossos, who were Greeks, assimilated many features of Minoan civilization, which had already exerted an influence on the centres of Mycenaean culture on the mainland. At the same time they contributed distinctly Mycenaean influences which grew in strength.

Probably at the end of the thirteenth century "one spring morning with a strong south wind", a fire broke out in the palace of Knossos, causing destruction on such a scale that it finally brought the era of the Cretan palaces

A detail of the fresco in the palace in Knossos showing a ceremonial scene. The spectators, seated under olive trees, watch a dramatic dance. Sketches of heads indicate their number. Crete, around 1500 B.C.

The gilded hilt of a ceremonial sword showing an acrobat bent over the blade. From the palace in Malia, Crete, 1700–1600 B.C.

Two acrobats performing in a meadow. A seal found near Knossos, Crete, around 1500 B.C.

to a close. The Minoan civilization was overshadowed throughout the Aegean by the Mycenaean culture, although it was undoubtedly less refined. Nevertheless some Minoan traditions persisted, especially in the religious sphere.[48]

The Minoan civilization was remarkably unwarlike; her strong fleet ensured mastery of the seas to Crete, for trading and cultural purposes, rather than for political advancement. Crete enjoyed regular contact with Egypt, and through Cyprus with Ugarit in Syria and Mari on the middle Euphrates, and over Rhodes to Miletus in Asia Minor. Domination of the seas protected Crete from attack, and so the original fortifications around the palaces were dismantled, and the weapons, which were originally worn for protection, became no more than elegant symbols.

Crete was also free from social disruptions; society was structured, indeed, but there were no sharp divisions within it. Women enjoyed considerable freedom and a position of respect. Power rivalries between the lords of the different palaces were not evident, nor were there despots; the lords were the representatives of the gods, and therefore never portrayed in art. Only Minos, the mythical ruler of Knossos, has left his name to Greek tradition, and indeed to the civilization of Crete.

The palaces were administrative units, which constituted the seat of the ruler, and the source of local administration, but they were also religious and economic centres of the region. The palace buildings were grouped round a central courtyard, with striking architectural features, colonnades, terraces, and facades surrounded by extensive gardens, and an intricate system of drains and waterworks operated. The whole was decorated in colour, with large frescoes and other adornments. The palaces were annexed to urban developments, sometimes of houses on several floors. The living rooms of the palace were served by bathrooms and dressing-rooms equipped with a very wide variety of cosmetics, mirrors and combs for complicated coiffures, and containers for different types of make-up. The most magnificent of the dresses depicted are long, decorative skirts, worn with the breasts uncovered. Archaeological finds of elegant, decorative table-ware suggest that high standards were set at meals. The greatest palace, and the most luxurious, was that of the "double axe-head", the Labyrinth of Knossos; there were almost 1,500 rooms and corridors arranged in a complicated design.[49]

No monumental war scenes can be found in Minoan art, and hunting only rarely, but the happy portrayals of entertainment and games are most striking. The vivid colours used, and the diversity of movement, shown in successive stages as though on film, contribute to the overall effect. Nature scenes, with wild creatures wandering free, are a frequent theme; the coloured frescoes present landscapes with wild roses blooming, crocuses and lilies, as well as parks with sparkling fountains. Live creatures abound − dolphins, sepia, monkeys, cats on the prowl, goats, and birds. On one of the frescoes from Thera a boy is carrying his catch of fish threaded on a string. Among the recent discoveries at Thera is a magnificent miniature fresco, of which six metres have survived, apparently depicting some historical event. The sea, full of dolphins, is shown and a landscape threaded with rivers, abundant with rich vegetation and all forms of animal life. Minoan boats, some under sail and others richly decorated, all fully loaded, are setting out for a distant land. The towns with their huge houses and colonnades are thronged with people, ladies in magnificent clothes sitting at windows and on terraces, others joining the men to welcome new arrivals, and children running excitedly all over the place.[50]

Children and adults are shown engaged in games of all sorts. In the palace of Knossos there are children crawling on the floor, throwing or pushing dice, and at Palaikastro a figurine of a child at play has been found. Adults sit at gaming tables. Various kinds of dice, draughts and other games suggest the popularity of such pastimes. A chequers board, richly inlaid with precious stones, ivory, gold and silver, was also discovered.[51]

The theme which dominates the frescoes and other art forms, however, is that of festivities. The very frequency of their occurrence confirms the important role these occasions played in Minoan life and civilization. Festivals were held at various stages of the vegetation cycle; they were religious in character, and were held in honour of the goddess − the mistress of the animal world or of the mountains, the queen of the Labyrinth or the Great Mother. Since no literary sources exist, it is extremely difficult to determine the religious ideas of the Minoans, manifest on such occasions. Certain elements seem to have been connected with Neolithic cults, particularly with the festivals held in Çatal Hüyük, while other features are quite novel.

The cult was originally based in caves and on mountain tops, and was later transferred to small shrines in the palaces, which were adorned with figures of the goddess and her symbols of trees, doves, snakes, the double-headed axe and bulls' horns. Members of the royal family, especially the queen, played an important part in the ceremonies. An alabaster throne can still be seen in the throne room of the palace at Knossos, where the queen used to sit as the goddess, accompanied by fantastic winged animals, griffins, painted on the walls.

The solemn processions were of great significance in the ceremonies. The corridor leading to the throne room in the palace at Knossos was decorated with frescoes showing over 500 life-size figures taking part in such

66

A "sports" rhyton from the palace in Hagia Triada. In the upper band a boxer in a helmet with a clearly visible glove on his right hand. In the lower band a victorious boxer with the defeated opponent at his feet. Crete, around 1500 B.C.

Right: A fresco of children boxing with gloves on their right hands. Thera, around 1500 B.C.

a procession, and carrying rich goblets and other gifts. Similar occasions can be seen on a sarcophagus from Hagia Triada, and in relief on a steatite vase which realistically depicts twenty-seven figures, singing and in an obvious state of joyful intoxication, during a procession in honour of the sowing or harvesting of the fields.

Young men, with well-developed muscles and wasp-like waists, were depicted, controlling their limbs, head and body in graceful movement. The backward S-bend of the trunk gave them even more spring. The girls, in festive dress, were bare-breasted. There were musicians in the procession, and the nobility were carried in litters, headed by the queen, who represented the goddess and was borne on a special throne. Cult boats, and chariots decorated with ivory and painting, were also brought along. Two chariots like this are shown in the procession on the Hagia Triada sarcophagus: one is horse-drawn, with two women driving; the other is drawn by griffins, but also with two women drivers, possibly goddesses. Both scenes testify to the significance of chariots in the cult; they were known on Crete from the end of the seventeenth century B.C.

Sacrifice was also part of the ceremonies − especially the sacrifice of a bull. The Hagia Triada sarcophagus shows a bull tied to a table, with blood flowing from a knife-wound in the neck into a pitcher, while a piper plays a double pipe. In another part of the same scene a priestess is pouring the blood of the sacrificed bull between two double-edged axes, while others are bringing more pitchers of blood. A musician is playing the lyre. Similar scenes can be found on gems and seals. The ritual culminated in the manifestation of the divinity. There are a number of scenes showing a figure descending from the skies, or divine symbols.[52]

Closely connected with the ritual were special ceremonial performances which took place inside the palace or in an olive grove surrounding it. The significance of these performances is indicated by the architecture of the palaces, which were arranged round a central courtyard with this end in view. In some cases, the palace of Phaestus for example, there were special grandstands round the courtyard; elsewhere windows and terraces served the same purpose, or the slopes of the gently rising olive groves.

The onlooker himself had a special role to play on these occasions, and the representation of the audience is one of the remarkable features of Minoan art. They are portrayed in various forms, as exemplified in the historical fresco at Thera, where there are innumerable onlookers, or a fragment from Knossos which depicts over three hundred and fifty people.

Left: Scene from the sacrifice. The bull is tied to the table and his blood flows into the vessel. A man is playing the double flute and a priestess stands in front of the altar, with the symbol of bull's horns. A sarcophagus from Hagia Triada, Crete, around 1500 B.C.

*Above: Noble ladies watching
a ceremonial performance. A fresco
from the palace in Knossos, around
1500 B.C.*

The groups of elegantly dressed women standing or sitting at their appointed places are treated with considerable realism, gesticulating and obviously talking animatedly, as though commenting on the performance. The majority of the onlookers' heads are only schematically outlined, but even here lively communication is suggested by the turn of their faces.[53]

The large number of spectators shows that the performance was a public one, open to both men and women, and to all social classes, so it would seem. They also prove that these festivals were a very important part of Minoan social life, and enjoyed great popularity.

The performance itself was a professional affair. Priestesses clad in ritual costume performed dances which seem to have been ecstatic in character, judging from the jerky movements of the dancers depicted on the Knossos frescoes. A small group of clay figures, representing four women dancing a round dance, has been found not far from Hagia Triada. Relief carvings and seals often show ecstatic dances. The excitement may have been enhanced by

69

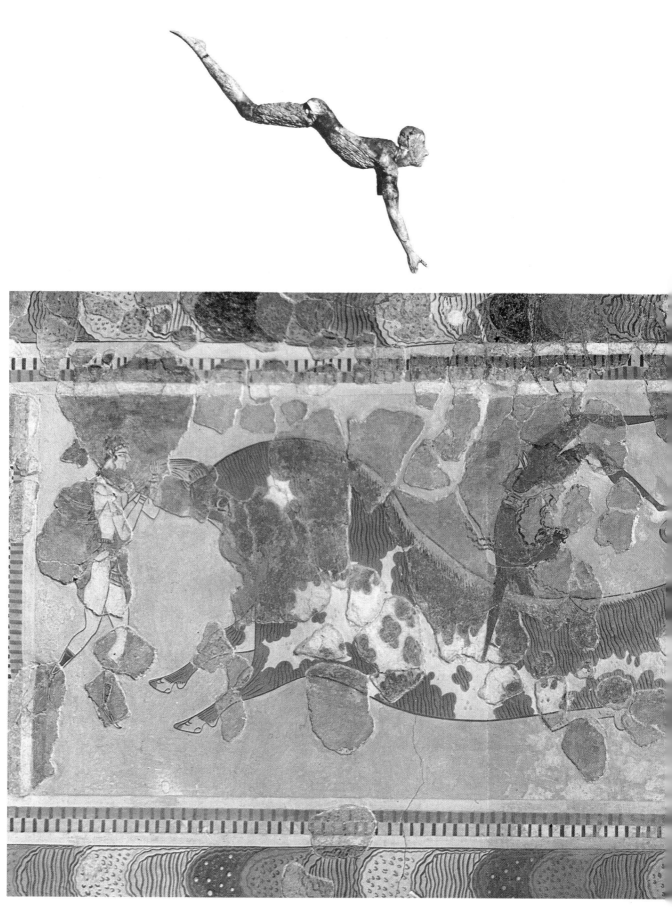

Left: A gilded ivory statuette of an acrobat at the moment of jumping the bull. From the palace in Knossos, around 1500 B.C.

Below: Fresco from the palace in Knossos, showing three stages of the leap over the running bull. Catching it by the horns, landing on its back, jumping off behind the bull. Crete, around 1500 B.C.

the use of drugs, in particular opium; this is suggested by figurines of women with poppy-heads in their diadems, as well as by a scene on a seal showing a priestess handing poppyheads to the other women. The large number of dance scenes shows how significant a role they played in Minoan ceremonial. The priestesses may have mimed a story as they danced, part of which would have been the evocation of the divinity and her epiphany.

Pairs of wrestlers also performed during the festivals, as can be seen on fragments of Knossos frescoes, but it was boxing that enjoyed the greatest popularity. A black steatite rhyton from Hagia Triada presents boxing matches in three of its four bands of carving, showing the successive phases leading up to the dramatic victory of one combatant and defeat of the other. The victor, still tense with excitement, is shown having delivered the decisive blow, and the defeated man is sinking to his knees, falling forward on to his head, or backwards to sit on the ground and use his feet in a last attempt at defence. He is seen shielding his head from the next blow, or sent somersaulting backwards by the final stroke. The boxers have athletic figures, and wear a metal helmet protecting the head and face, leaving only a narrow opening for their eyes. Their shoes are tied with leather straps up the calves, and they wear some kind of protectors on their hands, probably also leather straps. The fourth band of carvings shows boxers who are completely unprotected; the pillar which marks the ring and symbolizes the palace shows that these matches were part of the festival performances in the palace.

A fresco recently uncovered in Thera, in a room adorned with flowers and antelopes, illustrates the same subject. The fresco shows two children, probably about seven years old, a boy and girl painted life-size, with protective gloves on their right hands.[54]

Various acrobatic performances also seem to have been included in the festivities. A bronze sword was found in the palace at Mallia, with a gold relief ornament on the hilt. A plaque about 7 cm in diameter shows an acrobat bent so far backwards that his toes touch his head, possibly jumping over a sword, or somersaulting over the blade. Two acrobats are shown on a blue chalcedony seal found in Knossos. In Hagia Triada a clay figure was discovered, representing a woman in ceremonial costume swinging between two pillars, on which doves, the symbols of the goddess, are sitting. This seems to have been more than a display of skill, and by analogy with other instances all over the world it can be interpreted as a ritual act performed to awaken the earth's fertility. It is probable that other forms of physical activity

Bull jumping. Seal, Crete, around 1500 B.C.

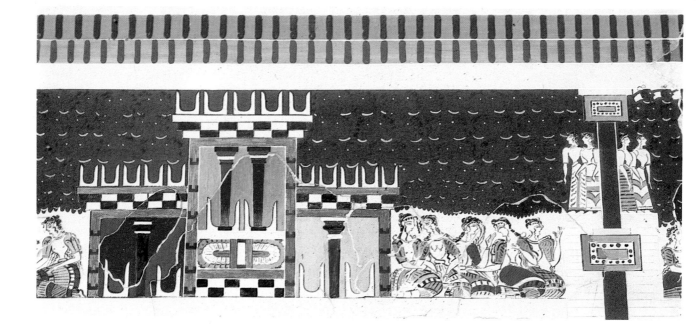

— wrestling, boxing and acrobatics — were also symbolic in different ways.[55]

The climax of the performances was undoubtedly provided by the bull sports, acrobatic leaps over the backs of the charging bulls; this was also the most characteristic feature of the Minoan festivals. The earliest evidence of the sport dates from around 2000 B.C., on a ritual clay rhyton shaped like a bull; the ornament shows three men, two of them swinging on a bull's horns, and the third held between the bull's horns, while the acrobat clings onto them. The earliest palace period has yielded a clay figurine of a bull with an acrobat leaping over it. The motif is repeated in innumerable variants throughout Minoan art.

To perform the more straightforward leaps, the acrobat approached the bull from the side, seized the horns and vaulted over to the other side. A seal stone shows this leap performed over a bull lying peaceably in the grass. This was either a preparatory exercise, or a simple and not at all dangerous form of sport. In more difficult versions the acrobat approached the bull head on, catching it by the horns; the animal threw its head back, lifting the man into the air to perform a somersault over its back. Another leap, probably the most frequently performed, was basically the same as the last, but performed in three stages: the acrobat seized the bull by the horns, was thrown into the air and landed on the animal's back either on his hands or his feet. The man then leapt up into the air again, performing another somersault, to land with arms outstretched on the ground behind the animal. A Knossos fresco shows all three stages of this leap, and similar examples can be seen on other fragments. The remains of these frescoes show that the palace of Knossos was originally decorated with several bands of stucco relief depicting these bull sports. Torsa of ivory and gold figurines, larger and smaller, have also been found there, representing acrobats at various stages of this performance. One of them portrays the taut body, and alert expression of a man at the climax of the vault, and there are similar moments preserved on seal stones.

These leaps were certainly dangerous for the performing acrobats, even if the bull was partially tamed and the horns filed down to minimize the risk. The Cretan artists did not hide the fact that a tragedy occurred fairly frequently. The artist who decorated the "sporting" rhyton with scenes of

A large audience sitting on the "grandstand" or standing on the terraces watch a ceremonial performance at the palace. Detail of a fresco from the palace in Knossos, around 1500 B.C.

Bronze statuette of a running bull with an acrobat landing on its back. From the palace in Knossos, around 1500 B.C.

An unsuccessful jump over the running bull. The acrobat is caught by the bull's horns. Detail from the "sports" rhyton from the palace in Hagia Triada, Crete, around 1500 B.C.

boxing matches immortalized one such moment in the second of his four bands of relief. The acrobat, facing up to the charging bull, was unable to complete his bold leap, and his body was caught on the horns of the enraged animal.

Formally speaking, these acrobatic leaps over the back of bulls, performed as part of the Cretan festivals, were derived from the practical skills of bull-hunting. The purpose of the hunt was to catch the wild bull alive and uninjured, and so lassoes and nets were used. Often, however, the skilled hunter would jump onto the bull's back, seizing the horns and twisting the head to one side, rendering the animal powerless. The shepherds of Thessaly, and probably others, used the same method to catch bulls. The Cretan hunters hung on to the bull until it was secured with cords, and a hunting scene of this kind is depicted on an ivory pyx and a gold Cretan goblet found at Vaphio, in Greece. On the latter the bull has been caught in a net, while a second is escaping and a third is charging the two men who are trying to catch it. It has shaken one of them off its back and is charging the other, its sharp horns goring the helpless body.[56]

In the Cretan festivals this sort of hunting was presented in the form of vaults over charging bulls, thus transforming a practical activity into a sport. At first the vaulters seem to have been skilled hunters, or shepherds and drovers; as the sport evolved and made greater demands on the performers, they must have been replaced by professional acrobats specially trained in the sport. Both men and women took part, and seem to have enjoyed considerable social prestige.

The Cretan bull sports were more than acrobatic performances however; they were a way of expressing certain ideas about the world, and presenting them in ceremonial form. They were religious in character, and to form some idea of their content a comparison can be drawn with the Neolithic cults illustrated particularly in Çatal Hüyük in Asia Minor, as well as learning from the art of the Minoans themselves, and clues in Greek mythology.

In the caves of Crete, which, together with the hill-tops, were the religious centres in Neolithic times, figurines of men and animals have been found alongside bulls' horns and the double axe. The history of these religious symbols dates back to the time of the Çatal Hüyük shrines. In the

Hunting wild bulls. The huntsman, who has leapt onto the bull's back to pull it to the ground by the horns, is falling. Another one is crushed by the bull's horns. Golden cup from Vaphio in Greece, Cretan work, around 1500 B.C.

palace shrines to which the religious ritual was transferred, however, new gods appeared, headed by the Mother Goddess.[57] Women were equally important in society and religion. The queen was the direct representative of the goddess, and the priestesses played an important part in the ritual sacrifices, danced ecstatic dances and drove ceremonial chariots in the religious processions. Women even took part in the acrobatic bull sports.

The Cretan Mother Goddess was closely linked to the animal world, especially to the bull, and this connection was preserved in Greek mythology. Minos, king of Crete, was the son of Europa, daughter of the Phoenician king, who was carried off from Asia to Crete by Zeus, in the shape of a bull. Pasiphaë, the wife of Minos, fell in love with the bull-god who came out of the sea. The fruit of this union was the Minotaur, half man and half bull, who lived in the palace of the double axe, the Labyrinth of Crete, and to whom human sacrifices were made. In both cases, a "sacred marriage", the physical union of man and god takes place. The God's assumption of animal form shows the influence of earlier hunting cultures. Women acrobats vaulting over the bulls may have been a symbol of this "sacred marriage", the form in which these ancient religious myths were handed down.

In Minoan religion itself, however, the bull was not worshipped; quite the contrary, in fact. The bull played a subordinate role in the ritual, as the beast of sacrifice and the participant in the ceremonial sports. This is reflected in the animal's form and function in Minoan art. The bull is never shown complete, but represented by the head or the horns, a symbol of the trophy remaining after sacrifice. The ritual utensils were shaped like bulls' heads or horns, and so were jewellery, vases, goblets and other articles of daily use. The horns — sometimes as high as two metres — were used in simplified form as a striking motif in architecture.

The special symbol of Minoan religion was the double axe, used as the ritual instrument when the bull was sacrificed, a fact which is stressed by the appearance of the axe between the bull's horns whenever it is depicted in connection with the animal's head. The double ax, the symbol of the sacrifice, was itself worshipped, and there are indications that it was also a personification of the god overcoming and killing the bull.[58] These developments seem to reflect the involved process by which the animal gods of hunting cultu-

Women in a chariot drawn by griffins. A religious scene from a sarcophagus from Hagia Triada, Crete, around 1500 B.C.

Emblem for chariot in the Linear B script. Detail of a clay tablet from the palace in Knossos.

res were displaced by the new gods of both the shepherds and farmers.

All these phenomena found expression in the programme of Cretan festivals. Unlike the Neolithic festivals of Çatal Hüyük, where the animal god, a giant bull, was the divine onlooker in whose honour the festival was held, in Minoan civilization the bull lost this privileged position and was merely a sacrificial animal. In the bull sports, too, it was subordinated to the role of vaulting apparatus for the acrobats. Leaping over bulls symbolized the hunting and taming of the wild animal, and the conquering of the old bull-god by new gods as well.

The same process is evident in the ritual sacrifice of the bull. In the "House of the High Priest", the decisive battle between the old and the new gods was fought out. The victory of the new gods was ensured by the binding of the bull, robbing it of strength; the decisive blow was struck with the double axe. The body was lifted on to the altar, and the blood, poured between two axe-heads, gave life to the new god. The sacrifice of a bull was an old form of expressing new ideas about the world and is attested in the religions of the Near East and Egypt.

Cretan bull sports seem to have evolved as the festival programme became richer; before being sacrificed, the bull was used for sport, and this in time became a performance in itself. The popularity of the sport was undoubtedly enhanced by the danger of the event, but neither death nor blood-letting was the actual point of the exercise. The performances were essentially displays of physical skill and beauty of movement. They came into being as an expression of Cretan civilization, and they passed with it.

These great public festivals were a striking feature of Minoan culture, and, despite their religious content, their primary function was as an exciting leisure entertainment. Their existence and their content reflected a society which was cradled in the enchanting environment of the Mediterranean. During its peaceful evolution warriors proved unnecessary, and women, the life-givers, were held in high esteem. The greatest enemy of this culture turned out to be the restless earth itself, with the dark blue waters of the sea around it, on which for centuries this mature civilization had been growing.

A warrior and driver on a chariot with two horses. From a tomb in Vaphio, Greece, Cretan work, 15th century B.C.

Right: Hunting with a chariot. Gold ring from a royal tomb in Mycenae, Cretan work, 15th century B.C.

THE GREEK WORLD

The Mycenaean Warriors

During the fourteenth and thirteenth centuries B.C. the focus of progress in the Aegean moved from Crete to the Greek mainland, where the Mycenaean civilization rose to its peak. Its centres were the palaces of Mycenae, Tiryns, Pylos, Thebes, Athens, Orchomenos and Iolcos in Thessaly. Settlements in the Mycenaean fashion are also attested on the islands of the Cyclades, Rhodes, and Cyprus, and on the coast of Asia Minor, at Miletus and Colophon. Strong Mycenaean influences can be traced in one of the strata of Troy (Troy VIIa). Mycenaean traders plied between Greece and Crete, Egypt, and in particular the Syrian-Palestinian coast and the shores of Asia Minor, whence they travelled inland as far as Babylonia and the Caucasus. Hittite archives refer to contacts with Mycenae, and the Ahhiyawa land is mentioned several times. In this name can be recognized the Greek term Achaeans, which was used at the time for all Greek tribes, bearers of the Mycenaean culture.

The culture was markedly military in character; the palaces, which later generations of Greeks believed had been built by mythical giants, the Cyclopes, were great fortresses protected by walls, built of huge stones. Here the kings, originally tribal chieftains, wielded absolute power over the surrounding countryside, and the monumental royal graves proclaim their might. The king of Mycenae held the supreme position among them.

Thousands of clay tablets, inscribed in Linear B script, have been found in the palace of Pylos, as in that of Knossos on Crete; the accounts recorded there show how the flourishing palace economy was run. Royal tombs, filled with gold, have been discovered, and masks, jewellery and painted vases. Among the principal finds were examples of the warrior's equipment – swords, daggers, shields, helmets, and armour made of bronze plates arranged in bands, to protect the whole body.

War scenes were a popular motif in the painted murals. The frescoes in the Pylos palace show well-armed Achaeans butchering a group of men clad in skins, and fighting groups and duels are often depicted on seal stones.

The meaning of the scene is not clear. It may show hunting with a chariot, but as it is a relief on a tombstone it may be a chariot race in honour of a deceased nobleman. A simplified visual treatment of war and later hunting with a chariot was widespread in the Near East. Here the dead warrior or animal under the horse are replaced by spiral decoration like the bird above the horse. Mycenae, 1580–1500 B.C.

Warriors in horse-drawn chariots are also represented. One of the most famous campaigns was the victorious siege of Troy at the end of the thirteenth century. A similar victory is dramatically portrayed on a rhyton from Mycenae, showing Achaean warriors landing and swimming for the shore to take the fortress by storm, while its defenders are firing at them with bows and arrows, and slings.

The war-like character of the Mycenaean civilization was also reflected in the religious thought, although marked traces of Minoan culture existed. Tablets from Pylos and from Knossos confirm that the Mycenaean Greeks were already worshipping some of the gods well-known in later Greek religion, including Zeus, Hera, Poseidon, Artemis, Athena, Dionysos, Ares and others. In Greek mythology many of these figures are closely bound up with the Cretan ambiance. Like the Minoans, the Mycenaeans followed the cult of the goddess called Mistress of the Horses on Pylos tablets. A goddess symbolized by a figure-of-eight or a bicircular shield on a mast was also worshipped. In frescoes recently revealed in Mycenae this is surmounted by a military helmet.

The noble huntsman on a chariot shoots the game with a bow and arrows, protected by a man with an axe. The wounded bull charges the chariot. An ivory pyxis from Enkomi, Cyprus, 13th century B.C.

Many features of the highly developed Minoan ritual were adopted in Mycenaean religion, including the shapes of ritual vessels and some of their religious symbols. The double axe, however, lost its sacral significance in this new environment and was regarded as no more than an instrument with which the sacrificial animal was killed. The rites themselves were performed by priests attired in rich vestments and priestesses wearing the ancient Minoan costume, leaving their breats exposed. On frescoes from Pylos, Tiryns and Thebes women are shown carrying various objects in religious processions; the influence of Minoan culture can be seen clearly in their shapes, their head-dresses, and their full skirts, with the chest uncovered.

Nevertheless, the Mycenaean ritual was a much simpler one, confined to the basic rites which culminated in sacrifice. The only form of physical activity which can be deduced from the fragmentary source materials is communal orgiastic dances, in which all present, both men and women, took part. The rites do not appear to have been great religious celebrations nor are there any portrayals in art of an audience or a performance, all of which suggests that public festivals were not an aspect of life in Mycenaean times.[1] Nevertheless it can be assumed that various simple forms of sporting competition were enjoyed by the people, as the communal ecstatic dances were, even if they had no place in religious ritual.

In addition to scenes of war, Mycenaean art is rich in representations of the hunt, and in many cases, the scenes decorating swords from Mycenaean graves for example, the two are combined. Hunting took place in horse-drawn chariots and also on foot; the hunter in his chariot shot at the game with bow and arrows. The stereotyped hunting motif of Near Eastern art reappears, and is particularly marked in a relief carving from Cyprus, in which the chariot is driven by a man with a whip, while the hunter standing in the chariot is accompanied by a man on foot, who is armed with an axe. Large numbers of game are fleeing before the chariot, including goats and cattle, and a bull, wounded by an arrow, is charging furiously at the moving vehicle, head down to attack.

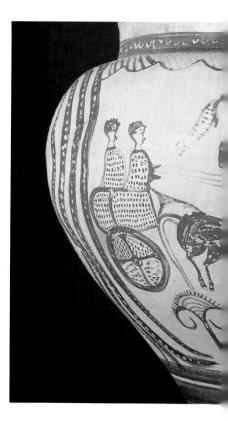

In some of these very sketchy treatments of the hunting motif, as on the Mycenaean steles, the chariots could also be racing, but this is by no means certain. There are frequent references to chariot races in Greek mythology, however, and Homer's epics provide plentiful evidence of their existence. The important place assigned to chariot races in later Greek festivals also indicates not only their popularity, but a long-standing tradition. It, therefore, seems reasonable to suppose that chariot racing was known in Mycenaean Greece.

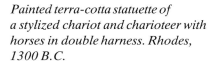

Painted terra-cotta statuette of a stylized chariot and charioteer with horses in double harness. Rhodes, 1300 B.C.

Below: A chariot with two charioteers. Painting on a Cypro-Mycenaean amphoroid krater. The vessel was found in a tomb and it may be that the painting shows a chariot race in honour of the deceased. Enkomi, Cyprus, mid 14th century B.C.

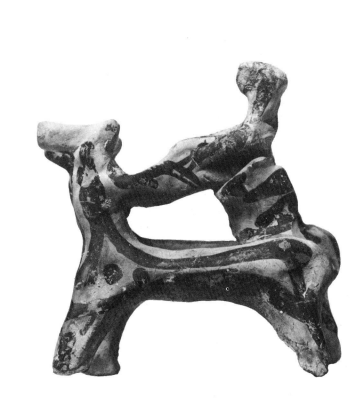

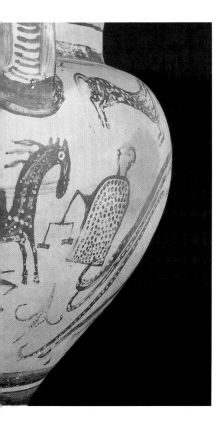

The essential technical knowledge certainly existed. The use of chariots drawn by horses, brought to the Aegean from Asia Minor as early as the turn of the seventeenth to sixteenth centuries, was wide-spread. They have already been discussed in the context of the religious processions of Minoan civilization, with women as chariot-drivers. In the Mycenaean world horse-drawn chariots were used primarily for war. The Knossos tablets record palace stores of over a thousand pairs of wheels and more than 350 chariots of two different types. There are also records of the recipients both of chariots and horses. The stores at Pylos contained over 200 pairs of wheels. Clay models of chariots have been found in Thessaly and elsewhere, which seem to have been children's toys.

The art of the region allows us to distinguish four types of chariot in use in the Aegean. There were chariots of Near Eastern, Hittite type, and there were also specifically Aegean chariots which apparently spread to the Near Eastern mainland at the same time. The commonest type was the two-wheeled chariot, like that used by the Egyptians, whose shape was adapted for the ideogram "chariot" in Linear B script. The fragmentary finds of chariots, in Mycenae and Tiryns, suggest that the light Egyptian Rosellini chariot was also known. Local breeders provided some of the horses but the standard was not very high, and it was necessary to import horses from the Near East, from Troy for example, and also from Thrace.[2]

Chariot racing, however, represents an intricate form of physical activity, which can only be the result of a long cultural tradition. In form it was derived from the aristocratic sport of hunting, with which it is linked by the use of horse-drawn vehicles. This close connection makes it particularly

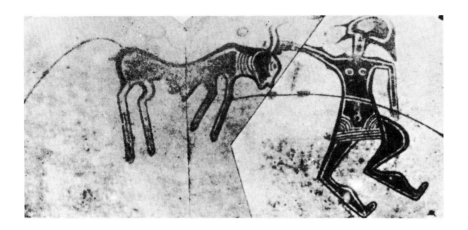

A bull-fight. Painting from Cyprus, beginning of the 1st millennium B.C.

difficult to distinguish between hunting and chariot-racing scenes. With racing, however, the significant difference was that the course was limited in space and time, and the competitive factor increased the speed. These changes moved racing still further from the reality of the hunt.

The Mycenaean Greeks adopted the aristocratic form of hunting in horse-drawn chariots from the cultures of the Near East; it is most unlikely that the transformation of hunting into a highly cultivated sport took place in Mycenaean civilization. It is much more probable that chariot racing, too, was taken over from the cultures of the Near East, particularly from Asia Minor and Syria. Mycenaean civilization, however, offered significant social conditions in which outside influences could be assimilated and further evolved.

The rulers of Mycenaean palaces formed a highly privileged and select social group within the Achaeans as a whole. Bound by ties of blood and marriage, they kept up lively social contacts and, of course, joined together in military ventures. Their social equality was a practical basis on which to compete in displays of prowess. Later Greek sources imply that they participated in varied forms of duel, and that chariot racing was another type of contest.

Painted sarcophagus. Lower left may be a scene from a chariot race with gesticulating spectators in the background. Hieropytna, Crete, 13th century B.C.

Boxers. Painting on a krater from Cyprus, 12th century B.C.

Like the hunt, chariot racing was a socially exclusive form of entertainment. It is clear from Greek myths, too, that races were used to settle disputes within this privileged group, and were also undertaken in honour of the memory of the dead.

Around the year 1200 B.C. Mycenaean civilization came to an end. Varied peoples, called in Egyptian sources the "Peoples of the Sea", poured into the Aegean, Asia Minor and Syria and even menaced Egypt. This vast migration of people is thought to have destroyed the civilization of Mycenae and cast Greece into darkness for about three centuries. The Mycenaean palaces were destroyed, economic life disrupted, and society disintegrated. People fled to the mountains or to islands, especially Cyprus, for refuge. Writing was forgotten, and thus the links with the past were broken.

Yet, in spite of this profound destruction, a certain continuity between the world of Mycenaean Greece and later Greek civilization persisted throughout these dark ages. It can be traced in pottery, where certain Mycenaean features were gradually transformed into the new Geometric style, but it was Greek oral poetry that forged the strongest link. Wandering bards, *aoidoi,* travelled all over the Greek-speaking world, telling of the glory of time past, of the lives and deeds of the heroic Achaeans.

Impulses from the Near East were particularly important for the new civilization now forming. Recent archaeological excavations in Northern Syria, the site of present-day Al Mina, have proved that close contact was established between the new Greek settlers and the mature civilization of Syria from the ninth century B.C. It was here that the Greeks learned new metallurgical skills, in particular iron-working, and were in touch with the rich cultural heritage of other lands of the Near East. The latest reports suggest that it may also have been here that eighth century Greeks became acquainted with the North Syrian Aramaic script that became the basis for their own new alphabet.[3]

Young man about to leap into the water from a boat. Painting on an Attic black-figure amphora, late 6th century B.C.

Homer's Sports Reporting

In the eighth century B.C., on the coast of Asia Minor, where new Greek settlements were gradually appearing, Homer gave epic form to the ballads of the *aoidoi,* in the *Iliad* and the *Odyssey.* Both poems are bound up with the Mycenaean Greeks' campaign against Troy. The life described by Homer is seen only superficially, and the distant past is mixed up with the far more primitive conditions of the poet's own day. Nevertheless, excavation of the Mycenaean palaces and settlements has confirmed that Homer's epics reflect the historical reality of a time long past.

His heroes are kings, *basileis,* who rule the different Greek tribes. Surrounded by their aristocratic followers they spend their days making war, hunting, drinking, dancing, listening to the *aoidoi* and contesting their prowess in sport. A lively piece of reporting in the *Iliad,* almost 700 lines long, describes in detail the sporting contests organized in mourning for the dead hero Patroclus.

The event took place on one of the last 35 days of the ninth year of the siege of Troy, the period described in the *Iliad.* After the ritual sacrifices and the ceremonial banquet, the dead body of Patroclus burned on its funeral pyre and a cairn was placed on the urn holding his ashes. The mourners were preparing to disperse when Achilles, "the fleet of foot", Patroclus' closest friend and the great hero of the Greeks, announced that races would be held in honour of the dead man − *Athla epi Patroklo.*[4]

On the plain near the sea, the aristocratic company took their seats and Achilles, who was both organizer and umpire of the races, had prizes brought, ready for the winners. These were the spoils of war − tripods, cauldrons, horses, mules, bulls, female prisoners, and "grey iron".

Chariot racing, two-in-hand, was first on the agenda. There were five competitors: Eumelus, Diomedes, Menelaus, King of Sparta, Antilochus of Pylos and Meriones of Crete. The name of each of the competitors is accompanied by a note on the origin of his horses. Before the race began, Nestor, the ruler of Pylos, gave his son Antilochus some final words of advice

– his horses, bred at home, were not of the best, and he would have to think out his strategy carefully if he wanted to win.

Then the competitors mounted their chariots and placed their lots in a helmet, from which Achilles drew the order in which they would line up for the start. Achilles also fixed the point round which they would turn their chariots for home. This was a narrow gully round a dried-out tree, against which two white rocks rested. Achilles appointed an umpire to watch the proceedings and see that all went well, and then the race began.

The drivers raised their whips, lashed their horses' backs with the reins and shouted as they set off. The horses' manes streamed in the wind and clouds of dust rose from their flying hooves. The whole group was drawing close to the turning point with its dangerous gully, and just before reaching it they all put on speed. The two fastest chariots shot ahead, those of Eumelus and Diomedes, and gained a clear lead over their rivals, Eumelus first and Diomedes so close behind that Eumelus could feel the horses' breath on his back. It looked as though Diomedes was about to overtake him, when he suddenly dropped his whip. His horses lost speed and Eumelus shot further and further ahead. Then he, too, met with an accident, the yoke broke, the shaft fell to the ground, and the horses scattered. In his fall Eumelus himself was injured in the elbow, nose, mouth and forehead. Diomedes took advantage of this situation to pick up his whip, drive round the broken chariot, and put on speed. This made his victory certain.

A tough fight for second place was being fought between Menelaus and Antilochus. Menelaus was ahead of Antilochus, who so longed to win that he threatened his horses with death on the spot if they did not manage to pass Menelaus. The two rivals were entering the gully at the turning point; Menelaus slowed down to avoid a crash, but Antilochus abused the situation and shot ahead, wildly ignoring Menelaus' warning not to overtake him at this dangerous spot. Antilochus gained a lead of "a discus throw", but the outcome was still uncertain. Menelaus had the better horses, and on the level stretch he soon drew close to Antilochus.

Meanwhile the onlookers were waiting for the first chariots to appear and a violent quarrel broke out as to who was the winner. Idomeneus, king of Crete, declared that it was Diomedes, while Aias of Locris swore that Eumelus was first and shouted insultingly at Idomeneus, calling him a fool, who was too old to be able to see so far. This naturally enraged Idomeneus, and he began swearing at Aias, saying he was the worst of all Greeks, and incapable of anything but quarrelling. He challenged him to bet a tripod or a cauldron on which of them was right. Aias sprang to his feet and made to attack Idomeneus, but Achilles intervened and told them to calm down, and to sit and watch instead of quarrelling, because the chariots were coming in.

Diomedes was the first to arrive, with his Trojan-bred horses. He dismounted, and flung himself on the prize awaiting him – a young woman prisoner and a Trojan cauldron. Antilochus came next, with Menelaus only a neck behind him. He had rapidly reduced the lead Antilochus gained by his unscrupulous behaviour at the turning point, and had the course been longer he would certainly have passed his rival. The fourth to arrive was Meriones, who was "a spear's throw" behind the rest, because, besides having the slowest horses, he was also the poorest rider. The last to arrive was Eumelus, on foot, dragging his broken chariot behind him and driving his horses in front of him. When Achilles saw him in this forlorn state he felt sorry for him and offered him the second prize, a mare in foal. This angered Antilochus, who had put so much into winning second place, and now started shouting that he didn't care a fig for Eumelus' broken chariot, nor was he going to be robbed of his rightful prize. Turning to Achilles, he suggested that if he was so

Two boxers. Painting on the neck of a Geometric vase, 8th century B.C.

*Detail from a funeral scene, showing either a procession or a chariot race in honour of a dead warrior.
A Geometric tomb krater from the middle of the 8th century B.C.*

84

sorry for Eumelus he should give him some of the loot which his tent was full of. Achilles laughed and did, indeed, give Eumelus a special prize — a bronze breastplate.

This argument settled, Menelaus began to attack Antilochus, accusing him of winning by cunning and saying that the second prize was his by right. He demanded that Antilochus should swear, if he could, that he had not held him up at the turning point, either deliberately or out of cunning. Whereupon, Antilochus, driven into this corner, began to back down, admitting that he had acted thoughtlessly. He said that he did not want to lose Menelaus' friendship, and he offered him the prize. Menelaus was touched; he admonished Antilochus not to try to "cheat the better man" next time, but he forgave him, and, to show his generosity, refused Antilochus' offer and took the third prize of a cauldron.

The fourth prize of two talents of gold was won by Meriones, while the fifth, a two-handled goblet, which was unclaimed as Eumelus did not finish the race, was given by Achilles to old Nestor. It was meant as a compliment to his wisdom and a consolation in his old age, which no longer allowed him to take an active part in such races. Thus, in spite of all misadventures, the race ended in general satisfaction.

Other disciplines followed: boxing, wrestling, running, spear duels, discus throwing, archery and spear throwing. The handsome, well-built young Epeius entered for the boxing match, taking immediate possession of the mule offered as the prize, and threatening any possible rivals that he would "tear their bodies into little pieces and break all their bones". After a long silence Euryalus of Thebes took up the challenge; the two men put on their soldier's skirts, twisted straps round their fists and started the fight. Before long Epeius landed a decisive blow on his opponent's face, and his friends led Euryalus from the ring, spitting blood, and his head sagging.

Odysseus and Aias of Salamis entered the wrestling match; they stripped and grappled each other "like roof timbers". Dripping with sweat, muscles bulging and bones cracking, neither could throw the other and thus claim victory. The onlookers were beginning to get bored, and so Aias tried to lift Odysseus to liven things up; Odysseus was not taken by surprise, however, and he kicked his opponent in the knee and tripped him up. Aias fell, but so did Odysseus. This woke up the spectators and so Odysseus tried to lift Aias; he managed to move him, but not to lift him, and so he tripped him up and again both fell to the ground. When they grappled for the third time Achilles called the indecisive match to a draw. This satisfied both the contestants and they peaceably divided the prize between them: a large tripod

Late Geometric kantharos from Kerameikos showing games held to honour the memory of a dead warrior. Athens, end of the 8th century B.C.

Centre left: Man and woman, duel between men with swords, two animals tear at an armed man, lyre player accompanies a round dance for women. Bottom left: Armed contest, boxing, lyre player accompanies a dance for men.

cauldron worth twelve cows, and a girl skilled in handiwork, worth four cows.

Odysseus, Aias of Locris and Antilochus entered the running race. They stood in a line and Achilles measured the course. At the start Aias dashed ahead, with Odysseus close behind him, encouraged by loud cries of "Faster!" from the onlookers. Aias held on to his lead until almost at the winning post, where an unfortunate accident befell him — he slipped on some cow dung which had lain there since the sacrifices. As a result it was Odysseus who won, while Aias, "nose and mouth full of dung" and "spitting", vainly complained that the goddess Athena had deliberately tripped him up because Odysseus had always been her favourite. This attempt to blame his failure on the goddess aroused much laughter. Nevertheless he was also given a prize, a large fat bull, and Odysseus won a beautiful large silver mixing bowl from Phoenicia. Antilochus, who came in last, was to have won half a talent of gold, but because he accepted his defeat, smiling and joking in appreciation of Odysseus' skill as a runner, Achilles gave him another half talent.

Aias of Salamis and Diomedes faced each other, fully armed, for the spear duel; the aim was to penetrate the armour until the spear touched the body, the duel ending with the first sign of blood. Each attacked three times;

Aias aimed at his rival's shield, which was not dangerous, but Diomedes aimed above the shield, right at Aias' throat, and the onlookers feared for his life. The duel was interrupted, and the two divided the prize between them – a spear, shield and helmet. However, Achilles gave Diomedes the great silver-ornamented sword of Thracian origin, which was to have fallen to the one who drew the first blood.

For the discus throwing contest Achilles had brought out a large iron disc taken from the Trojans; it was to be both discus and prize for the winner. This object seems to have been an ingot of iron which, according to Achilles, would provide the winner with enough iron for a good five years. Of the four who entered the contest the first to try was Epeius, but he was greeted with laughter when he swung and threw the disc. The second, Leonteus, was better, but Aias of Salamis, who was the third to throw, landed his disc beyond all the marks set up to measure the distance. Polypoites then picked up the disc, threw it lightly in the air, and the onlookers gasped in amazement as it flew, turning like a boomerang, and fell far beyond the marked circle. Polypoites' companions carried the ingot to his ship.

Achilles had a ship's mast set up in the sandy soil, with a pigeon tied to it by one foot, for the archery contest. The two entrants drew lots from a metal helmet, and Teucrus won first shot. His arrow hit the ribbon and the pigeon flew off. The second man, Meriones, snatched the bow from Teucrus and aimed at the bird, as it circled in the clouds. His arrow was so straight and swift that it struck the bird in the chest, shot right through its body and came down to bury its tip in the ground at the archer's feet. The wounded bird settled on the mast and then fell, dead, to the ground, watched by the admiring onlookers. So Meriones victoriously carried away ten double axes, while Teucrus was given ten ordinary ones.

The famous François vase was made by the potter Ergotimus and the painter Kleitias with scenes from the life of Achilles and his father Peleus: a Calydonian boar hunt, chariot races, the wedding of Peleus, procession of goddesses, the death of Achilles. Athens, 575 B.C.

Below: Detail from the François vase. Four-in-hand races held by Achilles in honour of the memory of his dead friend Patroclus. The cauldron and tripod under the horse's hooves are evidently prizes for the contestants.

Two competitors matched their skill in throwing the spear: Agamemnon, King of Mycenae and Commander-in-chief of all the Greek tribes besieging Troy, and Meriones of Crete. Achilles did not want the contest to take place, saying that everybody knew Agamemnon was better than all the others, and that he had so often shown his strength and proved his supreme skill with the spear. According to Achilles, he unquestionably had the right to the chief prize, which was a cauldron decorated with flowers, the value of a bull. Then, with Agamemnon's permission, Achilles gave Meriones the second prize, a bronze spear. When all the contests were over, Achilles presented a "lovely prize" to Menelaus' herald, Talthybius. When Menelaus had stood up after the chariot race to accuse Antilochus, Talthybius had

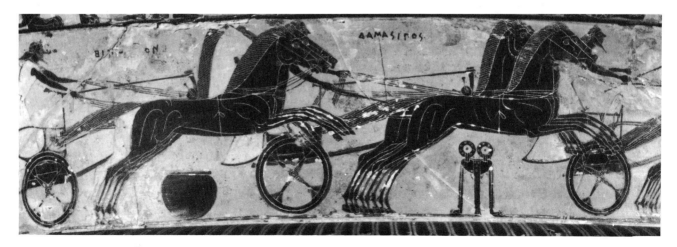

placed the sceptre in his hand and called upon those present to be silent for Menelaus to speak.

Today, almost three thousand years later, Homer's masterly description and the atmosphere of excitement he evokes are still fascinating. Dramatic incidents alternate with humorous episodes; the factual description of the course of each event is interspersed with poetic similes drawn from everyday life and work, and from nature itself.

All the contests are closely linked with military skills, yet there are already a number of features which point to the future development of individual sporting disciplines. The fact that the prizes were all drawn from the spoils of war is reflected in the general term *aethla,* or *aethlia,* from which the word for a match or contest, *aethlon* (s.), was derived, as well as the verb to compete, *aethleo* or *aethleuo.* In later Greek the word *athla* (abbreviated from *aethla*) was used for such contests, from which come the modern words, athlete and athletics.

Homer uses the word *agon,* a general term for a meeting place, in reference to where the contests were held. Nor does he distinguish between the area set aside for the onlookers and the place where the active participants performed. Gradually the word *agon* came to mean not only sporting contests but competitions of all kinds, in music, recitation, oratory, and so forth. The term has survived in modern European languages, for example in the word agonistic, meaning competitive.

Special terms were developed for certain contests: "wrestling", *palaismosyne;* "boxing", *pygmachie* or *pygme;* "running race", *dromos.*

In addition to the simple disciplines of wrestling, boxing and running, weapons and military skills were used in some contests, such as spear duelling and throwing, archery and chariot racing. In others there were special requisites, such as the iron discus, or a bird tied to a mast to serve as a target.

Scene from the funeral games in honour of the dead Patroclus. Two chariots are approaching the finish and the spectators on the graded stand show their excitement. The name of the organizer of the races, Achilles, can be seen above on the extreme right. Painting on a cauldron by the painter Sophilus. Athens, around 580 B.C.

Stand with excited spectators. Detail from the scene below.

Scene from a festival: Spectators watching the performance of acrobats on horseback accompanied by the music of a double flute. Painting on a black-figure amphora. Athens, middle of 6th century B.C.

In boxing, the military skirt was used for protection, as well as special straps of oxhide to cover the fists. Markers were used to measure the length of the discus throw and in chariot races the starting line was marked, as well as the turning point, round which contestants drove before returning to the umpires' stand. Foot races were run from one point, indicated by a column, to another.

Certain rules do seem to have existed. In wrestling the winner was the one who threw his opponent to the ground. In boxing, blows were aimed primarily at the face, and the match ended when either man was in no state to continue. The spear duel ended with the first blood drawn. The order of entry in chariot races, archery and also discus throwing was determined by lot.

Menelaus' accusation of unscrupulous behaviour on the part of Antilochus also suggests that some rules about fair play existed.

The contests which Homer describes took place after an official funeral ceremony, but it is clear from the way in which Achilles' proposal was so easily accepted, and from numerous references in Homer's epics and in Greek mythology, that games held in honour of aristocratic heroes were not unusual. The games in honour of Patroclus were personally arranged by Achilles, his closest friend, who was both patron and organizer of the event. It was he who set the course for the foot race and the chariot race, it was he who offered the prizes from his own war booty, and he who was the principal umpire. It was only for the chariot race that he appointed another special umpire.

The contests were essentially duels, and where there were more than two competitors, as in the chariot race, the foot race and discus throwing, the events were broken up into duels. An outright winner was not called for; a match could be stopped if it went on too long; the spear duel was interrupted for fear of mortal injury and the spear throwing contest did not even take place. No clear distinction was made between winner and loser as every entrant received a prize of some sort. The only exception was the discus throwing contest, in which the only prize offered was the discus itself. Moreover, the last man to arrive in the foot race was given a larger prize than expected for accepting defeat with such good humour. Similarly, Eumelus, who did not even complete the chariot race, was given a special award, and old Nestor, who took no part, also had a prize. Agamemnon, King of Mycenae, won first prize for his prowess in battle, and, unlike the umpire in the chariot race, who received no reward, Menelaus' herald was given a prize for a purely routine formality. The purpose of his prize was simply to enhance the royal glory of the king of Sparta, who was second in importance only to Agamemnon of Mycenae in the Greek army.

The games in honour of Patroclus concerned only a small social circle of kings and princes. They were primarily an occasion for a display of physical skills, by privileged actors, who were performing to an audience to gain admiration for their courage and expertise. The social equality of the performers made possible the contests of skill, but as soon as this was disturbed, no contest could take place. This was the case in the spear throwing contest, which the supreme commander of all the Greek armies entered, for there could be no equal partner to oppose him.

The agonistic principle led to greater and greater efforts to win, and increased the dramatic excitement. Although the performers represented the cream of Greek society, they were greedy to win and anxious for their prizes; impetuous, quarrelsome, vain, sometimes childlike in their naivety, sometimes good and wise. The same emotions swayed the spectators, too, human and divine. Not only did the gods follow the competitions, but they used their divine powers to intervene, for each one had a favourite among the performers; their protégés must be helped and their rivals hindered. It was Apollo, for example, who knocked the whip out of Diomedes' hand when he was leading; in revenge the goddess Athena broke up Eumelus' chariot and put him out of the race. She also gave nimbleness to the limbs of Odysseus and was the cause of Aias' fall. In the archery contest, Meriones promised Apollo a lamb, thus ensuring the god's aid and the defeat of Teucrus, who was neglectful of the gods.

Interpretation of the games is one of the problems connected with the Homeric epics. It is difficult to distinguish between the poet's invention and features which reflect the reality of the Mycenaean world, to trace the influence of Near Eastern cultures and finally, to determine how far the poems reflect the realities of Greek life in the eighth century B. C.[5]

The prizes given to the competitors, for example, show a high level of metal-working skills; in Homer's day these were centred in Urartu, which had rich mineral deposits. Besides the traditional artefacts of gold, silver and bronze, the new products made of iron were very highly valued indeed. The iron tripods and cauldrons, which can also be seen on Late Geometric Greek vases, seem to have been much in demand among the aristocracy of the period. The iron ingot which served both as discus and as prize in the discus throwing contest in the *Iliad,* illustrates the gradual spread of knowledge of the metal.

As for the sporting events themselves, the tradition of some of the activities seems to go back to the time of the Cretan palaces. The Cretans were regarded as exceptionally good dancers, as well as fast runners. The description of the games in honour of Patroclus, and several other such passages in the two Homeric epics, testify to the popularity of sporting contests for occasions other than funeral ceremonies, and for different social groups.[6] In the *Odyssey,* for instance, the festival staged by Alcinous, King of the Phaeacians, in honour of Odysseus, included contests in running, jumping, throwing the discus, wrestling and boxing. The competitors were drawn from the leading Phaeacian families, while the spectators came from all classes. Skill in one or other of the disciplines was taken for granted.[7] Again, when Odysseus returned to his native Ithaca disguised as a beggar, he was challenged to a boxing match by another beggar, Irus, and fought for the very plebeian prize of a blood sausage. In this eposide, boxing is presented as a sport for commoners.[8] Many scenes on Late Geometric vases show that in Homer's time sporting contests in similar disciplines were popular.[9]

The matter of chariot races is more complicated. There are several refe-references to the sport in the *Iliad.* Nestor, King of Pylos, tells how his father sent a four-in-hand to Elis in order to compete for a prize there. He himself was beaten in a chariot race as a young man, by twin brothers who rode together, one holding the reins and the other whipping up the horses, and his words of advice to his son, Antilochus, suggest experience of similar races in Pylos. Homer also mentions races held in Thebes, after the death of King Oedipus.[10]

In the games held in memory of Patroclus, the chariot races seem to have been the most attractive aspect of the whole event; they were held first, and attracted the greatest number of competitors. The description of them is also given prominence and takes up 373 lines, a good sixty per cent of the whole account. Homer's account seems to bring evidence that chariot racing was already known in Mycenaean times; his detailed and lively portrait, on the other hand, raises the question of whether he is describing more than just an orally preserved tradition. Chariot racing demanded a high degree of technical skill, and during the "dark centuries" the chariot itself fell into oblivion, which must have meant that not only the exact appearance of the vehicles, but the course of chariot races as well, were forgotten.

From the time of the destruction of the centres of Mycenaean civilization, throughout the period from the eleventh to the eighth century B.C., there is no evidence of the use of horsedrawn vehicles anywhere in the Aegean, except in Cyprus. They do not reappear until half way through the eighth century B.C. painted on Late Geometric vases. At first they are shown very imprecisely, which suggests that they were neither widely known nor used. It is not until the end of the eighth century B.C. that the chariot is shown realistically. At present the general opinion among scholars is that the Late Geometric chariots were not a development of the old Minoan-Mycenaean type, but a new vehicle of light construction, adopted by the Greeks, during the eighth century, from the Near East.[11]

The fall of the Mycenaean civilization and the disappearance of the

Achilles with his team of horses. Fragment of a black-figure kantharos made by the potter and painter Nearchus. Athens, 560–550 B.C.

chariot obviously brought an end to racing, although an awareness of the existence of the sport persisted in oral poetry. It was revived when the new type of chariot became common, and, here too, there would seem to be a Near Eastern influence at work. This influence can be traced in the proposal that the chariot races, held in honour of Patroclus, should take place on the old Trojan race track, in awareness of the old Trojan tradition of horse-breeding, and the fact that the victor, Diomedes, was driving Trojan horses.

Asia Minor and Syria also suffered from the invasion of the "Peoples of the Sea", who are believed to have overturned the Mycenaean civilization about the year 1200 B.C. and at the same time to have brought down the Hittite Empire and destroyed the coastal towns of Syria. Nevertheless, the links with the rest of the Near East helped to maintain cultural continuity and speeded up renewed economic and cultural advance. Important new states were formed in Asia Minor, first the Phrygian kingdom, and after its downfall, that of Lydia.

It was in Asia Minor and Syria that new riding techniques evolved during the eleventh and tenth centuries B.C., gradually superseding the use of chariots in wartime throughout the Near East. It seems clear, too, that it was from this region that the Greeks adopted the light racing chariot in the course of the eighth century, as a result of their close contact with the cultures of the Near East.[12] It has already been concluded, more than once, that this region is where chariot racing originated. It is, therefore, possible that it was here that the Mycenaean Greeks, like the Greeks of Homer's day, became familiar with the sport.

Homer's lively and colourful reporting of the games, especially his dramatic account of the chariot race, suggests that his exact and detailed description was more than the reflection of a centuries-old tradition; that it was an eye-witness account, by one who had ample opportunity to witness such races in his birthplace in Asia Minor.

The Ideal of Harmonious Personality

In the eighth century B.C., Greece witnessed the birth of a new stage in its evolution, one of peace, after centuries of upheaval and confusion. There were local wars, of course, but up to the year 500 B.C. no foreign invader threatened the independence of the country. The skill of writing was restored, and the haze of oblivion lifted. Creative impulses were once again free to develop, and in the course of the three dynamic centuries, known as the Archaic period, new forms of society were evolved.

In place of the royal palaces of Mycenaean Greece the city state, or *polis*, emerged. Independent city states grew up in the fertile valleys between the mountain ranges, urban centres with public and religious buildings, closely linked to an agricultural hinterland. At first, government was in the hands of the aristocracy, who had overcome the power of the kings, and the townspeople were craftsmen and tradesmen, whose numbers were constantly increasing. The *polis* was the source of dynamic evolution, influencing the character of Greek ideas, and creating the conditions for the emergence of the harmonious personality as the ideal.

In the sphere of Greek religion, men were already free agents. The gods ruled over nature and mankind, but they were by no means despots; they were in constant touch with human beings and themselves possessed many human features; they left man with enough freedom to act on his own. From the eighth century B.C. onwards, the appreciation of human individuality is evident in the increasing numbers of poets, artists and philosophers who emerged from obscurity to become household names.

In the early Archaic period, the eighth and seventh centuries B.C., physical culture was the privileged monopoly of the aristocracy and was similar in character to the culture of the Homeric kings. It was only the aristocrats who had the opportunity, and therefore the right, to acquire an all-round physical culture; they alone had the time and the means to enhance their physical strength and skill by purposeful training, to become expert in the use of weapons on horseback, or in a chariot. Exceptional physical fitness

Warriors and riders. Black-figure column krater in the Late Corinthian style, first quarter of 6th century B.C.

was necessary for an aristocratic way of life, filled as it was with preparations for war, hunting, duelling and racing. It was also a feature which distinguished the aristocracy from the rest of the population, an expression of their social superiority.

The language itself bears witness to this: an aristocrat was described as *agathos,* originally meaning "prepared for battle", and hence "brave". This bravery was the product of his training, his command of the most up-to-date weapons, and the speed of movement conferred by the use of a horse. The antonym was *kakos,* an "ordinary man", "untrained", and therefore "cowardly". Besides the word *agathos,* there were stronger terms, *agathos ex agathon,* "brave among the brave", and *aristos* (the superlative form of *agathos,* from which our word aristocrat is derived), "the bravest", which gradually came to mean "the best", in the sense of high-born.[13]

The qualities of such a hero were summed up in the word *arete.* Homer applied this word exclusively to the qualities attributed to a warrior, among them physical strength, skill in the use of weapons, and heroism in the fight.

Besides these physical qualities, psychological traits were also stressed, especially by Homer, like the cunning of Odysseus or the wisdom of Nestor. In the passage describing the education of the young Achilles, his tutor Phoenix claimed to have taught him not only the arts of war, but eloquence as well. Mentor, the tutor to the son of Odysseus, taught his charge moral behaviour and good manners. These qualities were not included in the idea of *arete,* but they were highly prized not only by Homer, but in the ranks of the Greek aristocracy as well.[14]

In the course of the seventh and sixth centuries B.C., profound changes took place in the social structure of the Greek city states. The aristocracy lost their privileged position and unlimited political powers. Changes in fighting techniques, causing the close formations of infantry, hoplites, to become the basis of the army, meant that they also lost their importance in this sphere. As a result of these changes, the aristocracy adopted a new life-style, which led to the emergence of a new set of values in this social class.

As the aristocracy could not assert itself in the new social reality it turned to alternative spheres. Physical culture became a tradition and one of the outward signs of social status. Skills which could no longer be proved in battle found their raison d'être in sporting contests, especially in such exclusive disciplines as equestrianism and chariot racing.

The majority of aristocrats, particularly the young ones, now lived purely private lives. Their free time was spent in exclusive clubs, *hetairiai,* at

banquets, *symposia,* with song and dance and love affairs, and in discussions about the meaning of life and the structure of human society. Their thoughts were now concentrated on man himself, his joys and sorrows, and they contemplated the human spirit. The new concepts of love and happiness found expression in lyric poetry with love verses and drinking songs, and meditative elegiac verse. A group of poets — Archilochus, Alcaeus, Sappho, Simonides, Xenophanes and many others — gave, through their poetry, a new dimension to the old aristocratic ideal of *arete*. Besides the cultivation of physical skills, it now incorporated refined social behaviour as well — the arts of conversation, recitation, song, dancing and the playing of musical instruments.[15]

The earliest Greek philosophers had tried to find an answer to the question of how the world came into existence, by the rational observation of natural laws; they also studied man and the evolution of society. Greek philosophers increasingly emphasized the importance for both man and society of such moral and spiritual qualities as justice, generosity, nobility of mind, and learning. These qualities were also brought into the meaning of the term *arete,* and considerably added to its significance.

The new conception of *arete* became the foundation of the education of aristocratic youth. At the end of the sixth century B.C. the philosopher and mathematician Pythagoras founded a school at Croton, where not only scientific research, but systematic physical education was part of the curriculum. This meant regular physical training, especially foot races and wrestling, as well as a special diet.

In the course of the seventh and sixth centuries, therefore, a new aristocratic ideal evolved, which called for a balance between physical and mental cultivation to ensure the development of the complete human personality. The ideal of *kalokagathia* was born, *kalos* meaning "beautiful", *agathos*, "good", "noble", and "learned". The ideal is first documented in the verse of the female poet Sappho, and later in the writings of Xenophon, Isocrates, and Herodotus, among others.[16]

When the rule of aristocrats ended a new phase of social and political development began, which made it possible for the aristocratic physical culture to be applied to other social conditions. This process took different forms in different city states, and the greatest contrast emerged between Sparta and Athens.

The Dorians, the last of the immigrating Greek tribes to reach the Peloponnese, settled in Sparta during the "dark ages". The newcomers destroyed the civilization they found and enslaved the native population; during the eighth century they continually attacked neighbouring Messenia, subjugating its inhabitants and turning them into helots.

Sparta itself remained an odd-man-out among the evolving city states of Greece. The breakdown of tribal society did not proceed as fast there as in other cities; the aristocracy was weak and the power of the kings persisted. The helots, several times more numerous than the Spartans proper, gave Spartan development a still more divergent character. An important role here was played by the Second Messenian War in the middle of the seventh century, when the Messenians rose in revolt against the Spartans to assert the independence of their own city state, as well as to recover their personal liberty. The revolt was all but successful and the Spartans had to exert an extreme effort to regain control of Messenia, mobilizing a large proportion of their own menfolk of all social groups and organizing them in a new form of military formation. This consisted of a phalanx of heavily-armoured foot-soldiers, or *hoplites*.

This battlefield solidarity had a direct effect on Spartan society. The aristocracy lost the few privileges it had and the idea that all Spartans were equal, as they had been in tribal society, gained a new lease of life. In the sixth century the principles of equality and unity, expressed now in terms of stern discipline, produced a thoroughly militaristic regime. The ideological herald of this development in the preceding century had been the poet Tyrtaeus, who formulated the Spartan variant of the concept of *arete*.

Tyrtaeus addressed the *hoplites* in verses which may in fact have served as marching-songs for the phalanxes. He called upon them to wage pitiless war against the Messenians and their struggle for liberty. Physical prowess in racing or wrestling, beauty, wealth and eloquence meant nothing to him; the one essential quality was courage on the battlefield, with no mercy for the foe. This for Tyrtaeus was the only true *arete*. Another *leitmotif* in Tyrtaeus' poems was the firm bond that ties the individual to his native community – Sparta. This was a combination of patriotism, awareness of common destiny, dependence on the collective, and the unconditional requirement to obey it and serve its interests. The highest expression of the individual's link with the *polis* was to die in its service. The *polis* in turn rewarded every such heroic warrior with its highest token of esteem – assured glory and immortality.

Successive wars, and the elevation of courage in battle to the paramount value in Spartan society, led to a peculiar system of state-sponsored physical training for the young, the *agoge*. The entire male youth of the city was organized into groups, which were subdivided according to age, and given

Spartan girl running dressed in a light sports tunic. Bronze statuette, Sparta, around 550 B.C.

Spartan girl running.
Her lively expression is typical in
Spartan art at the end of the Archaic
period. Bronze statuette, Sparta,
around 500 B.C.

special names. Carefully selected men of honour were entrusted with their training. Within each group senior boys, between the ages of fourteen and twenty, called *eirenes,* took charge, and the subdivisions of each year were put under lads of the same age. All the older menfolk of the city had the right to take part in the training, to watch, advise and even administer punishment.

The basic disciplines in this physical education were running, wrestling, discus-throwing and javelin-throwing. It is interesting to note that girls were subjected to similar training, aimed at making them fit mothers of the next generation.

The boys' education also featured a variety of hunting and war-games. Pausanias describes the organized contests among *eirenes* in a place called the *Platanistas:* "In fighting they use their hands, kick with their feet, bite, and gouge out the eyes of their opponents. Man to man they fight but in the mêlée they charge violently and push one another into the water."[17]

Later on ball-games were added to the system. In one kind of game two opposing teams struggled to get hold of the ball, in another they used special bent sticks. It was the older boys in particular who took part in them and their enthusiasm can be judged from the fact that they came to be called *sphaireis,* from *sphaira* meaning ball.

Another essential part of Spartan training was a variety of round dances and group dances accompanied by flute-music. One of the most celebrated, the *pyrrhiche,* was a battle-dance executed in full panoply with mock attack and defence, shooting of arrows and hurling of javelins.

In the earliest period the exercises took place in an open field outside the city. This was called the *dromos,* and since the word originally signified "running" one can infer that racing was one of the oldest sports. Later an arena was set up inside the city; this was termed the *palaestra;* its name indicates that *pale,* "wrestling", and other disciplines had now been added.

All-round toughness was one of the prime objects of Spartan education, as a passage in Plutarch testifies. He describes the training of the boys on the basis of rules ascribed to the legendary Spartan legislator, Lycurgus: "Their training was calculated to make them obey commands well, endure hardships, and conquer in battle. Therefore, as they grew in age, their bodily exercise was increased; their hands were close-clipped, and they were accustomed to going bare-foot, and to playing for the most part without clothes. When they were twelve years old, they no longer had tunics to wear, received one cloak a year, had hard, dry flesh, and knew little of baths and ointments; only on certain days of the year, and few at that, did they indulge in such amenities. They slept together, in troops and companies, on pallet-beds which they collected for themselves, breaking off with their hands − no knives allowed − the tops of the rushes which grew along the river Eurotas."[18]

The physical standards of the young men were assessed at festivities amounting to initiation, where their fitness to enter the society of mature citizens was put to the test. The rites were conducted at the temple of Artemis Orthia, a fertility goddess of ancient tradition. Remains of this temple, whose foundations have been assigned by archaeologists to the ninth century B.C., are still to be found in a remote clearing, now overgrown with vegetation, on the marshy bank of the Eurotas. In the course of the ceremony a group of youths would try to snatch a cheese from an altar defended by an opposing group, and whichever ended up in possession of the cheese was declared the winner. At a later period the young men were subjected to merciless whipping as a test of bravery.[19]

Another trial of this kind was the *krypteia.* Young Spartans were supposed to demonstrate their courage and maturity by attacking and killing some of the enslaved helots at night.[20]

In the late seventh and sixth centuries B.C., as Spartan society was progressively militarized, the training system was extended to adult men. They were subjected to severe exercises aimed at maintaining and enhancing

Left: Scene from a palaestra. Two pairs of young men, their hands tied with thongs, box under the supervision of a coach. One young man shows by raising his first finger that he is giving up. Painting on a black-figure cup by the painter Douris, Athens, around 470 B.C.

Ball game. The seated coach about to throw a coloured ball to three pairs of young men. Black-figure amphora, Athens, 540 B.C.

Three young men practising javelin-throwing under the supervision of a coach. Detail from a red-figure amphora from the potter Nicosthenes' workshop. Athens, around 525 B.C.

the physical strength and stamina acquired in youth. Spartan men spent most of their lives doing military training and were virtually professional soldiers.

The evolution of a militaristic regime had many remarkable consequences. The technical standards, toughness and above all variety of physical training methods produced a high level of individual efficiency, while the corporate discipline strengthened the collective. The power of Sparta accordingly grew apace and in the course of the sixth century B.C. she came to control almost the entire Peloponnese. By the end of the Archaic period Sparta was indisputably the strongest state in Greece.

The same system, however, placed severe limits on the individual's freedom, hampering his activity and nipping creative energies in the bud. Warfare became the only free field for initiative. The whole regime was held back by the petrification of the surviving elements of the tribal system and the suppression of any tendency towards the creation of private property. The use of coins made of precious metal was forbidden and contact with neighbouring cities prevented. The result was a decline in the crafts, fine arts and culture in general. From the sixth century B.C. onwards, despite her military power, Sparta began to lose her leading position in the economic and cultural progress of Greece.

The one-sided concentration of Spartan education on physical training, and its complete neglect of the intellect, was a factor leading to the stagnation of society. More significantly, stagnation started to affect the physical aspect of Spartan life as well: from around the turn of the seventh and sixth centuries the population began to fall. The constant wars that cost so many lives were clearly one reason, but another was the steady decline in the birth rate. Long-term military service undoubtedly produced a male society of extraordinary cohesiveness, which provided the basis of Sparta's strength. But it interfered with the natural rhythm of life and by disrupting the family unit did grave damage to the fabric of society. A paradoxical situation arose in which young women were trained to produce strong and healthy progeny, yet the number of children born was very low. Between one and two children was the family average and not even legislation exempting fathers of three from military service, and fathers of four from civic duties of any kind, could halt the downward trend of the population.[21]

Even the physical training system itself was far from ideal. The specific conditions of Spartan society, notably the artificial reduction of social

Running race with armour. The second runner has lost his shield. On the left a supervisor with a staff and a stick. Painting on a black-figure kylix, middle of 5th century B.C.

differentiation to a minimum, gave physical education a truly universal character. The other side of this coin was of course the fact that the Spartans themselves were a ruling group, enabled only by their physical training to maintain their exclusive control over a far more numerous oppressed and enslaved population.

Notwithstanding, the writers of the ancient world, particularly the historian Thucydides and the philosopher Plato, justifiably regarded Sparta as the cradle of physical training in all Greece. Almost all the city states adopted features of the Spartan system; its closest imitator, to judge from the fragmentary evidence, was another Dorian vity, Gortyn, on the island of Crete. There, too, boys and young men were divided into age groups and given an education consisting largely of exercises, wrestling, races of various kinds, hunting and war-games with and without weapons. Significantly, young and old were distinguished by names relating to running: adult men were called *dromeis* or "runners" to show that they could take part in the

Young men in a palaestra after training: One of them is having his injured foot treated by a boy, another is pouring oil from a vessel into his hand to rub it all over his body, a third is about to put on the clothes handed to him by a boy. Painting on a red-figure krater by Euphronius. Athens, around 510 B.C.

public races, while adolescents were *apodromoi,* who had to remain "outside the running". If skill in running was the chief criterion of maturity it must have played a major part in physical training.[22]

Even in those Greek city states where there was no state-organized physical education, such as Sicyon, Naxos, Croton, Athens and elsewhere, the example of Sparta influenced the technique of training; throughout the Greek world it served as a precept and incentive.

The militaristic character of Spartan physical education, with its exclusive aim of preparing men for war led, however, to a rejection of everything outside this aim, even of the sporting element. The ideological spokesman for Spartan militarism, the poet Tyrtaeus, had already relegated sport to a subordinate place in physical culture. This was clearly demonstrated at the ceremonial pageants of sporting prowess that were already being held in the Archaic period − the Olympic Games. Whereas throughout the seventh century B.C. Sparta's primacy in systematic training won her contestants the prize on almost every occasion, a sharp change occurred at the beginning of the following era. No sooner had the militaristic regime been perfected than Spartans disappeared from the lists of winners. By a dialectic contradiction, the very exclusiveness of Spartan concentration on military training, to maximize physical skill and resistance, undermined the city's progress in competitive sport. The moment when Sparta, in the sixth century B.C., attained the pinnacle of her expansion and power was also the moment when she began to lose her economic, cultural and even in part her political influence among the Greek city states, together with her long primacy in physical culture.[23]

From the late seventh century and especially the early sixth century B.C. onwards, it is Athens who is in the forefront of Greek progress, bringing new and remarkable innovations in many fields.

The history of Athens exhibits from the early times a significant continuity with the Mycenaean age. Even today one can see remains of Cyclopean walls on the Acropolis and Mycenaean motifs persisted for a long time in Athenian pottery. Their simplified primitive patterns changed in the middle of the eleventh century B.C. into the Protogeometric style which is

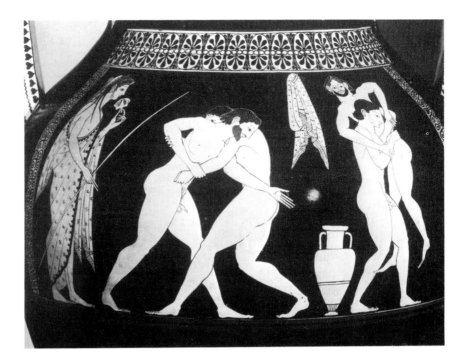

Wrestlers. Detail from the painting on a red-figure amphora from the potter Andocides' workshop. Athens, 520 B.C.

the direct ancestor of the Geometric ceramic art of the early Archaic period. However slender the cultural thread that extended back to the Mycenaeans across the dark ages, it made for faster progress in Athens and continuity with the past.

As for her political development, Athens had abolished the kingship at the start of the archaic period and all power became concentrated in the hands of the aristocracy. The social tensions that built up in Athens through the second half of the seventh century B.C. because of the city's rapid expansion and consequent social differentiation, were solved in a way almost exactly contrary to Sparta's. Where that city tried artificially to put a brake on natural progress, Athens witnessed the release of new forces claiming their rights and demanding to see them implemented in political life. The process naturally involved a certain amount of tentative experiment and severe internal conflicts.

Pankration. One of the pankratiasts seems to have kicked his opponent who has caught his leg and is tilting him backwards. A further part of the scene shows the supervisor with a stick following the match. Painting by the painter Epictetus II on a Panathenaic amphora from the potter Kleophrades' workshop. Athens, 500—490 B.C.

One way of liberating these forces was through reform. Its greatest and most typical exponent was the thinker, poet and statesman Solon. Elected archon, the highest official in the state, for the year 594 B.C. Solon used his position to bring about profound changes in the political and social structure of Athens. He classified the citizens of Athens not according to social origin, but to property, under four separate categories. This enabled wealthy citizens to participate in political power, while ensuring at least minimum rights for the poor citizens. His reforms affected only citizens of Athens, of course, and were not applicable to women, foreigners, and, least of all, slaves. Solon advocated the harmonious development of society within a framework of law and order and opened the way for a novel form of society — Athenian democracy.[24]

The result of Solon's reforms was a sudden outburst of creative energy in which physical culture held an important place. On the technical side many features were taken over from Spartan physical training, but the underlying principles were very different, being derived from the new aristocratic ideal of *arete*. Besides physical prowess, this ideal comprised a number of moral and spiritual qualities, and it was the Athenians who stressed these moral aspects of *arete*.

As the aristocracy lost its privileged position and political rights were granted to all Athenian citizens, the aristocracy also lost its monopoly of physical culture; this right, one of the aspects of political privilege, now belonged to all citizens. Slaves, who had no political rights, were, however, also excluded from this sphere. One of Solon's laws states explicitly: "Slaves should not undergo training, nor anoint themselves with oil in the palaestra."[25]

Only fragmentary evidence exists of how this right to physical education was actually implemented in the sixth century B.C. Although it was the right of every citizen, it can be assumed that only the affluent exercised it. These were the men who had access to political office and could afford the expense of education for their sons, for Athens differed from Sparta in that it made education the private responsibility of the parents.

The *palaestrae,* where this education was offered, were probably private schools set up and run by specialized teachers, *paidotribai.* Particularly wealthy citizens may have had a *palaestra* of their own, at home, for their sons; Athenian girls were allowed no part in these activities.

In addition to the *palaestrae* there were *gymnasia,* a name derived from *gymnos,* which Homer used to mean "unarmed" and later came to mean "without an outer garment", and ultimately, "naked". At first, boys exercised lightly clad in the *gymnasium,* later they were naked. Unlike the *palaestra* the *gymnasium* was a public institution, supervised a *gymnasiarchos* who was responsible for its proper conduct and was rewarded with public honours for good administration. These *gymnasia* may have been designed for military training; they were certainly used to prepare young men for public appearances of various kinds. Their association with religious rites is confirmed by their siting near temples and centres of religious worship in the cities.

The evidence supplied by archaeological excavation and literary research places the first Athenian *palaestrae* and *gymnasia* in the sixth century B.C., and indeed the three oldest *gymnasia* are known by name — the Academy, the Lyceum, and the Cynosarges.[26]

From the middle of this century onwards the development of physical culture in Athens can be followed in a different medium, the fine arts, vase painting in particular. The scenes here preserved compensate in some measure for the patchiness of the literary evidence, and offer a vivid picture of life in the *palaestrae.* They portray trainers with long staffs, supervising and

An athlete with halteres in his hands and the wreath of victory on his head. Painting on a red-figure vase, Athens, 510 B.C.

Scene showing contestants in various
branches of sport: a jumper with
halteres, a man about to hurl
a javelin, a discus thrower and
another javelin thrower.
Panathenaic vase from the potter
Euphiletus' workshop. Athens, 520 B.C.

Two teams of young men playing
a ball game with bent sticks. Relief
on Themistocles' wall, Athens,
around 510 B. C.

instructing their pupils. Wrestling is the sport most often illustrated, while
other disciplines appear more sporadically — running, running in armour,
discus throwing, jumping, boxing and the *pankration,* a combination of
boxing and wrestling. Paintings of public contests feature chariot racing and
horse racing most frequently.

The increasing number of such records, and the frequency of *palaestra*
scenes amongst them, testify to the growth in popularity of physical exercise.
Yet the sixth century B.C., the concluding phase of the Archaic period, saw
only the first stages in the evolution of physical education, and physical
culture in general, in Athenian life. Its slow growth clearly reflects the fact
that physical exercise was only one aspect of the education of the young in
Athens. The progress towards a democratic form of society required that
young people of the upper classes should be prepared for exercising political
functions in the city. Hence the special emphasis placed on intellectual
training, above all on learning the laws of the city, but also on all-round
political and cultural awareness. The Athenian educational system, while
attending to the special needs of the new rising social groups, preserved some
of the elements of aristocratic culture such as instructions in music, singing
and recitation.

In this period there is also evident in Athens an appreciation of the
importance of leisure. It was Solon again who introduced this idea. For, in his
view, social improvements and prosperity were essential conditions for
human happiness; it was happiness which constituted true fulfilment in
a man's life.

For Solon happiness meant above all love (in the sense of aristocratic
love of boys), possession of horses for racing and dogs for the hunt, and
a supply of friends for hospitality on one's travels.[27] He stipulated happiness
as a human requirement, to include competitive sport, and considered
leisure, well-spent, as the most proper employment of human life.

Athletes training: a runner at the
start, wrestlers, a man with a spear.
Marble relief on Themistocles' wall,
Athens, around 510 B.C.

The Panhellenic Games

Games, organized as part of the religious ceremonies in honour of the gods, played a significant role in the development of Greek physical culture. Greek religious ideas were influenced not only by those of the Mycenaean Greeks, but also the Minoans, as well as the cultures of the Near East and the old hunting cultures, which persisted in religious ritual. Every Greek *polis* had its sacred grove, usually on the site of ancient cults. Here the new gods of Olympus were worshipped in the open air, until monumental temples were set up later on.[28]

The ritual ceremonies included not only processions and sacrifices, but also sporting contests, in which the competitors offered themselves, their skill and their physical prowess to the gods. Thus everyone who took part in the festivals could play an active part in the ceremonies. The sporting contests were entertainment for human onlookers and gods alike, and they took the simplest forms of dancing, running and various kinds of wrestling. The most popular ceremonies of all, those in honour of Dionysus, included foot races. Military games were held on the feasts of Zeus. A hymn to the god Apollo describes the ceremonies arranged in his honour on the island of Delos. "There the Greeks gather in long *chitons,* together with their children and their respectful women, to pay thee honour; every contest which they organize is for thy delight: boxing and dancing and singing." Sailors organized foot races round the altar of Apollo, who was regarded as the god of sporting contests. In Sparta, and also in Megara, special sports events, *gymnopaidiai,* were arranged in his honour.[29]

Some of the local festivals outgrew their original purpose and acquired a wider significance, such as the Olympic Games, and the Pythian, Nemean and Isthmic Games. They comprised various sporting events as well as competitions on different musical instruments, and poetic and recitation

Olympia. The gate, through which the contestants came into the stadium during the Olympic Games.

contests. The term *agon* was used for all these entries. The musical *agon* consisted of musical and recitation contests, while the sporting *agon* was divided into two special sections — the simple sporting disciplines, which were called the *gymnic agon,* and the chariot races, which were known as the *hippic agon, gymnos* meaning "naked" and *hippos,* a "horse".

According to mythology, the races organized at religious festivals were decided by the gods, and gods and heroes were the first privileged performers. One of the most ancient of these festivals with a sports competition was held in the north-west of the Peloponnese, in the area sacred to Zeus, known as Olympia. The recorded history of the Olympic Games starts in the eighth century B.C. but myths, supported by recent archaeological finds, point to much earlier origins.

The earliest evidence shows that Olympia was already inhabited in the third millennium B.C. In the stratum corresponding to the second millennium extensive foundations were found of a building 10.5 metres (35 feet) long by 3—4 metres (10—13 feet) broad, plus an apse, devoted to the cult of nature, fertility and vegetation gods. In the Mycenaean period, from the middle of the sixteenth to the twelfth century B.C. the whole area was densely settled, centering round the royal Mycenaean household at Pisa. The old religious site was now dedicated to new gods and the hero Pelops, after whom the whole peninsula was named.

When the Dorian tribes overran the Peloponnese after the fall of the Mycenaean civilization, they brought with them the worship of Olympian Zeus, who became the ruler of the old religious centre and gave it the new name of Olympia. At first he was worshipped in the open air; sacrifices were brought, and the ashes piled up on the altar. Nevertheless, older gods continued to be revered, and in the oldest part of the sacred site devotion was paid to Kronos, the god of nature, and to the earth goddess Gaia, goddess of fertility. The memory of the hero Pelops was honoured at his tomb, the Pelopion. An important place was also accorded to Heracles, who was believed to have set up the original altar to Zeus. He was regarded as the patron of the contests dedicated to Zeus which were held there, and thence called the Olympic Games.

What these Games were like in the earliest period is still a matter of dispute. They first emerge from the mists of antiquity when the first victor was recorded, in 776 B.C. But even this date is primarily a traditional point of reference, rather than a historical fact. This uncertainty applies equally to the dates of subsequent Olympic Games. The basic date was established by Hippias of Elis in the fifth century B.C. and was calculated on the assumption that the Games were held regularly every fourth year. Contests had of course been held before that time, at shorter, perhaps annual intervals.[30]

From the point where written records (mainly the names of the winners) are available we find ourselves on firmer ground. The data are still fragmentary and imprecise, but they help to establish in outline the genesis of the Games. The first Games in 776 B.C. were of purely local significance. They lasted one day and served a ritual purpose — sacrifices followed by racing. The *agon* was a simple running race, likewise of religious character, but the fact that the victor, Coroebus of Elis, was recorded proves the degree of lay interest in the race. Recording the name of the winner, which now became customary, reflects a general tendency of the time — the effort of the individual to transcend anonymity by exceptional physical performance, and to secure lasting fame by winning.

The popularity of sports competitions was reflected in the gradual amplification of the sports programme. While the sacred rites stayed more or less unchanged, more and different contests were added. According to tradition, at the fourteenth Games in 724 B.C. a two-lap race, *diaulos,*

Men's running race. Painting on an amphora, 520—500 B.C.

there-and-back along the track, was instituted in addition to the original one-length race, *stadion*. At the fifteenth Games (720 B.C.) an endurance race over a long course, the *dolichos*, appeared. The five-discipline *pentathlon* — running, jumping, discus-throwing, javelin-throwing and wrestling — was first included in 708 B.C. Twenty years later, at the twenty-third Games, boxing made its appearance, and chariot racing (with four horses) at the twenty-fifth Games in 680 B.C. New items at the thirty-third Games (648 B.C.) were horseback riding and the *pankration*. This virtually completed the evolution of the Olympic programme. Innovations during the seventh and sixth centuries were only modifications of disciplines already included: running, wrestling, pentathlon and boxing for boys, and running with weapons.

An account of the history of the Games by the Greek writer Pausanias in the second century A.D. suggests, however, that the chronological sequence given above is not exact, and that the range of disciplines was more varied from the very beginning.

It is clear from this survey that the original Olympic Games were simple sporting disciplines — the *gymnic agon*. It was not until the programme had considerably broadened that chariot races were incorporated. The oldest Greek myths link these races with the hero Pelops, who was believed to have become ruler of Mycenaean Pisa after defeating old King Oenomaus in a chariot race, thus winning his lovely daughter Hippodamia as bride. This is possibly the reason why festivals incorporating chariot races were held under the patronage of the rulers of Pisa.

These legends are one of the sources which support the view that chariot races existed in Mycenaean times, and disappeared with the destruction of the Mycenaean culture. The subconscious knowledge of their existence, which can be traced in oral poetry, is also apparent in the votive models of two-wheeled chariots with drivers, dating from the ninth century, which were excavated by archaeologists in Olympia. In the eighth century, the time when the Olympic Games were taking shape, such figurines are no longer found.[31] The festivals organized by the new inhabitants, took the form of simple contests, at first only foot races, but it seems clear that chariot racing was cultivated by the Greek aristocracy, which had adopted the life-style of the Greek kings, *basileis*. Chariot races continued to be arranged as a traditional ceremony in honour of deceased members of this aristocratic society. The numerous scenes on Late Geometric vases, which depict funeral rites, show not only chariot races but communal dances of men and women, boxing, armoured duels and sword duels.[32] At the beginning of the seventh century, chariot races were included in the Olympic Games, but as a socially exclusive discipline. In the past, chariots were drawn by two horses, but now the races were for four-in-hand chariots. Horse racing gradually took its place by the side of these races. The classification of such contests under the separate title of *hippic agon* itself shows how they differed from the simple sporting disciplines.

As the programme became more varied, the length of the Games increased. There are no exact figures, but it was probably a two-day affair by 688 B.C. (the 23rd Games) or by 680 B.C. (the 25th Games), when boxing and four-in-hand chariot racing were added. Later on, the duration was extended to four or five days.

As time went on the sporting contests completely overshadowed the sacral element and became an autonomous component, if not the chief concern of the Olympic festival.

The gradual severing of links between religious and athletic events is well illustrated in the history of the stadium at Olympia. In the earliest period, the stadium formed part of the sanctuary; the western side, which was

The palaestra in Olympia, where wrestling matches and other sports were held and watched from the colonnade.

the starting point for the races, was left open, so that there was direct access to the stadium area from the great altar of Zeus. The other three sides were built on an incline to provide seats for the spectators. Later, the stadium and the sanctuary were separated by the building of the stoa of Echo and the construction of a fourth slope on the western side of the stadium.[33)]

As the sporting programme became more varied, so the range of participants enlarged. The records of victorious athletes show how fast the list of cities sending their representatives to Olympia had grown. During the first fifteen Games, up to 720 B.C., the champions came exclusively from the city states of the Peloponnese; participation was still fairly limited and the local character of the Games corresponded to the programme of simple foot races. In addition to contestants from Elis (at that time in political control of Olympia), Messenians appear among the early victors, carrying off the prize at the third and fourth Games, and at the seventh through to the tenth. But from the last third of the eighth century B.C. onwards, Messenia was fully employed in fighting Sparta and could not spare time from her war of liberation to attend the Games at all. Between 716 and 684 B.C. there was only an occasional prize for a Messenian, and when their country was again defeated and enslaved by the Spartans the Messenians were out of the Olympics for good. Sparta's enhanced power was equally reflected at Olympia, where it won nearly all the events in the seventh century.

From the end of the eighth century both the variety of events and the catchment area of the Games expanded. Competitors were now coming in from more numerous and further-flung cities. At the beginning of the seventh century B.C., the first occasional mentions appear, of winners from Athens and Thebes, and in 688 B.C. the boxing champion hailed from Smyrna in Asia Minor. From the early sixth century Spartan victories became a rarity and the southern Italian city of Croton came to the fore, along with

The struggle between the hero Heracles and the giant Antaeus. The girls are showing their enthusiasm. Painting on a krater by the painter Europhronius. Athens, 510 B.C.

Boxers. The bronze tripod between them is the prize. Detail of a black-figure vessel from the middle of 6th century B.C.

A javelin thrower and a jumper with halteres facing a supervisor. Black-figure vase, 540–530 B.C.

Young men with javelins and discuses. Detail from a red-figure amphora, around 500 B.C.

Athens, Miletus in Asia Minor, and the island of Naxos. The Olympic Games were now a sporting event of the first order, drawing entries from all over the Greek world.[34]

In the sixth century B.C., however, other festivals also began to transcend their purely local significance, notably the Pythian festivals at Delphi, associated with the cult of Apollo. These also went back to legendary beginnings. The most widespread story concerned Apollo's victorious duel with the great dragon Python. At first the festivals were held every eight years; the musical *agon* was the first to be incorporated (musicians playing religious music, and poets reciting hymns to the god Apollo). Early in the sixth century (582 B.C.) the festivals were held every four years, and the programme was modelled on that of the Olympic Games. It included athletic exercises and later, horse racing as well, but the main event remained the

Boxers fighting with their fists protected by straps. One is bleeding from the nose. Painting on an amphora from the potter Nicosthenes' workshop. Athens, around 525 B.C.

Racing two-in-hand with a charioteer sitting on the box. Painting on a Panathenaic amphora. Athens, around 550 B.C.

musical *agon,* and this was later expanded. The prizes awarded to the victors were originally objects of intrinsic value, but were replaced later on by sacred laurel-wreaths.

Like the Olympic Games, the Pythian festivals were held at midsummer. How long they lasted we cannot be sure, but they were certainly extended to several days. The first three days were probably devoted to musical competitions, followed by athletic and equestrian events. Finally, one day at least was reserved for the ceremonial procession and sacrifices to Apollo.[35]

Another series of all-Greek festivals began in 573 B.C. – the Nemean Games held in the north-eastern part of the Peloponnese. They were originally mourning ceremonies in honour of a nature divinity who died in each annual vegetative cycle, either in the winter or in the summer drought.

Scene from a boxing match. The kneeling man admits his defeat by raising his forefinger. His second informs the referee standing behind the group with the same gesture. Painting on a red-figure amphora, 530–520 B.C.

Pankration. The lower pankratiast is conceding defeat by tapping his opponent on the shoulder. Painting on a cup (scyphos). Athens, late 6th century B.C.

An athlete holding the discus in his left hand. Bronze statue, around 500 B.C.

These festivals, too, were originally interwoven with a mythical narrative in which Heracles, among others, appeared as the founder of the *agon*. In the historical period the Games were dedicated to Zeus, to whom a temple was set up and surrounded with a sacred grove. They were held in the summer in the second and fourth years of each Olympic cycle, and comprised an athletic, an equestrian and a musical competition. The athletic events were similar to those at Olympia; records tell of running races for men and for boys, wrestling for men and boys, a *pentathlon* and *pankration* for both classes. There is also mention of boxing, and a running contest for entrants wearing full armour. The winner of each event was originally given a garland of olive branches, replaced later by one of fig-wort. Most of the time the Doric city of Argos was the most influential in organizing the Games, but Athens gradually came to occupy an important position too.[36]

In 572 B.C. the Isthmian Games also became a regular Panhellenic event. Like the Nemean Games these took place about every second and fourth year of the Olympic cycle, but in the early spring, perhaps in April. These Games also had ancient origins, around which all kinds of myths were woven. According to the oldest story they were founded by Poseidon, the god of the sea, and all the great heroes took part in them. Castor was said to have won a running race, Orpheus a lyre-playing competition, Polydeuces the prize for boxing and Peleus for wrestling, while Theseus was champion in running, or perhaps wrestling, in armour. Phaëthon came first in horse-riding and Neleus in the four-horse chariot race. According to another version the festival originated in funeral ceremonies.

These myths show that the Isthmian Games, too, included athletic, musical and equestrian events; on the athletic side there are records of men's and boys' running-races, both one-way and two-way; of men's and boys' wrestling and boxing matches; and of men's *pankration* and *pentathlon*. The fullest lists of names preserved are those of outstanding boxers and *pankration* winners.

The contests were preceded by sacrifices to Poseidon. In the earliest years the champions were adorned at the end with wreaths of fig-wort. Later on, however, the wreaths were made of fir branches, to symbolize the god Poseidon.[37]

All four festivals described here attained sufficient popularity to rank them as Greek national events, but the Olympic Games transcended all others in importance.

The elaborate preparations devoted to all these Games are proof of their prestige. Messengers were despatched, well in advance, throughout the Greek world to announce their exact date, as this varied. The messengers would invite the various city states to take part both passively, as spectators, and actively. In view of the incessant local disputes and wars between Greek states, it was essential to guarantee safe passage for those attending or returning from the Games, as well as the safety of the Games themselves. The envoys therefore announced a sacred truce or *ekecheiria* wherever they went, a truce which varied in length according to the distance the participants had to travel and the duration of the Games themselves — sometimes a month, sometimes three. Any violation of these sacred truces, which secured direct protection by the god in question for every participant, was severely punished.

Only free citizens of Greek blood were permitted to take full part in the Games. Barbarians and slaves were allowed to watch, though not to compete; Greek married women could not even be spectators, under pain of punishment that extended even to the death penalty. This evidently stemmed from an ancient taboo; the veto did not apply to unmarried girls. All women were normally excluded from any sports competitions, but while the Olympic

The young athlete has just received the wreath of victory from the coach with a stick. Detail from a red-figure amphora, around 410 B.C.

Games were in progress special races for girls were held nearby as part of the festival of the goddess Hera, called the Heraia. These races were dominated, like the Olympics, by Sparta up to the early sixth century, which reflects the Spartan concern to involve women in the state educational system.

A further category banned from the Panhellenic festivals were those who had spilt blood and whose guilt had not been expunged. Consideration of such cases was entirely in the hands of umpires, the *hellanodikai,* against whose verdict there was no appeal. Those who had committed theft in temples were likewise barred, and not only individuals but whole cities could be excluded in this way. In the beginning the umpires themselves could take part in the Games, but in the Classical period this too was prohibited.

All competitors had to arrive at Olympia by a stated time; latecomers were banned, and no excuse, not even a storm at sea, was accepted. It was up to every contestant to see that he set off in good time. In the later years entrants were required to make special preparations for the occasion and even to go on a diet; for this purpose they had to turn up a full month beforehand and undergo intensive training before the Games started.

The *hellanodikai* exercised strict control over all the contests. At

118

A young rider in ceremonial dress at the prize-giving after winning a horse race. The naked young man is bringing the prizes — a tripod and a wreath. Attic vase, 6th century B.C.

Olympia there were originally two, but the number later grew to nine. They drew lots to assign the entrants to the various elimination heats and had the last word in deciding which should be classed as men and which as boys. They also conferred the prizes in each discipline. At Olympia the winners were crowned with a wreath made from wild olive branches, which had to be cut from the sacred tree with a golden knife, by a youth whose parents were still living. Not only was the wreath a great mark of distinction, but the Greeks believed that it possessed magic power and secured for its wearer the protection of the Olympian Zeus. Equal importance was attached to the laurel, fig-wort and fir garlands employed at the Pythian, Isthmian and Nemean Games.

On the last evening of the Games the champions would sit down with their relatives, friends and fellow-citizens to a solemn supper which marked the conclusion of the festival. As time went on the celebration of the victors grew more and more ostentatious; they would receive ovations during the course of the Games and be showered with honours when they returned home. Their native cities were regarded as sharing fully in their glory and were recorded alongside the names of the winners in the final lists.

Particular esteem was accorded to the *periodonikai,* who had won prizes at all four Panhellenic Games. Famous among these was Milon of Croton, known as the "King of Wrestlers". This most celebrated athlete of the ancient world first won the Olympic wrestling prize in 540 B.C. at the age of fourteen; in his adult life he gained the Olympic wreath seven times, and also won seven times in the Pythian, ten in the Isthmian and nine in the Nemean Games. His strength and skill were legendary, and there is reliable evidence that he remained in peak form until the age of forty: his last recorded victories date from 516 B.C.

119

It is equally significant that Milon owed his successes to training, which included abstinence and dieting, undergone in the school for aristocrats run by Pythagoras in Milon's home city, Croton. He also played a prominent role in its political life, embodying in some ways the aristocratic ideal of *kalokagathia.*

The lists of victors show that the contestants in the Panhellenic Games were drawn from the rich classes that came to power in the city states during the seventh century. In Sparta, thanks to her military system, all Spartans constituted a privileged caste *vis-à-vis* the subjugated population.[38]

The exclusively upper-class origin of the contestants was an inevitable consequence of the length and costliness of the journeys involved. The requirement of prior training in the case of the Olympics also limited entry to those who could afford it. In contrast to the purely local festivals, where commoners could hold their own by dint of native strength and agility, the Panhellenic Games were a demanding business where only well-prepared competitors of outstanding talent could hope to stand the pace.

The Panhellenic Games were very important for the entire Greek world in many ways. Their emergence and the significance they gained were a reflection of the high level of physical culture in the Greek states. Even if the contestants at the Panhellenic Games came largely from the upper strata of the population, sport in ancient Greece must have been widely practised at popular festivals.

The Panhellenic Games were also of great economic significance. It became necessary to provide housing and provisions for increasing numbers of visitors, so that merchants from far afield would pour in during the festival season and large market-fairs were organized. The places where the Games were held grew wealthy from the rich gifts brought by delegates from all the city states as sacrifices for the gods in whose honour the festivals were held, the gifts being stored in special treasure-houses set up in the sacred places.

The political prestige conferred by the Games was another prime factor. From the time when they acquired a Panhellenic character, that is, from the sixth century B.C. onwards, Olympia was, for example, a venue for the signing of inter-city treaties and other public documents.

The sites of the four main Games thus became focal points for the whole Greek world. Amid the fertile variety of the city states, free of pressure from any central power, it was here that a sense of national identity arose in a purely natural and spontaneous way, through awareness of a high level of shared culture both intellectual and physical, and through a sense of superiority over the slaves and over the neighbouring barbarians. The outward symbol of this superiority was a strong, tanned, well-developed naked body. It became an ideal for all Greeks, distinguishing them from other peoples, and an object of admiration at all Panhellenic festivals.

In the oldest times Olympic runners were clad in loincloths. During the fifteenth Games in 720 B.C., however, one of the contestants lost his loincloth in mid-race; he ran on regardless, and won. From that time on nudity was increasingly favoured and at some point in the sixth century B.C. it became general behaviour.[39]

The cult of the naked body, strong and sun-tanned, was reflected in Greek art as well. Through the whole Hellenic area — on the mainland, the islands, in Asia Minor and the colonies — sculptures were created that were later labelled "Apollos" or *kouroi* ("young men"). Whether they were meant to represent divinity or human beings, their nature was indisputably athletic. In every case we see the same effort to bring out the muscles of the male form and to depict its sheer strength, something that distinguishes the art of the Archaic period from all subsequent fashions. The Panhellenic athlete was that kind of man, and in that form the contemporary artist portrayed him.

Part of the stadium in Delphi. On the right the ruins of the seats for the supervisors — hellanodikai. In front are the starting blocks for the runners. The spectators' stand can be seen opposite.

*A charioteer in a long white robe driving a racing
four-in-hand approaching the turning point of the race at full
gallop. Panhellenic amphora from the late 5th century B.C.*

Charioteer from Delphi, winner of the chariot race in the Pythian Games. (continued on page 124)

Classical Beauty

At the beginning of the fifth century B.C. the Greek world stood at a crucial point of its history. A powerful foe had struck at the Greek mainland – the Persian Empire, heir to the territory and civilization of the ancient Near East, a world power controlling not only that whole area, including Egypt, but part of Central Asia and India too. In the middle of the sixth century B.C. the rulers of Persia also dominated one portion of the Greek world, namely the Greek city states on the coast of Asia Minor.

Around 500 B.C. these Greeks of Asia Minor revolted against Persian rule, receiving support from European Greeks and particularly from Athens. But the rebellion was ferociously put down and the Persian Empire made a retaliatory attack on Europe; numerous Persian task-forces drove into Greece itself in 490 B.C. and again ten years later.

Split up as they were among rival city states, the Greeks seemed like powerless pygmies in the face of the giant Persian Empire. They had little experience of large-scale land campaigns, and naval warfare was completely unknown to them. Yet the unexpected happened. The first wave of Persian forces was defeated by the Athenians at Marathon and the second assault lost momentum thanks to the Spartan hoplites at Thermopylae, whereupon the Athenian navy destroyed a Persian fleet off Salamis. A year after that, in 479 B.C., Greek soldiers scattered the rest of the Persian land force at Plataea, and the Persians were forced to evacuate the country. The independence of Greece had been saved against multiple odds, and after all these centuries we can still only ask in amazement how this was possible.

An advanced economy, particularly in the crafts, assured the Greek warriors a supply of first-class weaponry. Their bodily fitness was maintained by a high standard of physical culture, and their strength and agility put to continuous test in competitive sports. Well-trained limbs were capable of carrying weapons and wielding them in battle. The heavily-armed Greek hoplites were far more than a match for the Persian infantry and could even worst their cavalry. Skill in building and sailing ships enabled the Greeks to create a war navy in an amazingly short time. Their intellectual resources, fostered in conditions of freedom, further tipped the balance, outweighing their quarrelsomeness and mustering the nation's power in defence of its liberty. These were assets that far transcended the vast size of the Persian forces, controlled as they were by a despotic regime that made the development of creative personalities impossible and spread a sterilizing pall over its own resources.

Victory over the Persians proved a vital factor for Greece's own future. The life-and-death struggle was a warning experience that taught the Greeks to be ready for another assault, and it led to a suspension of the rivalry between Athens and Sparta, even if shortlived. While the militaristic regime in Sparta became less oppressive, Athens embarked on a new, expansive foreign policy, exerting her influence in southern Italy, Egypt, Cyprus and along the Syrian-Palestinian coastline as well as in northern Greece and the Peloponnese. All this strengthened the primacy of Athens among the Greek states and was reflected in her internal development.

The awareness of danger survived made the Athenians more appreciative of their own freedom and democratic institutions. The experience of war involved wider circles of the population in the city's political life. Landless peasants who had played their part as oarsmen in her maritime victories demanded a share in government. Far-reaching reforms were accordingly carried out in the middle of the fifth century B.C. that gave all citizens, regardless of property status, the same rights to take part in running the state. In this context *arete politike,* "civil qualities", took on exceptional significance; this was the term applied to the qualities and activities through which an individual showed that he was a good and valuable member of society. This new political *arete* also found its place in the ideal of *kalokagathia.* Athenian democracy had reached its pinnacle and Athens attained its high point of evolution in political, economic, social, scientific and artistic terms alike. This culmination is associated with the name of Pericles. He made Athens the centre of contemporary culture, art and scholarship. The sculptor Phidias, the tragedian Sophocles, the historian Herodotus and the philosopher Anaxagoras are only four out of many great names linked with this golden age.

The glory of Athens in this early and high Classical period of the fifth century B.C. was also reflected in many aspects of its physical culture. The fitness of the body was something that the Persian wars had endowed with increased importance. But the activities of the philosophical schools led to a demand for systematic intellectual education as well. The internal democratization of the city state had also produced a clearer realization that

A statue over six feet high, representing either Zeus hurling a thunderbolt, or Poseidon throwing his trident. The whole position of the statue is an exact representation of an athlete about to throw the javelin. The forefinger of the throwing hand is cocked so that it can hold the leather loop common in Greek javelins. Attic bronze statue, around 460 B.C., found in the sea near Artemisium on the island of Euboea.

(continued from page 123) *The statue was part of a group which included the owner of the chariot as well as the four-in-hand and a slave boy. According to an inscription this owner was Polyzalus, a tyrant from Gela in Sicily, who dedicated the whole statue to the god Apollo in gratitude for the victory. Bronze statue, 477 B.C.*

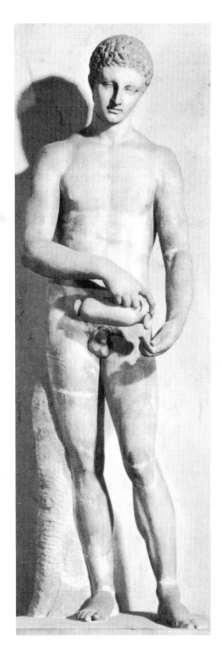

A young man pouring oil into his hand to rub over his body. Marble statue, beginning of 4th century B.C.

mental, as well as physical, improvement was a basic right of all Athenian citizens which the community was in duty bound to bring within their grasp.

The educational system in the Classical period rested on similar foundations as previously. There was still individual tutoring for the rich, who could afford special teachers for their children, send them to private schools or to special teachers called sophists who gave all who had political ambitions the necessary training in rhetoric, law, history, philosophy and the natural sciences.

In addition, however, a system of general education, financed and protected by wealthy citizens, was introduced and provided elementary schooling for the poor citizens of Athens.[40] The three principle subjects were *grammatike, mousike* and *gymnastike;* the first covered reading, writing, arithmetic and learning by heart the poems of Homer, Hesiod, Solon and other writers. The second subject, *mousike,* centred on music, which was regarded as the best method of refinement for the mind and the emotions. The third subject, *gymnastike,* concerned the all-round cultivation of the body, and included both active sports such as running, wrestling, boxing and ball games, and general hygiene, baths, steam baths, massage, and the anointing of the body with perfumed unguents.

This system of universal education meant that in the fifth century B.C. practically all Athenian citizens were literate, had a general knowledge of Greek history and culture, and were well-trained and cultivated from the physical point of view. Thus the originally exclusive aristocratic ideal of *kalokagathia* was realized throughout the structure of Athenian society, at the height of Athenian democracy.

The gymnasiums, now larger and more elaborately equipped, became centres for the training of the mind as well as the body, each one including a *palaestra* reserved for its original purpose, wrestling. Other areas were set aside for ball-games, and for boxing lessons there was a room with a ball, or bag filled with sand or wheat, suspended in the air, for testing strength, agility and different types of blow.

At the same time there was a development of such facilities as swimming-baths, steam-baths and halls for massaging and applying ointments.[41] There is no record of the inclusion of swimming in the training schedules, but in describing the battle of Salamis, Herodotus mentions that the Athenians were able to survive by swimming when their ships sunk, whereas many Persians drowned because they did not know how to. And the contemptuous Greek phrase, "a man unable to read or swim", shows how much both skills were taken for granted.[42]

Boys and young men underwent their physical exercises naked. They began by oiling their bodies; before wrestling they would also dust themselves with powder to make the skin less slippery and afterwards scrape themselves clean with special implements that were available, along with jars of oil and ointment, in every gymnasium. It was also part of their training to harden themselves against both harsh weather and sun.

It can be gathered from piecemeal evidence that the training both of boys and young men was closely related to the various sporting disciplines at the public Games. Of these the most highly esteemed was the *pentathlon,* which with its combination of running, jumping, wrestling, discus and spear-throwing formed an ideal basis for all-round physical exercise.

Training also included a number of preparatory exercises, such as forcing one's partner from his stance with the pressure of one hand or finger. Standard positions and movements in wrestling were practised, and how to hold the arms in defence and attack. Attention was given to the maintenance of degrees of muscle tone; exercises in climbing, rope-pulling and skipping were recommended, and various kinds of ball-games particularly encouraged.

The instructors carried long sticks; physical punishment was inflicted to preserve discipline, but pain was in any case regarded as an effective means of moral and intellectual stimulation. The right to chastise was enjoyed not only by all teachers, *paidotribai* and *gymnastai,* but also by their assistants, the *paidagogoi,* often slaves entrusted by rich parents with the constant supervision of their sons.[43]

As Greek power and prosperity grew in the wake of the victories over Persia, so the prestige of the Panhellenic Games reached its zenith. The treasure-houses of Olympia and Delphi were crammed with magnificent gifts. New structures were erected at Olympia and the sacred site in the centre was rebuilt. Plane trees and olives were cut down to make way for a splendid new Temple of Zeus, where Phidias's impressive gold and ivory statue of the god sat on his throne. At Olympia, too, a huge new stadium was designed with seats for spectators, a system of baths, living-quarters for the athletes and a rebuilt gymnasium. For the horse and chariot races a special course, the hippodrome, was created. No remains of this have been found, but Pausanias gives a fascinating account of the mechanism by which a bronze eagle was launched into the air as a starting signal.[44]

There are many fifth-century inscriptions which throw light on individual champions. The number of *periodonikai,* prize winners at all four Panhellenic Games, increased sharply at this time. One of these, Theogenes, secured 1,300 prizes during the course of his life; another, Diagoras of Rhodes, fathered a whole family of athletes. All victors were acclaimed as heroes in their native cities.[45]

Another reflection of the Greek triumph over Persia was the emergence of further festivals with a racing element. In the immediate vicinity of the Marathon battlefield the shepherd's god, Pan, had been worshipped since 490 B.C. After the Athenian victory in which Pan was thought to have lent a hand, Pan's Cave became the site of annual celebrations in memory of the battle and an *agon* in the form of a torch-race formed part of them.[46]

Again at Plataea, the site of the victory of 479 B.C., festivities with a sports component were inaugurated. According to Plutarch: "After this, there was a general assembly of the Hellenes, at which Aristides proposed a decree to the effect that deputies and delegates from all Hellas convene at Plataea every year, and that every fourth year festival games of deliverance be celebrated — the *Eleutheria* [Liberty]." The Eleutheria consisted primarily of a procession and sacrificial ceremony, in which the fallen warriors were honoured through the flesh and blood of a bull. The sacrifice was made on the altar of Zeus the Liberator. After the sacrifice the *archon* of Plataea, as master of ceremonies, poured a libation with the words: "I drink to the men who died for the freedom of the Hellenes."[47]

Of the race that followed we have few details. Pausanias tells us however that "great prizes are offered for running. The competitors run in armour before the altar", so the main event was evidently a race in full armour. He also records that the athlete Euchidas, at the first such ceremony, brought fire from as far away as the temple at Delphi. After running the distance of one thousand *stadia* (182 kilometres or 114 miles) from Plataea to Delphi and back in a single day, he fell exhausted and died.[48]

Alongside these new, politically inspired festivities, the traditional ceremonies also enjoyed a great revival throughout Attica. There were, for example, the Thesmophoria held in honour of the goddess Demeter and her daughter Persephone, with much dancing and special Games. Zeus himself was honoured with horse racing and military contests at ceremonies called Olympia. At the Piraeus, the principal harbour of Athens, boat-races were organized in honour of the same god, while the festival of the sea-god

Scene from a race with torches. Painting on a red-figure krater, Athens, 450–425 B.C.

Poseidon, centred on the temple whose remains still stand on the cliffs at Sunium against a backdrop of blue sea and sky, featured races between triremes, naval vessels with three banks of oars. The Hephaestia, celebrating the blacksmith god Hephaestus, included torch-races and musical contests.

The hero Theseus, whose identity became merged with that of Heracles, was regarded in the fifth century B.C. as the friend and protector of the Athenian democracy. His temple was a sanctuary, particularly for slaves. The festival held here comprised a banquet and a variety of sports events, notably a torch-race, and torch-races along with musical performances marked the yearly festival of Prometheus, symbolizing that hero's bravery in stealing fire from the gods and giving it to the human race.

In Athens, among many other sports festivals, honours were paid to Hermes as the special god of gymnastic proficiency. Such ceremonies were held in the *palaestrae* and gymnasiums, and statues of Hermes were to be found in most institutes for physical training.[49]

Another type of festivity that gained increasing following through the fifth century was one which gave rise in due course to a novel form of Greek popular entertainment — the theatre. This was associated with the ancient god of the vine, Dionysus. His festivals — the Dionysia — sometimes centred around running races, sometimes round wine-drinking contests, but they also featured, amid scenes of ribald jollity, group dances accompanied by choral singing. From this emerged, back in the Archaic era, the new literary genres of tragedy and comedy, and thereafter these two competed with sport for public favour. In Athens a special semi-circular auditorium, the *theatron,* was built on the slopes of the Acropolis. The three greatest dramatists of the Classical world, Aeschylus, Sophocles and Euripides, writing in Athens in the

Young men in a palaestra. Having laid aside their clothes, they are about to scrape off the oil from their bodies with their strigils. An oil vessel hangs above. Painting on an Attic vase, around 460 B.C.

*A horse race. A painting on
a Panathenaic amphora by
Eucharides' painter, 500−480 B.C.*

*Racing four-in-hand. Over it floats
the winged goddess of victory with
a wreath for the winner. Coin from
Syracuse in Sicily, 412−400 B.C.*

fifth century, gave Greek drama a new character, and at the turn of the fifth to fourth century Aristophanes exerted the same influence on Greek comedy.

Among the events which have been mentioned, however, the greatest glamour was attached to a festival called the Panathenaea, held in Athens in celebration of the city's protectress, the goddess Athena. She was in her origins the goddess of the clear skies (of the ether), bringer of light, warmth and moisture, goddess of the dew whose cooling drops fell on clear nights, freshening the earth and all growing things. But since, according to myth, Athena had sprung from the forehead of the thunder-god Zeus, she was also the goddess of wisdom, of victory in war and of fructifying peace. Ceremonies in her honour went back to the earliest times.

When Solon's reforms at the start of the sixth century opened the way for democracy in Athens and that city came to occupy a new position in the evolution of Greece, the Panathenaea underwent a profound change. It was in 566 or 565 B.C. that its programme first included racing, and then musical contests. As the power and wealth of Athens grew throughout the Classical period, so the festival waxed in fame, magnificence and variety. A number of temples were erected in Athens to provide a suitable background to the festival, and a special building, the Odeion, was put up on the slopes of the Acropolis for musical and singing performances.

The festival was held every year, but with special emphasis on every fourth year, when the Great Panathenaea took place, a six-day occasion noted particularly for its horse-and-chariot races, accompanied by various acrobatic feats. Great favourites were the *apobatai,* drivers naked but for shield and helmet who would leap down from their chariots at full speed, run for a given distance alongside them and then jump on again. Similar exploits enlivened the equestrian races, with much acrobatic byplay.

These races were followed by others, evidently of similar kinds to those cultivated at the Olympic and other Panhellenic Games. The torch-race was one speciality, starting immediately after dusk on a moonless night. It was run by *epheboi,* a team of young men representing respectively the various *phylai,* "districts" of Attica. The *epheboi* began by running to the altar on which the fire of Prometheus blazed, lighting their torches from it and making off towards the altar of Athena on the Acropolis. As they went they would

Horse riders throwing javelins at a target in the form of a round shield. Painting on a Panathenaic amphora, late 5th century B.C.

129

pass on their torches to successive runners from the same *phyle*. The first to reach the altar won the prize, and his *phyle* was declared victorious.

Trireme races also formed part of the Panatheaea, ships and oarsmen being provided again by the individual *phylai* and competing against one another in what amounted to a parade of Athenian might.

A further attraction was provided by dance companies who performed war-dances — *pyrrhiche* and other rounds — adopted from the Spartans. A male beauty competition was another event, each *phyle* entering the strongest and handsomest men it could muster.[50]

All arrangements were entrusted to ten officials elected for a four-year period. Winners of musical events received money-prizes and golden wreaths, athletic champions a quantity of oil from the sacred Athenian olive-groves. The considerable amount involved was all the more valuable for being presented in elegantly designed vessels, with a portrait of Athena fully armed, over the inscription "From the Athenian Games", on one side, and scenes from the various contests depicted on the other. In the popular nautical event, the *phyle* whose trireme came first was presented with a large money-prize.

The climax of the Panathenaea was a splendid procession through the richly decorated city. The sheer beauty of the procession was a matter of great prestige; in this respect, too, the individual *phylai* vied with one another, and the best display received a prize in cash.

The splendour of the Great Panathenaea reflected the splendour of Athens itself, as the statesman Pericles proudly declared: "...our government is called a democracy... not only in our public life are we liberal... we have provided for the spirit many relaxations from toil; we have games and sacrifices regularly throughout the year... For we are lovers of beauty yet with no extravagance and lovers of wisdom yet without weakness... we shall be the wonder not only of the men of today but of after times."[51]

This remarkable address formulates the striving for harmony and balance in every aspect of Athenian life, an extrapolation of the ideal of *kalokagathia*. As in Solon's time, the stress is laid on the importance of leisure, with festivals and races specified as ways of employing it. Further evidence of this awareness of the importance of spare time is furnished by the emergence in the early fifth century B.C. of a special term for it — *schole*. It now comes to be considered as the portion of men's lives which is most truly human, in contrast to the time spent in work, *ascholia*.

The classic age of the fifth century saw the climax in every way of competitive sports throughout Greece, but in Athens *par excellence*. Physical training was now the very basis of education, Athenians devoted their spare time to sport, and contests were not merely included in most festivals but became their chief content. It is not surprising, then, that the prestige of sport should be reflected in the art and literature of the time.

Poets frequently acclaimed the victors of the races and competitions and sang the glory of their native cities. The most effective exponent of this literary genre, the *epinikion* or triumphal ode, was Pindar, who celebrated Panhellenic champions in countless verses. Even in the sixth century sporting motifs had appeared on vases. Now they became the commonest subject of all works of visual art: painted vases, coins and above all sculptures.

Vases showing scenes from the Panathenaea, or incidents in the *palaestrae* and gymnasiums, provide vivid glimpses both of sporting events and of the training that preceded them. Young men jumping with special *halteres*, throwing the discus, or engaged in boxing and wrestling are exceedingly frequent. Wherever runners are depicted it is easy to distinguish the short-distance style from that of the long-track endurance contests. In the young men's schools training is often accompanied by flute-playing

Young riders in procession during the Panathenaic festivals. Detail of a marble frieze on the temple of the goddess Athena (Parthenon) by the sculptor Pheidias. Athens, around 440 B.C.

Top left: Statue of a young man throwing the discus — called the Discobolus — by the sculptor Myron. Athens, around 450 B.C. (Roman copy)

Below left: Bronze statue of an athlete with a beautifully developed body. Second half of the 5th century B.C.

and the instructor with his long stick is frequently shown urging his charges to greater efforts. There are many scenes from the baths, while others show wrestlers oiling themselves before the fight or scraping off the oil and dust afterwards.

As well as supplementing our knowledge of physical training among the Greeks, these images remind us of an incidental purpose which the *palaestrae* and the ever more popular gymnasiums came to serve, namely as centres of social intercourse. The gymnasiums were open to all men: anyone could join in the contests or watch others doing so. This in turn was a stimulus to art, for artists could spend hours there observing the naked human body, either at rest or in complex motion. It was in these "studios" that the Greeks achieved technical perfection in depicting the nude, and the mastery that we now so much admire would have been impossible without them. Moreover, the development of so many branches of physical exercise was bound to enhance the sheer beauty of the well-trained body that is so striking in the art portraits of the Classical period.

Whereas in the late sixth century B.C. physical strength had received the main emphasis in sculptures and the other arts, in the following century stress fell on the aesthetic attraction of the athlete's form. Mere technical improvement in the art of representation may have played a part, but there is a marked shift of interest from the inherent power of the male body and the basic musculature to portrayal of the well-trained body, deliberately and artificially cultivated and brought to a consummate pitch of harmonious beauty. By the fifth century B.C. nudity was the rule in public races as well as in school training. Even charioteers and horse-riders were naked. In this respect the Greeks had no sense of modesty, not merely because their

Ganymede shown as a young man playing with a hoop, holding a cock which he has been given by Zeus. Painting on a red-figure krater by the Berlin painter, Athens, 475 B.C.

training developed fine figures, but because they took nakedness to be a sign of a degree of civilization and felt scorn for the barbarians' awkward and untanned bodies. Physical shame, indeed, was for them a hallmark of barbarism.

Nudity, by contrast, was for the Greeks a statement of individuality. Their view of the world and of man's place in it was far removed from theocratic ideas. Seeing the body as the fount of vital energy and joy and the basis of human existence, they devoted special attention to its wellbeing.

In social terms, nudity was felt to distinguish the Greeks not only from the barbarians but from their own slaves, who were not allowed to share in physical training. Nudity was furthermore a link that bound all Greek citizens together. Just as the Athenian democratic system gradually overcame distinctions based on birth and wealth, so the discarding of clothes meant a nakedness that was common to all.

Athenian fifth-century art portrays, then, the free bodies of free citizens. The victory-wreaths which Athenians were so regularly winning in their own games and at all the Panhellenic festivals provided the best evidence that bodies appreciated and fostered in this spirit also performed best in sport. In a famous address, Pericles claimed that in spite of their free life, Athenians were as strong as the Spartans who had been subjected to hard drill from their childhood.

It is surely significant that whereas the appearance of the Spartan warriors left no artistic heritage in their culturally sterile city, the bodies of the free citizens of Athens are immortalized in countless portraits. These are not only an expression of delight in beauty, but an identification of the naked body as the basis of human personality and a symbol of inner democracy.

A victorious young athlete with his right hand raised in greeting. Fragment of a marble stele from the shrine of Athene in Cape Sunium, around 460 B.C.

*Below right: A young man in
a dynamic position just before
throwing the discus. Painting on
a Panathenaic vase, 450 B.C.*

Anonymity, either of model or of artist, is accordingly abandoned in the Classical period. This in turn must have stimulated the fashion for sculptures in honour of victorious athletes, so that not only their names, but also their bodies would attain immortal fame.

While artists concentrated so effectively on the rest of the body, the face was relatively ignored. Fifth-century portraits reveal no effort to catch individual features and in vase-paintings particularly faces are often reduced to an insignificant stereotype. Vase designs being admittedly concerned mainly to record incidents such as physical training scenes, there is often little individuality in the rest of the bodies either, though the inscribed names show that real persons are depicted. As for sculptures, it may be that the apparent lack of facial differentiation means only that most athletic models were young *epheboi,* whose features were still unmarked by experience.

Of the hundreds of statues of naked athletes that were produced, only a few have survived; later copies are not so rare. Those that remain show a progressive abandonment of the rigidity of the Archaic period and an increasing determination to hew out of marble forms lifelike in action as well as shape: a runner straining to set off, a ball-game in progress, a discus-thrower, a wrestler planning his attack. The supreme depiction of movement is no doubt Myron's Discobolus, the young discus-thrower seen at the last moment of arm-extension before releasing the discus. The perfect portrayal of a perfect body is enhanced by the choice of this particular moment when every muscle is tensed in preparation for the throw, in an extraordinary unison of utter rest and dynamic motion.

As well as striving to reproduce movement, fifth-century sculpture seems also to aim at establishing an ideal type of male beauty. In this it reflected the tendency of physical training with all its various disciplines to produce a standardized male body. The supreme achievement in this respect was Polyclitus's Doryphorus, a young man bearing a spear, which embodied in marble the ideal of *kalokagathia.*

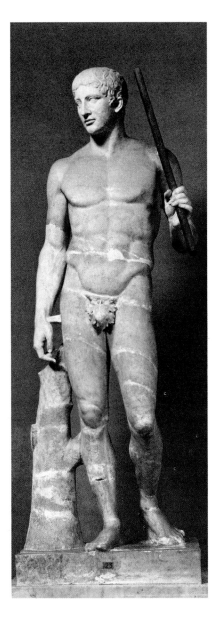

*Doryphorus — a young man
with a spear. The sculptor
Polycleitus created him as the ideal
of a masculine body — the Canon,
5th century B.C.*

*Group of men and youths holding
a discussion in a gymnasium. The
setting is suggested by the strigil held
by the man in the middle. Red-figure
painting on a cup, 475 B.C.*

Scientific and Professional Gymnastics

In the shadow of the classical ideal of *kalokagathia*, something new was emerging that in the fourth century would break up the cherished harmony, a rival tendency promoted in part by internal evolution, in part by outside forces.

The Athenian democracy that reached its pinnacle in the fifth century B.C. was accompanied by a political and economic expansion leading quite logically to differentiation and specialization in every sphere. Of the external factors, a paramount one was the defeat Athens sustained at the hands of Sparta in the Peloponnesian War of 431-404 B.C. Though the victorious Spartans did not manage to destroy Athens and her system, that city's leading position in the Greek world was severely shaken and the strength of her democracy gravely sapped.

Social contrasts were heightened when the war was over. The social basis of Athenian democracy was narrowed and the state ceased to support its poorer citizens on the old scale. These citizens were excluded from political life, the educational system of the Classical period broke down, and the poor thus lost the possibility of acquiring an elementary education, and with it the chance to hold public office. A marked polarization ensued between the wealthy classes on the one hand, and the ranks of the poor on the other, swollen by an influx of country-people from backward areas. The social polarization was emphasized by contrasting life-styles and values.

The upper classes continued to live in the manner of the Classical era. Their sons received an all-round education in the gymnasiums and their traditional physical education was now enhanced by a scientific appreciation of its value. For the last years of the fifth century saw great advances in the field of medicine, and medical literature paid close attention to the value of physical culture for a healthy life. Medical writers formulated the scientific principles of physical culture and a new discipline was established, called at first *gymnastike* and later *hygieine*. The foundations were laid for a branch of science that was to show remarkable success — therapeutic gymnastics.

135

The first to study these matters was the physician Herodicus of Selymbria, who had gained useful experience by serving as a *paidotribes*. He was interested in the theoretical aspects of training and diet, and was the founder of therapeutic gymnastics, designed not only to cure illness but to prevent it.

It was Herodicus's teaching that inspired another physician, Hippocrates (460-370 B.C.), whose voluminous writings were one of the foundation-stones of Greek medicine. Thanks to him, religious and magical explanations were finally abandoned and every disease was now seen as the outcome of rationally determinable processes. Much attention was now given to the aim of preventing illness and to the prophylactic value of physical exercise. Hippocrates also sought to establish rules for a healthy way of life, and concluded that its basis was a balance between diet and exertion. On this theory he drew up carefully designed daily regimes comprising regular morning and afternoon exercise, proper diet and a whole ethical system of body-management.[52] Throughout the fifth and fourth centuries, medical doctrine encouraged the exercising in due degree of every part of the body, and so gave support to the old ideal of *kalokagathia*.

Upper-class Athenian youths now found their education affected by the new role of the gymnasium as a training ground in philosophy, where the most advanced ideas of the age were dangled before a fascinated audience. Here the sophists defined man as "the measure of all things"; here Socrates preached his philosophy of morality, the first true humanism, and his death opened the way to free inquiry into everything. Plato taught his pupils at the gymnasium named after the hero Academus, the Academy, while Aristotle held classes at the Lyceum. Small wonder that with such instructors, education not only became the new ideal of the affluent youth, but added a new dimension to the whole life of Athens.

All these philosophers proclaimed the need for a harmonious development of physical and mental powers. Socrates warned against neglecting bodily exercise and himself practised rhythmic gymnastics and dancing up to an advanced age. Yet he was opposed to any element of excess or eccentricity in athletic training, and preferred discussing philosophy to hearing about the finest running or horse-riding competition.

Plato likewise placed considerable value on physical training, stressing its utility as part of military education in his concept of an ideal state. Here he took as his model the harsh training methods of warlike Sparta. Yet in general he advocated a harmonious balance between music and physical exercise, the one to rid the soul of coarseness, the other to preserve the body from effeteness. He was concerned, however, that physical training should not be overdone. He referred to a man who was interested in nothing but sport as a victim of the one-sidedness that rules out an appreciation of the full variety of life.[53]

A thorough discussion of the subject is provided by Aristotle, for whom gymnastics are part of the education of the young. Though he favoured the regulation of education by law, making it a public concern as in Sparta, he strongly rejected the rigidity and utilitarianism of the harsh Spartan system and insisted that physical training should aim at fostering not only manliness, but also beauty. He condemned the tendency towards excessive exercise because it "damages the figure and healthy growth", and stressed: "For until puberty we should apply lighter exercises, forbidding hard diet and severe exertions, in order that nothing may hinder the growth; for there is no small proof that severe training can produce this result in the fact that in the list of Olympic victors one would only find two or three persons who have won both as men and as boys, because when people go into training in youth the severe exercises rob them of their strength."[54]

136

Young men debating in a gymnasium. The place is indicated by the oil vessel hanging on the wall between the first and second figure. Detail of a painting from a red-figure amphora, the work of Peleus' painter. Athens, middle of the 4th century B.C.

A young man holding a strigil and a slave bringing a vessel of oil and the athlete's clothes. Marble tomb relief, Athens, around 400 B.C.

Aristotle was also concerned with the use of spare time. He divided the whole of human life into working, *ascholia,* and free time, *schole.* While both were necessary, he considered *schole* the more desirable. *Schole* implied for Aristotle time free from work, care and suffering, time suited therefore for the pursuit of cultural interests, for the acquisition of knowledge and the development of the spiritual side of the personality. He accorded a special place to music which, like Plato, he found important for building the character, in opposition to physical training which "builds the body".[55]

Games as a leisure pursuit were rejected by Aristotle on the grounds that their purpose is merely recreation during a break in work. To devote one's spare time to sport would amount to making it the purpose of life, which is something else — albeit connected with leisure. For spare time in his eyes was the opportunity for self-fulfilment in society, or perhaps for work dedicated to society. But manual work was rigidly excluded, the only two forms of activity worthy of a free citizen being scientific research and public service.

Clearly, Aristotle's concept of spare time is quite contrary to what Solon thought. Though like him Aristotle saw free time as the most crucial part of human life, he differed completely about what it should be spent on: in place of hunting and sports he put the accent without hesitation on intellectual activity.

It is quite clear from these examples that all the fourth-century philosophers, representing the greatest achievement in thought in the ancient world, demanded a balance between training of the body and education of the mind. In this sense they linked old tradition and the findings of the new medical science. In contrast with the past, however, physical fitness gave way to intellectual maturity as a social criterion.

The philosophers' ideas moulded the life-style of the rich young people who sat at their feet. The young continued to exercise in the gymnasiums, hardening and caring for their bodies. But their attitude to this training was purely individualistic. The exercises were still designed to turn out strong, lithe and healthy bodies, but what the pupils were increasingly concerned about was the education of the mind. Interest in sport, especially in its social form of competitive racing in the *agon,* dropped into the background.

At the end of the fifth, and the beginning of the fourth century B.C., the father of comedy, Aristophanes, was already pouring ridicule on the sophists' pupils as pale, thin creatures who never ventured outside their "thinking-houses". In his play *The Clouds* he complains that while the *palaestrae* are empty, the sophists' lecture-halls are crammed with young listeners. The satirist's picture is no doubt overdrawn, but it certainly reveals a change of attitude toward physical training among the children of wealthy families.

Vase-paintings tell a similar story. While in the fifth century exercises in the *palaestra* and gymnasium are among the favourite motifs, from the end of that century such scenes practically disappear. An object hanging on the wall may indicate that the incident depicted is taking place in a gymnasium but, far from exercising, the young men are usually shown fully clothed, in groups — deep in discussion.

In the fourth century B.C., education came for such youngsters to seem not merely a necessity in life, but a symbol of their social superiority and exclusiveness. The old concept of *arete* was thus greatly modified. The original idea of physical strength and courage that in the sixth and especially in the fifth century B.C. had become refined into that of *kalokagathia,* harmonious growth of body and spirit, swung in the fourth century B.C. toward greater emphasis on the mind. The initial aim of political *arete,* mastery of everything necessary for the running of the state and particularly

Bronze statue known as the Anticythera youth. In his right hand he probably held the palm of victory. Middle of the 4th century B.C.

An athlete scraping the dust from his body with a strigil. Bronze statue, Ephesus, Asia Minor, middle of the 4th century B.C.

knowledge of the law, was eventually supplanted by the aim of acquiring knowledge in general.[56]

The new sense of exclusiveness enjoyed by the educated rich was a side-effect of intensified social distinctions and a diminution of Athenian democracy. The restless history of the whole country during the fourth century contributed to this, with Sparta displacing Athens from her leading position among the Greek cities after defeating her in the Peloponnesian War. Sparta's own regime now grew considerably less militaristic, but still stood in marked contrast to the democratic system, however enfeebled, of Athens, and the example of Spartan power inevitably affected developments elsewhere.

Spartan hegemony also proved impermanent, however. It was succeeded for a short time by that of Thebes, and the Classical age ended in mutual hostility among the various city states.

The continuous warfare of the fourth century inevitably led to a general coarsening of life, to an erosion of social links and to a deepening of internal conflicts. The qualities of education that distinguished the wealthy classes in Athens and later in many other cities tended to deflect them from the problems of contemporary life. They felt apathetic towards the endless inter-city quarrels and retreated from political activity into the exclusive concerns of their class.

One result of the individualistic approach to physical culture and the depreciation of its social function was a growing disinclination to fight. Disputes and constant hostilities nevertheless increased the importance of the arts of war, which at the same time became more sophisticated and called for protracted specialized training.

The solution to all this was the creation of an army of professional soldiers, paid by the state and subjected to tough training. In warfare, where the only issue was the predominance of one state over another, such men proved more serviceable than a citizen army.

Recruitment brought into the new mercenary army large numbers of strong and able countrymen from outlying backward areas like Thessaly and mountainous Arcadia. They were happy to earn a livelihood in this way and they received tough military training, as well as special physical preparation.

Just as the spiritual side of the ideal of *kalokagathia* took on extreme forms as a result of the prime value attached to knowledge, so the physical side found its extreme expression in professional sport, which became a feature of Greek development throughout the fourth century. There can be no doubt that specialist sportsmen had existed before now, performing at public festivals and showered with public admiration and respect, such as Milon "King of Wrestlers" in the sixth century B.C. In the fourth century B.C., however, the numbers of these professionals increased remarkably, and their social background changed, along with their character. The majority were now recruited from the mercenary army, which therefore meant from lower social groups and from parts of Greece which had never before been at the centre of development. They were known as *athletai*, and were trained long and thoroughly in a single branch of sport, to take part in public contests.

Their trainers were also professionals who devised systems of instruction, deciding what their charges should eat, what they should avoid, where they should sleep. Apart from exercise, diet and sleep were the main factors in an athlete's regime, and in his comedy *The Peace* Aristophanes mentions as a common phrase "to eat like a wrestler", in reference to the vast amounts such men consumed.

As already indicated, medical science condemned this kind of one-sided

Boxers with their hands bandaged with thongs up to the forearm. Painting on a Panathenaic amphora, 366 B.C.

specialization. Some doctors, however, must be assumed to have played a part in working out the training regimes.

Few details of the training have been preserved and these mainly in accounts attacking their over-specialization. The physician Galen in the second century A.D. was scornful of the system, which involved a repeated four-day cycle. The first day, devoted to rapid and energetic movement in short bursts, was a preparation for the second day when the wrestlers underwent trials of strength; the third was again spent in continuous movement and the fourth in the most intensive tests of all. The death of one Olympic champion in the course of training, as mentioned by Philostratus in the third century A.D. suggests how hard a school it was.[57] The contests for which these athletes were trained included above all wrestling, boxing and the *pankration*, which now came to dominate all sporting events.

From the fourth century B.C. onwards not only the performers, but also the spectators and their tastes changed. The wealthy classes were becoming gradually less interested in watching, as well as in competing, so the festivals developed into a form of entertainment designed for the poorer part of the population, who even in Athens no longer received basic education in reading and writing, music or gymnastics. Political chaos and constant warfare had coarsened the taste of the spectator public. The *pentathlon,* the exacting test of all-round skill, had ceased to be the supreme attraction and ideas of harmonious bodily development had lost much of their old appeal. Races turned into a spectacle where the onlookers hungered for dramatic and exciting moments.

All-round harmony gave way to specialization; brute strength was valued above beauty, and heavy athletic disciplines, especially wrestling, found the most favour. The rules were simple. The wrestler's aim was to throw his opponent to the ground; to do this three times was to win the match. Boxing also achieved great popularity in this period. The rules prescribed that blows should be aimed only at the head and face. Pausanias, in the second century A.D., describes a match between Damoxenus of Syracuse and Creugas of Epidamnus. It was hotly contested and for a long time points were equal, until Damoxenus urged the other to cover his head; as he raised his arms to do so, Damoxenus hit him so hard in the belly that he died. The unfortunate Creugas was nevertheless declared the victor, on the grounds that he had succumbed to a foul.[58]

Injuries to the hands from striking the head rapidly led to the introduction of soft thongs for protection. There were various devices for this purpose, including different styles of binding. At first only the fingers and wrists were covered, but later the whole forearm, so that a kind of gauntlet was evolved. Then the straps might be studded with hard objects, or something like a miniature dumb-bell would be lashed to the palm, with metal balls protruding at each side. More frequently, several thick rings would be strapped round the knuckles to intensify the effect of a blow. A further device, which became quite common in the late Hellenistic and Roman periods, was the *caestus*, which comprised a series of sharp metal points that stuck out of the leather-bound fist — a fearsome weapon capable of inflicting severe and even fatal injury.[59]

In defence, boxers aimed chiefly to protect their heads, the main target of the opponent's blows; they wore specially constructed helmets, and ear-covers became increasingly popular.

Boxing between professionals was a ruthless matter; there were no breaks and the match ended when one contestant was totally defeated or, as more frequently happened, declared himself exhausted. To indicate this he would raise one hand outspread, or concede defeat with a shout.

The third heavy athletic discipline, *pankration*, was a combination of

A naked girl acrobat being watched by a seated man and figures with grotesque masks. A scene from a south Italian farce.
Painting on a krater by the painter Asteas of Paestum, around 350 B.C.

140

A match between pankratiasts under supervision. Painting on a Panathenaic vase, 4th century B.C.

Pankration. On the left a supervisor, on the right a man encouraging the pankratiasts. Painting on a Panathenaic amphora, 330 B.C.

wrestling and boxing. Unlike wrestling, the fight continued on the ground after a fall; scratching, biting, strangling, eye-gouging and mouth-gouging were all permitted. Blows could be aimed at any part of the body with the fist or open palm, but the hands were never protected as in boxing. The match ended with the elimination of one contestant who would signify surrender with a formal tap on his opponent's body.

Even contemporaries regarded the *pankration* as something in between bad wrestling and bad boxing, attracting men who lacked the strength for the one and the height and reach for the other. But the public seems to have enjoyed the unbounded ferocity of it.[60] The more pain the contestants inflicted on one another, the more furious the fighting became, and the more exciting and successful the show.

The head of a professional boxer with ear protectors. Detail from a marble grave-stone relief, 4th century B.C.

Pictures of wrestlers on coins from Aspendus, a Greek town in Asia Minor. From 400 and 373 B.C.

The changed character of the contests in this period was reflected in the outward appearance of those who took part. Sports festivals were no longer a parade of harmoniously developed bodies but of muscular colossi, mountains of trained flesh. Sheer strength was the only qualification for victory.

Representations of these professional athletes in the art of the period are highly revealing: huge bodies with muscle-bound limbs, disproportionately small heads and vacant stares. The finest and saddest is perhaps the statue by Apollonius of the first century B.C., showing a seated boxer with boxing gloves, torn face, broken nose and swollen eyes.

These professional fighters, coarse-grained and uneducated, born in poverty or in the primitive conditions of remote and backward areas during a troubled age and excluded from any intellectual activity, were made still more savage by their training and by the contests themselves. They would travel with their trainers from one engagement to another, showing off their hard-won skill to pitiless, sensation-hungry spectators. Neither danger, nor injury could deflect them from their career, for the constant surveillance of their instructors excluded them from any normal life and they were, indeed, incapable of other work. Ancient writers testify that they were not even serviceable as soldiers, so one-sided was their training. Unused to normal conditions they were not really hardy, and subjected to any deviation from their standard routine of diet, sleep and exercise they very quickly became ill.

Not that such men sought a different livelihood. They enjoyed benefits which, considering their humble origins, no other way of life could have given them. Every victory brought a princely reward, and the money in turn brought them in touch with higher social strata; from paupers and simple countrymen they became respected citizens, enjoying popularity and fame.

Even in earlier periods sporting champions had enjoyed boundless admiration, the acclamation of poets and the attention of sculptors who immortalized their bodies in stone; they were usually honoured as heroes in their native cities. Their professional successors were not honoured in that fashion, but the applause they won from their supporters was even more vigorous. The new type of spectator identified with his favourite combatants, seeing in them the fulfilment of his own private ambitions. Most of the public were now deprived of access to physical education themselves; they were described, from the end of the fifth century, as *idiotai*, that is, laymen without the benefit of training. In the writings of Aristotle and later authors this term invariably refers to people of common birth. These onlookers, unable to take an active part in sport, were all the more enthusiastic as fans. Watching matches was the most popular form of leisure activity, providing escape from daily cares; crowds encouraged the fighters, despised the losers and cheered the winners with fanatical zeal.

These changes had their effect on the Olympic Games, whose old glamour faded and Panhellenic character diminished. The victors' lists show that the exclusive four-horse chariot races drew considerably fewer entrants from Greece proper. These contests won increasing support, on the other hand, from aristocratic circles in the fringe areas around Greece where Greek culture was influential, especially in Macedonia whose power was now growing. King Philip of Macedonia was himself an equestrian champion several times over, winning in the horse-riding event in 356, in the four-horse chariot race in 352, and in the two-horse chariot race in 348 B.C. According to the athletic contests the Games acquired an increasingly regional flavour, and from the fourth century B.C. onwards, more and more of the victors came from the immediate neighbourhood of Olympia.[61]

A further by-product of professionalism, particularly noticeable at the Olympic festivals, was corruption. The first case recorded was at the ninety-eighth Games in 388 B.C., when the boxer Eupolis of Thessaly paid three rivals to let him win. The attempt was a fiasco, however. The fine imposed on the offender was so high that it financed the erection of six statues to Zeus, known in the local dialect as *Zanes*; inscriptions carved on their plinths reminded passers-by that victory in the races had to be achieved by strength and proper training, not by bribery.

A similar case occurred at the 112th Games (332 B.C.), when an Athenian, Callippus, successfully bribed his opponent to lose. When this became known the Athenians refused to pay Callippus's fine for him and the whole city was excluded from the Games. Only the intervention of the Delphic oracle settled the matter: the Athenians eventually paid the fine, which again was used to erect half a dozen statues of Zeus. More of these *Zanes*, or statues paid for out of fines, were put up later, until there was a long row of them at Olympia.[62]

As the fanaticism of the spectators and the corruption grew, critical voices were heard more and more openly inveighing against professional sport. They had indeed been raised earlier, starting with the poet-philosopher Xenophanes's ridicule of the adulation of champions at the turn of the sixth and fifth centuries B.C. His attack was that of a proud aristocrat, concerned chiefly to ensure the well-being of the city state. His poems are the first recorded expression of the new concept of *arete* that was to become normal in the upper classes by the fourth century B.C. — the idea that intellectual values were superior to physical ones.

What critical comments have survived from the fifth century B.C. are likewise aimed at the over-estimation of sport and particularly at the adulation of champions. An interesting critique comes from the dramatist Euripides, who in the fragment of the satyr-play *Autolycus* asks what use to the fatherland are sporting feats rewarded with garlands, and whether athletes can drive the enemy from their soil with their fists or with the discus.

By the fourth century B.C. systematic criticism is already found directed chiefly at professional athletes. Medical writers, valuing physical exercise as they do, are unanimously opposed to the unbalanced and abnormal way of life these men lead and insist that far from improving the body's health, it undermines it. Philosophers join in the same chorus, regarding such regimes as contrary to their own call for harmony between body and spirit and describing it in many cases as one of the greatest evils in the country[63] There can be no doubt that professionalism in athletics had many undesirable features; on the other hand, it was most effective in furthering the search for very varied forms of training, and their trial in practice.

The fourth century B.C. heralded the decline of overall physical culture in ancient Greece. In parallel, however, the rapid development of scientific research during the same period laid the foundations of purposeful, rational care for the human body and of human health in general. Even the much-maligned professional athletes were instrumental in this process, their experiments with a variety of exercises making an important contribution to the establishment of a system of scientific gymnastics, doubtless one of the great achievements of Greek civilization.

A coin of Philip II of Macedonia. On one side is the head of Zeus with an olive wreath, on the other a horse racer with the palm of victory in his hand. Macedonia, around 330 B.C.

Olympia. The road leading to the entrance gate to the stadium. On the pedestals stood the Zanes, statues of Zeus, financed from fines for bribing competitors during the Olympic Games.

The Greek Tradition

The Greek gymnasium in the town of Salamis in Cyprus.
Left: The palaestra. Above: A part of the gymnasium decorated with Roman statues.

Below left: A marble statue of two pankratiasts in the final phase of the match, the winner having dislocated his rival's right shoulder. A.D. 245.

The rivalry between individual city states of Greece, which marked the decline of the Classical period in the course of the fourth century B.C., was finally ended by a foreign conqueror. The invader was backward Macedonia, equipped with a strong army. The Macedonian victory at Chaeronea in 338 B.C. terminated the freedom of the Greek city states, and Greece, now under Macedonian rule, embarked on a new phase of her history, known as the Hellenistic period.

Under the leadership of Alexander, the Macedonian forces followed up the conquest of Greece with an attack on Asia Minor and Egypt, and then defeated the Persian Empire, which controlled the whole of the Near East. Alexander made Babylon the capital of this vast Empire, and so revived the glories of that old culture. This colossal power structure, however, was short-lived, and after the death of Alexander it was split into three parts: Greece and Macedonia, Egypt, and the Asian dominions of which, in the end, only Syria remained. Each area developed along its own lines, under local kings, until in the course of the second and first century B.C. they were all conquered by Rome and incorporated into the Roman Empire.

Alexander, and the regional kings who succeeded him, accepted the way of life of oriental rulers, surrounded by a vast court, magnificent trappings and the halo of divinity. They also adopted the royal chariot hunt as their exclusive form of amusement. Yet the dominant feature which unified the whole of this vast area was the process of Hellenization, the intense penetration of Greek culture into local life. Alexander himself pioneered this trend, for as a disciple of Aristotle he wanted to use the culture of Greece to unite the heterogeneous parts of his vast domain, and after his death the trend was continued by his successors, who were all of Macedonian descent. Greek became the official language, facilitating communication throughout the Hellenistic world.

In some parts, of course, Greek influence had been present since the early period of colonization, but Alexander's campaign gave that a new

147

A winning athlete. He held the wreath of victory in his raised right hand. Bronze statue by the sculptor Lysippus. Around 310 B.C.

intensity. Throughout the Near East and Egypt new Greek cities were founded, as the loss of political freedom set in motion a strong and long-term movement of emigrants to new lands, where they introduced the high standard of Greek economic, scientific and cultural life. Economic prosperity soon converted many of these cities into great urban centres; Pergamon in Asia Minor, Antioch in Syria, Alexandria in Egypt, were only the greatest of hundreds of cities now being revealed by archaeological excavation.

These new Greek cities maintained close contact not only with the motherland of Greece, but with each other as well. This was kept up by merchants and by the pilgrims who went to consult the oracle at Delphi, but also by professional sportsmen and Greek intellectuals – engineers, architects, judges, teachers, musicians and poets – who moved from city to city, seeking more or less permanent employment. They all brought with them personal messages, news of events, and fresh ideas.[64]

This new situation had a marked effect on Greek attitudes and thinking. Traditional bonds with the native city remained strong, but the Greek now felt his roots in the whole of the Hellenistic world, which was seen as a single unit dotted with Greek centres.

The conditions in which the new Hellenistic cities were developing, however, differed from those of the old city states, particularly in their lack of political freedom. Although the inhabitants of the new cities were free, and the cities themselves enjoyed some sort of autonomy, no real political power was invested there. The cities were only components of a great centralized empire, and this stifled their individual political development.

The lack of freedom, loss of their homeland, and the need to settle down in an alien environment encouraged a feeling that the world was in a constant state of flux. Belief in the old gods of Olympus died, and was replaced by philosophies which attempted to rationally explain the world and human life. Man with his passions and emotions occupied the centre of the stage, and life and art concerned themselves primarily with the microcosm of daily life. Instead of the beautifully developed bodies of the Classical period of Greek art, which represented a well-balanced attitude to life, scenes depicting human passions and figures destroyed by the lives they had lived were familiar in Hellenistic art: love scenes, orgiastic dance scenes, drunken old women, hunchbacks and professional wrestlers, crippled by their work.

At the same time, however, Hellenistic Greek culture drew new inspiration from the ancient cultures of the Near East. This was particularly fruitful in scientific matters – mathematics, astronomy, medicine and

Right: Professional wrestlers fighting. Alexandria, Egypt, second half of the 3rd century B.C.

A young wrestler preparing to attack his opponent. Bronze statue, around 300 B.C.

technical skills. The loss of personal faith and deepening scepticism brought some sections of Greek society into contact with mystic oriental cults and rituals; these rituals embraced the cult of the rulers, who thereby increased their hold over the people.[65]

Close contact with non-Greek cultures led on the one hand to increased tolerance and humanism in the Hellenistic world, and on the other to a strengthening of the desire to preserve specific traits of Greek culture. The old traditions were fostered, and ancient myths and institutions preserved. In this context Greek physical education played an important part. Its new social function was seen in the disappearance of the previous polarity. Greek athletics were no longer the domain of professional athletes on the one hand and aristocrats on the other, and all strata of Greek society began to take an active part in physical training. Even the character of the architecture provides evidence of this, as the gymnasium acquired the same dominant position as the *agora* and the theatre. The wealth accumulated by the new empire made possible the erection of monumental public buildings, luxuriously furnished and providing a high degree of comfort.

During this period the gymnasium became a complex of buildings and arenas inside the city itself. Covered running tracks were built, as long as 200 metres, where the various kinds of racing were practised: simple *(stadion)*, double *(diaulos)* and long distance. In some centres, like Pergamon, there were special courses for running up and down steps. The *palaestra* — for boxing matches, wrestling and the *pankration* — were a traditional feature of the gymnasium. The areas set aside for body-care were also extended — swimming baths, hip-baths, steam-baths, massage chambers, and places for rubbing oil on the skin and relaxing. From about 100 B.C. the gymnasium was equipped with a form of central heating, the *hypocaustum*. There were always numerous rest-rooms and comfortable chairs where one could watch the more active gymnasium activities, as well as colonnades for promenading and discussion.[66]

The size of these complexes is an indication of the important role they played in the Hellenistic cities. Columns were set up there, engraved with Greek moral maxims, and have been found in Thera, in Miletopolis in Mysia, and even far away, in what is now Afghanistan — in Kandahar and Ai Kham. The gymnasium was also used for lectures, and festivals of different kinds were held there.[67]

The principal significance of the gymnasium, however, was its role as the centre of traditional Greek education of the young. It was here that young men studied Greek literature, rhetoric, mathematics, and were given systematic physical training. The latter was part of a tradition, valued all the more highly by Greeks living in foreign environments and received special emphasis within the general education framework.

With Greek emigrants waxing rich on the fruits of Greek expansion, the numbers of wealthy young people increased. Special care was devoted to the upbringing of the adolescent *epheboi*, including their physical training. Their instruction was public and their tutors, the *paidotribai*, enjoyed increasing prestige. From the second century A.D. onwards their appointment was for life.

The *epheboi* were given duties to perform in religious ceremonies and had to take part in the races held during festivals; on these occasions their training records would be reviewed, the best would be rewarded with gold wreaths, and their instructors publicly commended.[68]

At first only Greek citizens were accepted in the gymnasium, but the barriers which had previously existed were removed, so that in time Greek women were also admitted, as well as, eventually, freed slaves.[69] Although the gymnasium and traditional physical culture played a crucial role in

149

preserving Greek culture among the Greeks in the Hellenistic world, they were ultimately of equal importance in propagating this culture among the non-Greek peoples. At first it was the prerogative of Greeks only to enter the gymnasium, but this slowly changed. Wealthy members of the non-Greek population were allowed in, and thus acquired the all-round Greek education, mental as well as physical. All those who completed this education were considered "culture Greeks" and demonstrated their adherence to the Hellenistic world by adding new, Greek names to their own. This trend continued even when Rome dominated the Hellenistic world.[70]

The response to Greek culture varied according to local tradition and from class to class. In some cultural spheres, especially in science, the Greek influence was welcomed and led to fruitful collaboration. On the other hand, in matters in which the irrational prevailed, in particular, the native peoples tended to oppose it. Religion was the prime example, but resistance also developed when the traditional forms of society and life style were threatened by Greek control. The response to Greek physical culture was also mixed, and was more readily adopted in areas with a tradition compatible with sport.

It was the coastal region of Asia Minor that felt its influence most. There were, after all, old Greek cities here through which Greek culture had percolated into the whole hinterland for centuries. Ephesus, Miletus, Halicarnassus and many others can be counted among them, and in the Hellenistic period dozens more were founded, all of them with gymnasiums.[71]

The same was true for the region of Syria, where Greek and Near Eastern civilizations converged. Many new Greek cities were founded here during the Hellenistic period, and many Syrian cities underwent Hellenization. Syrian intellectuals not only acclaimed Greek literature; many of them made a name as writers in Greek. One such was the poet Meleager, whose epitaph says that he was a Syrian, but having been born human, he regarded the whole world as his fatherland.[72]

As part of the Hellenizing process, Greek gymnasiums became an integral part of public life in Syria and thousands of young Syrians underwent the Greek system of physical training. Nevertheless, one of them, the polymath Posidonius, wrote that Greek physical culture remained alien to them. They regarded the gymnasium as a place of idleness, and physical exercise as a waste of time.[73]

Pankration. The standing wrestler has applied an arm-lock to his rival's elbow and shoulder. Hellenistic bronze statue.

Greek physical culture found a warmer response in Egypt, where it could build on elements of native tradition. Despite nationalist enmity towards Jews and Greeks, and the xenophobia cultivated particularly in the religious shrines, Greek gymnasiums spread throughout the land. Indeed, they became an inseparable feature of the great Egyptian cities; the gymnasium of Alexandria was outstanding, but facilities for Greek-style education could also be found in the centres of Adada, Ptolemais, Omboi and the Nile island of Elephantine. There *alumni* – "those from the gymnasium" – formed organizations to promote the Greek way of life, which served as clubs for those who had been educated in the Greek manner.[74]

Mesopotamia presented a more complex picture. A number of Greek settlements were founded in Babylonia, and there were Greek quarters containing gymnasiums in ancient native cities like Uruk and Babylon itself. Yet, in spite of Alexander's efforts, there was no real blending of the two cultures. There is no evidence that Greek culture had any real attraction for the people of the region, in whose own civilization nothing analogous had existed.[75]

In Palestine, too, there were many Greek and Hellenized towns. Jerusalem had a Greek gymnasium. In the second book of the Maccabees it is

The stadium in the Greek town of Aphrodisias in Asia Minor. The stone seats were built on artificially raised slopes. On the far side the entrance gateway for the contestants can be seen.

written that when Jason-Joshua sought to displace his brother as high priest in the Temple of Jerusalem (175 B.C.) he directed his request, accompanied by a gift of money, to King Antiochus IV, promising further gifts if he were allowed to set up a gymnasium in the city. His request granted, he immediately set about introducing Greek ways: not only did he start a gymnasium, but he made it compulsory for young Jews to exercise there. The people of Jerusalem, we are told, "at the call of the discus would take part in the illicit entertainments of the *palaestra*", and belittled the customs of their fathers. However, the originators of the way of life they were imitating failed to acknowledge the compliment; Jason-Joshua was removed from office in due course and led the struggle against the Seleucids. The inhabitants of Palestine then fought as doggedly against Greek customs as they did against Greek political hegemony, regarding the gymnasiums and physical exercise as significant aspects of the Hellenizing process.[76]

A professional boxer resting. His bandages reach up to his forearm and his fists are reinforced with metal. His cheeks and forehead are covered in scars, his nose is broken, his ears deformed. Bronze statue by the Athenian sculptor Apollonius, 1st century B.C.

151

The considerable Jewish population outside Palestine, however, in Asia Minor, Syria and Egypt, thus came into contact with Greek physical culture and was more influenced by it than the Jews in Palestine itself. In Priene in Asia Minor, where a large sports stadium has been excavated, together with a gymnasium, washrooms and changing rooms, the boys who trained there have left their names scratched on the walls. One of the names, to emphasize that the boy was Jewish, is accompanied by the figure of a menorah, the seven-branched candlestick that served as a national and religious symbol of Jewry. The Jewish philosopher of the first century A.D., Philo of Alexandria, also used a large number of expressions in his writings which are drawn from the sphere of sport, which confirms his close connection with Greek physical culture.[77]

The degree to which Greek physical culture found its way to the local peoples through the influence of the gymnasium clearly differed in various parts of the Hellenistic world, and was generally limited to the wealthy non-Greek stratum. Nevertheless, the gymnasium usually played a significant role in the process of Hellenization, and the numerous and complex sports grounds throughout the Near East were focal points in this process.

The sports festivals of Greece were of exceptional significance in spreading the ideal of Greek physical culture. The traditional festivals, headed by the Olympic Games, not only kept their primary place in Greek culture, but carried their fame into the new sphere of the Hellenistic world. In the new Greek cities different Games were initiated, some of which (known as Isolympia) were equated to the traditional Olympic Games. So far, almost three hundred have been documented.[78]

Victory in the Games, and particularly in those regarded as equal to the Olympic Games, was highly rewarded. Monuments were set up to the victors in their home towns, recording their successes, as can be seen from the late-second-century inscription found on the site of Cedreae in south-western Turkey:

"The Confederation of the peoples of the Chersonese salutes Onasiteles the son of Onesistratus, victor in the furlong race three times in the boys' category at the Isthmia, in the beardless category at the Nemea and at the Asclepieia in Cos, in the men's category at the Dorieia at Cnidus, at the Dioscureia and at the Heracleia, in the boys' and the ephebes' category at the Tlapolemeia, victor in the furlong race and the two furlong race in the boys' category at the Dorieia in Cnidus, in the ephebe category at the Poseidania, in the furlong race and the long race in the men's category twice, in the torch race 'from the first point' in the men's category at the great Halieia and twice at the lesser Halieia, twice at the Dioscureia, twice at the Poseidania, in the furlong race and the race in armour, in the men's category."[79]

This inscription is informative about the number of festivals held in various places in the Hellenistic world, and also about the athlete himself. He was obviously a Greek by birth who specialized in running races and had taken part in various disciplines from boyhood onwards. This, and the fact that he competed in the category of the *epheboi,* shows that he had been trained in a gymnasium. Afterwards he seems to have become a professional athlete.

Professionalism was a characteristic feature of the Hellenistic civilization, in military matters, where mercenaries predominated, and in civilian professions, the crafts, the arts, trade and athletics. Members of different social classes seem to have been able to become professionals in the sports, ill-educated and even illiterate men of the lower orders who were barely able to sign their names, and probably even former slaves. Yet there were among them educated men of the upper classes who had been educated in the gymnasium, particularly the elite *epheboi*. People other than Greeks also

Young men with the wreaths of victors on their heads. Marble statuette from the 1st century A.D.

gave their athletes, not only for local games, but for the Olympic Games and other Pan-Greek festivals. The Hellenistic rulers themselves endeavoured to glorify their reputations by sending their athletes to the Panhellenic Games, especially their chariot drivers.[80]

Professional athletes, like their counterparts in other fields, moved from city to city, from festival to festival, performing at their best. They were accompanied by trainers, who were professional *gymnastai* and saw that they exercised properly, as well as watching their diet and giving medical attention, to keep them in good shape. The athletes were specialized in the various disciplines, but some of them, wrestlers, boxers and specialists in the *pankration,* were particularly popular.

Successful athletes were rewarded very well financially, but there were other material advantages available, including high office. All of them bathed in glory and enjoyed immense popularity. The most popular champion of the era was undoubtedly Leonidas of Rhodes, who won twelve prizes at four Olympic Games, on each occasion the prize for three track events: the single and double races, and racing in armour. At two successive Olympic Games the victor in the running races was Pythagoras of Magnesia in Asia Minor, who also qualified twice as *periodonikes* by winning at all four Panhellenic Games. Philinus, from the island of Cos, came first at three Olympics. Alexandria put an exceptionally large number of champions into the field; the Ptolemaic dynasty invested heavily in the training of athletes and set store on bringing in as many prizes as possible. It provided competitors for both the two-in-hand and the four-in-hand chariot races, and these frequently carried off the coveted olive-branch.[81]

Professional athletes had their own organization to protect and further their interests. In the late first century B.C. there seems to have been a special organization of the élite victors in the Panhellenic Games, alongside the ordinary athletes' organizations.[82]

During the Hellenistic period all limitations on those watching the games seem to have been dropped. The Greeks apparently formed the majority of the spectators; it was their traditional form of entertainment and one of the ways in which they demonstrated their "Greekness". Nevertheless non-Greeks seem to have taken part in growing numbers. The fascinating and exciting spectacle offered by the Games undoubtedly attracted them, and the festivals in which sports played an essential part therefore became a most effective way of propagating Greek physical culture, and a means of general Hellenization.

In 146 B.C. the Romans destroyed Corinth, and Greece became part of the Roman Empire. As a symbol of this victory, the Roman leader had twenty-one shields, which had been looted in Corinth, hung in the Temple of Zeus in Olympia. A few decades later the Romans carried off the temple treasures and tried to bring the Olympic Games to an end by transferring them to Rome. Although this plan was never fully realized, towards the end of the second and the beginning of the first century B.C. the Olympic Games lost their significant position and became once again a local sporting event, as they had been in the beginning.[83] The other Panhellenic Games lost their importance at the same time. When Greece itself sank low at the end of the Hellenistic era, it was Egypt and the Near East that carried the dynamic traditions of Greek physical culture into the whole of the ancient world.

Top left: A professional athlete with over-developed muscles and low intelligence. Hellenistic terra-cotta statuette.

Below left: A side view.

*Scene from a festival: A girl dancer,
a man dancing to the
accompaniment of a double flute,
a match followed by a supervisor.
Mural from a tomb in Chiusi,
around 500 B.C.*

THE ROMAN EMPIRE

Etruscan Games

In the course of the first millennium B.C. the Apennine peninsula came into the theatre of ancient civilizations. The region was settled by Greeks in the south and became a part of the Greek world. In the central and northern regions of the peninsula a mature culture developed, that of the Etruscans. During the eighth to sixth centuries B.C. the primitive Villanovan villages were rapidly replaced by large well-built Etruscan towns, such as Veii, Caere, Tarquinia, Vulci, Vetulonia, Populonia and many others. These towns had monumental temples, a complex administration, an advanced economy based on metal-working, the crafts, and trade, and even sewage systems. The Etruscans maintained active contact with the Greek towns in the south, as well as with the Greek mainland cities, especially Corinth, with Phoenician Carthage on the African continent, Egypt, Cyprus, Phoenicia and other centres in Asia Minor. Many oriental and Greek influences can be traced in Etruscan culture, but it was a separate civilization, which reached a high stage of development.

The history and ethnic connections of the Etruscans are still matters for debate, partly because their language remains undeciphered.[1] Some scholars believe Etruscan culture developed from the Villanovan culture which preceded it in this region, while others favour the view that the Etruscans came to Italy from Asia Minor and combined the culture they had brought with them with elements of the Villanovan culture they found there. This latter view would accord with the statement by Herodotus that the Etruscans originally came from Lydia in Asia Minor.[2]

Besides references to the Etruscans in the works of Classical authors, the principal sources of information about this culture are the burial-grounds; these were established beyond the city bounds, each a self-contained world of the dead, exactly constructed to a detailed plan. The earliest shaft graves were succeeded by great circular structures in which a series of smaller tombs were arranged under a vast tumulus of clay of imposing dimensions. Each tomb was furnished with a wealth of everyday objects and many were adorned with

wall-paintings, which are helpful in providing at least a rough idea of the lives of the aristocrats, for whom the tombs were intended. A high standard of living is evident from the rich garments and the wealth of gold jewellery found in some of the women's tombs. The principal subject of the paintings was the way in which the aristocrats entertained themselves. Both men and women were shown reclining at banquets, at low tables laden with food. Silver utensils of the most varied shapes also suggest a high level of culture.

Music played an important part in Etruscan life, and Aristotle tells us that the flute was played in Etruscan ritual ceremonies, as well as on many different occasions, such as boxing matches, when slaves were flogged, when food was being cooked, and during hunting expeditions. There are many scenes of ecstatic dances, showing both men and women taking part, and also special dances performed by armed men.[3]

Scenes performed in public were a characteristic feature of Etruscan life; they were religious in nature, and formed part of the cult. They were carried out in honour of the gods, but apparently also in honour of dead members of the aristocracy. The most important element in the plays was physical displays of various kinds. Scenes of running, dancing, wrestling and boxing occur, with discus and javelin throwing, jumping, swimming and diving; they are found not only on the walls of tombs, but on vases, in relief carvings, bronze figurines and many objects of daily use. Most of the finds date from the sixth century B.C.

In 1958 a tomb was opened at Tarquinia where the rich decoration aroused great excitement when it was discovered that the paintings were devoted exclusively to sporting themes. It is now known as the "Tomb of the Olympic Games", and the walls are covered with brightly coloured portrayals of young athletes racing, jumping or preparing to throw the discus. In another tomb one scene shows a group of runners with their trainer, and a man vaulting over a wooden hurdle, while his trainer stands by protectively. Runners also appear on relief carvings, and are usually shown towards the end of the race. The "Tomb of the Monkey" depicts a wrestling match in which one contestant has just thrown the other to the ground, while an umpire, stick in hand, looks on to see that the rules are observed. There is another wrestling scene in the "Tomb of the Augurs", where the naked wrestlers stand with feet apart and heads touching, grasping each other's

Dancing women. Relief on a sarcophagus, Chiusi, end of the 6th century B.C.

Bronze statue of a girl acrobat made to form a lid of a decorated vessel, around 500 B.C.

Right: Scene from a festival: Two wrestlers are about to start fighting. The three vessels between them are prizes for the winner. Painting from the "Tomb of the Augurs", Tarquinia, second half of the 5th century B.C.

Scene from a festival: Two riders perform acrobatics and a wrestling match is watched by a supervisor. One of the wrestlers is about to throw his opponent to the ground. Fresco from the "Tomb of the Monkey", 6th century B.C.

hands in the final moment of concentration before the match begins.

Bronze statues of wrestlers are also frequent, and of later date (the end of the fourth or beginning of the third century B.C.) statues of men wrestling with women. A statue of a woman scraping the dust from her body after a match shows that women were active in the sport. Besides wrestling, Etruscan art also depicts armed combat, which seems in some cases to have ended in the death of both men. Boxers are often shown, too, with one hand, or both, gloved or grasping some device for making the punch more effective. Some boxing figures are shown wearing a protective helmet. An exceptionally fine bronze statue shows an athlete about to hurl a javelin; another represents a naked swimmer preparing to dive. Many vessels are decorated with figures of men and women athletes. Acrobatics on horseback also seem to have been popular, leaping on and off the horse's back.[4]

Chariot races are frequently depicted on vases and the walls of tombs. In the "Tomb of the Olympic Games" four two-in-hand chariots are racing, the fragment depicting one of the drivers holding the reins and looking back to see how far his rival has fallen behind him. The man is leaning forward, his hair flying in the wind, his face full of tense excitement. The third chariot is shown overtaking the second, while the fourth is experiencing an unfortunate

moment, as the horses shy and the driver falls backwards. In the "Tomb of the Bigae" at Cornet, three chariots are depicted, each a two-in-hand, at various stages of the race. One chariot is still stationary, and the driver is holding back his impatient horses. A second has just set off, while the third is being driven at full gallop past the spectators' stand.

The frequency with which such races are illustrated, the dynamic nature of the scenes and the wealth of dramatic detail all suggest that chariot racing was widespread and extremely popular. The question inevitably arises of the origin of these races, which demanded a high degree of skill and technical pre-conditions. The chariots illustrated are similar in type to those used by the Greeks on the coast of Asia Minor, although some technical details, including the harnessing and control of the horses, are reminiscent of Assyrian chariots. This confirms that Etruscan horsemanship was of earlier date than that of the Greeks in Asia Minor, and independent of them in its evolution; the Etruscan chariots, like those of the Greeks, were developed from Asian types.[5] Once again, the conclusion drawn is that the continent of Asia served as an important source of innovation for both Greeks and Etruscans. This is also compatible with the explanation given by Herodotus, that the Etruscans came from Lydia in Asia Minor, the region which from ancient times held a tradition of horse-breeding and chariot driving, and which, as indicated already, was the cradle of chariot racing. It is fair to assume that the Etruscans brought these skills with them to their new home in Italy.

Bronze statuette of a man wrestling with a woman. Handle on the lid of a vessel, 350–330 B.C.

Besides sporting races other matches were arranged during the festivals, in which prisoners of war were used as performers. In the earlier stages, these prisoners were killed, and sacrificed as part of the ritual honours paid to dead Etruscan warriors. The motif of human sacrifice appears frequently on Etruscan vases, and Classical authors also refer to the sacrifice of as many as several hundred prisoners of war. The killings seem to have been a form of public entertainment, judging from Herodotus' report that after the battle of Alalia the Etruscans took a large number of their enemies out of the city and stoned them to death.

In the course of time, this custom seems to have been superseded by organized combat, which offered an exciting and dramatic episode to the festivities. Victory in the contests meant a chance of survival for the prisoner. The prisoners were allowed to keep their arms — spears, shields, daggers or swords. Relief carvings and wall paintings show duellists covered with blood and wounds, or at the moment when the death blow was delivered. They are frequent motifs in Etruscan art, not only in Etruria itself but also in Campania and Lucania.[6] In these regions, which were under Etruscan influence, the forms of combat portrayed seem to reflect earlier local traditions.

Games involving animals were also important in Etruscan festivals. The animals are sometimes shown in combat, sometimes with an official umpire. There are also frequent depictions of men fighting beasts. The "Tomb of the Bulls" at Tarquinia shows bulls and men, and although interpretation is difficult, the scene may represent a bull-fight. The motif of a man fighting a bull appears, for instance, in the figural decoration of Etruscan tripods. In the "Tomb of the Olympic Games" a contest takes place between a blind man and a wild animal, who is tearing him to pieces. A scene from the "Tomb of the Augurs" presents a masked man, who appears in other scenes as well, and is called Phersu. He wears a short red jacket, sewn with tiny scraps of light-coloured material, and breeches. His head is hidden beneath a mock bonnet like a Phrygian helmet with raised vizor, lateral head-pieces and ear-pieces. Below is a dark-coloured mask, to which a long black beard is attached. The other man has his back turned to him and is wearing nothing but a belt round his waist and a cloth, or piece of leather, over his head. He is

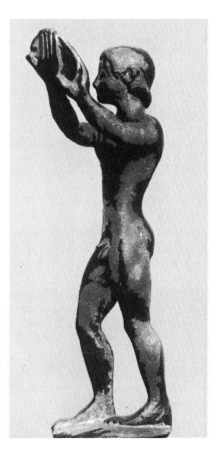

Bronze statuette of a boy about to throw a discus, around 500 B.C.

158

Detail of a chariot race.
Mural painting from the "Tomb of
the Olympic Games" in Tarquinia,
second half of the 6th century B.C.

Boy about to jump into the water.
Bronze statuette from Perugia,
beginning of the 5th century B.C.

being attacked by a dog, whom he has to fend off blindly, with a club in his right hand. His wrist, however, is held by a rope which passes round his left leg and is held by the masked man, who is thus in a position to hamper his movements or even trip him up. He also has a lead fixed to the dog's collar, with which he can egg the animal on. Phersu is, therefore, clearly in charge of the contest, responsible for maintaining the excitement and the subtleties of the fight between man and beast. The figure of Phersu passed through various transformations into the Latin dramas and thence to the Italian Renaissance commedia dell'arte; his name survives to this day in "person", in Latin the mask, and later the actor who wore it. The Latin word for an actor, *histrio,* is also of Etruscan origin, deriving from the word *ister.*[7]

Pictures of Etruscan festivals are frequently filled out with eager onlookers. In the "Tomb of the Olympic Games", for instance, the spectators are shown watching a chariot race. As one of the chariot drivers falls, the women desperately clutch their brows. In the "Tomb of the Bigae" there is a very detailed illustration of the spectators on the grandstand. It is a kind of theatre-box supported on wooden columns, with the onlookers sitting on backless wooden benches, the interior lined with red coverings and surmounted by a canopy against the sun. The spectators, of both sexes, are festively attired, the men in blue, red or white, the women in red, white or dark-coloured *chitons* with red or blue cloaks over them.[8] The painting, however, also shows a very different group of spectators, who are sitting on the ground beneath the grandstand, naked or casually attired. They are evidently members of the lower classes, and in contrast to the excitedly gesticulating aristocrats, they appear to be paying scant attention to the spectacle — perhaps because it was hard to see from their position.

Inclusion of a motif of this kind is highly unusual, and it proves therefore that Etruscan sports were not organized for the exclusive benefit of the aristocracy. The Roman architect Vitruvius in the first century B.C. drew attention to the remarkable ground-plan of the Etruscan towns. They were centred round an open oblong area which accommodated the Games and enabled large numbers of people to watch them.[9]

These scenes and other works of Etruscan art give an indication of the significance of the human body in this culture. It is clear that the higher social groups demonstrated their status by wearing rich, brightly coloured garments. Nakedness — as in all the ancient cultures of the Near East — was the sign of subordinate social standing. The naked body as a subject was

not given prominence in Etruscan art, and much greater care was devoted to the face and its expressions. The body was treated schematically, in smaller proportion to the head, as was the case in the art of the Near Eastern cultures.

Similar distinctions were made between the performers at the festivals. Again nakedness represents lower social position, usually, for example, men engaged in armed combat, or fighting animals, and in all forms of athletics. Certain differences are noticeable, however. Those taking part in bloody encounters or fighting animals wear a loin-cloth, as do athletes, unless they are wearing breeches, as in the murals in the "Tomb of the Olympic Games". Those performing in athletic races, however, are completely naked, which is a clear sign of Greek influence. A higher degree of interest in the body is apparent in these scenes, and many of them seem to have been painted by Greek artists. This differentiation between performers may, of course, have been the expression of different status; the men fighting duels, or struggling with wild animals, were prisoners of war without any rights, while the athletes may have been Etruscans of the lowest social order, who were given some degree of training to enable them to enter festivals as professional performers.

Drivers in chariot races are all shown fully clad, in long simple garments which cover the whole body. These scenes are larger compositions, in which attention has been paid to detail, to the individual features of the men, and to the intensity of emotion they experience during the race. All this suggests that the chariot drivers belonged to a superior social class, and were Etruscan aristocrats. In the dance scenes, too, the men and women performing the dances are dressed in rich, coloured robes, a sign of their privileged status.

Public festivals, including many kinds of physical activities, formed

Dancers entertain people at a feast. Mural painting from the "Tomb with a triclinium", Tarquinia, 5th century B.C.

Scene from a festival: A man fighting a dog. The "Tomb of the Augurs", Tarquinia, 6th century B.C.

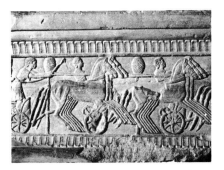

Three-in-hand race. Relief on a sarcophagus from Chiusi, 6th century B.C.

Scene from a struggle between animals, directed by two supervisors. Relief, 6th century B.C.

Scene from a festival: Spectators sitting on the stand with sacks full of awards for victors under the seats. In front is an armed athlete and a girl dancer, accompanied by a double flute. Relief on a sarcophagus, Chiusi, 6th century B.C.

a significant part of Etruscan culture. Two interesting references to their origin were made by the historian Herodotus. On one occasion he says that "the Lydians themselves claim to have invented them, as well as the games now organized by the Greeks and by themselves". They invented dice games, ball games, and "all such similar amusements", apparently in order to forget the hunger they suffered for many years, and which finally drove them out of their own country and brought them to the Apennine peninsula. Herodotus' comments suggest that public games were an important part of life in Lydia, and throughout the region of Asia Minor, where there was a tradition of contact between Greek and Asian culture.

The second reference made by Herodotus concerned the origin of the races held during the Etruscan festivals, and fills in the report of the stoning to death of the prisoners of war. According to Herodotus, the Etruscans were severely punished for this barbarous act; every living thing — small animals, livestock and human beings alike — that passed the spot where the dead bodies lay, was crippled or fell down unconscious. In order to purify themselves the Etruscans appealed to the Delphic Oracle, and were instructed to "arrange a great sacrifice to the dead men, including *gymnic* and *hippic agon*".[10]

The custom of human sacrifice gradually came into conflict with new social norms, and was replaced with symbolic activities, various sporting contests. In an analysis of the programme of the public festivals, the connecting link between the original human sacrifices and the later sporting events seems to have been the bloody combat and fights with wild animals.

The evidence seems to suggest, therefore, that Etruscan festivals embraced a number of heterogeneous elements. Some of these originated in the cultures of the Near East, some with the Greeks, and the rest in local cultures in the Apennine peninsula. They represented different stages in the evolution of Etruscan society, making it possible to trace the genesis of specific forms of physical activity and reveal Etruscan culture also in this respect as an important link in the development of the ancient world.

The Colosseum was built in Rome in the second half of the 1st century A.D. by Roman emperors for 50,000 spectators. Nearby there were four schools for 10,000 gladiators.

Gallery of the Colosseum with entrance gates for thousands of spectators.

Roman Festivals

In the eighth century B.C., the town of Rome, built by the Etruscans, replaced the Latin village settlements in central Italy. Etruscan kings ruled here until the end of the sixth century B. C., when they were driven out, and Rome became an aristocratic city republic, ready to embark on far-reaching campaigns of expansion. The Etruscan towns in the north, and the Greek towns in the south, all came under Roman domination, and in the third century B.C. Rome expanded beyond the Apennine peninsula, thereby weakening Carthage in North Africa; by the middle of the second century B.C. Rome was master of Macedonia and Greece, and then, by degrees, of the Near East, Egypt, and Western Europe from Spain to Britain. A world power had emerged. At the end of the first century B.C. the republic became an empire, and this form of government was maintained until the Roman state collapsed towards the end of the fifth century A.D.

The far-reaching and continuous policy of military expansion left its mark on the main features of Roman civilization; it formed the basis on which society rested, moulded its scale of values and was reflected in physical culture, in Roman festivals and games.

The highest place in Roman society was reserved for the aristocracy, originating with tribal leaders who had perhaps created privileged armed retinues in the monarchical stage. As the tribal system began to disintegrate, the aristocracy was comprised of groups who owned the most land. In republican times the military leaders and the highest officials came from this class, and representatives of the ordinary people gradually found admittance too. The right to establish an army, to command it and lead a military campaign, *imperium,* was the basis of both military and political power. It was exercised by those in high office − the consuls, praetors, and dictators. In imperial times this power passed to the Emperor.

The core of the Roman army was formed by the infantry legions, to which were added small élite cavalry units. To serve in the army was the right and the duty of every Roman citizen, and they were divided into five classes according to property. The wealthiest and most politically influential citizens formed the first class, and were recruited for the best-equipped units, as mounted and foot soldiers, with armour, a metal shield, spear and sword. The fifth class, in contrast, were merely stone-slingers, and the landless poor, who had no property other than their progeny *(proles),* had no military duties.[11]

Military training varied according to class. Fragmentary comments existing from later authors suggest that only the sons of aristocratic families were properly trained, outside the city walls on the site dedicated to Mars, the god of war − the Campus Martius. Their training included running, wrestling, boxing, throwing the spear, archery, swimming and ball games.

The cavalry underwent special training, and as their horses were

Scene from a chariot race at the circus following a collision at the turn round the spina (the three columns on the left). The charioteer is lying on the ground behind his car. Roman relief.

provided by the state, and maintained at state expense, they were known as *equites equo publico;* the members of this caste had their own organizations for young men, *collegia iuvenum.*[12] These young riders trained on the Campus Martius in equestrianism and chariot racing, and displayed their skill before the public on the feasts of Castor and Pollux, their patrons, held on July 15 in the Roman Forum, from 304 B.C. onwards. This was called the *equorum Romanorum probatio* (or *transvectio*). On other occasions they would present a military game, the *lusus Troiae,* in which they enacted a battle, and this was possibly of Etruscan origin.[13]

The military character of society gave birth to an ideal of the Roman citizen whose prime virtue was courage − *virtus* − a compound of military and personal discipline, and *pietas* − devotion to the gods, to Rome and to his fellow citizens.

From the end of the third century B.C. when Rome was beginning to expand overseas, Roman society underwent a fundamental change. The short summer campaigns over the Apennine peninsula were succeeded, after the Punic Wars against Carthage, by long wars which made greater demands both on military training and on organization. A professional army was gradually built up, employing volunteers who signed on for sixteen to twenty years. In addition to Roman citizens, volunteers were gradually accepted

Coin from the reign of Emperor Domitian with a relief of an amphitheatre crowded with spectators. Rome, A.D. 88.

Scene from a chariot race in the circus. A four-in-hand comes up to the spina round which the course turns. The charioteer has the reins round his waist. Roman relief.

from the conquered peoples, and these brought their traditional weapons with them: archers from Crete, stone-slingers from the Balearic Islands, and mounted troops from Numidia, Iberia, Gaul and elsewhere.

This professional army, the body of which consisted of mobile, well-organized and highly disciplined cohorts, required specialized training, an outline of which has been left by Vegetius, writing in the fourth to fifth century A.D. It can be assumed that the mercenaries underwent similar training even earlier, in the transition period. The basic training was preparation for long and fatiguing marches of fifteen to twenty kilometres a day, and "great marches" of considerably longer duration. In addition, the soldiers were trained in running, jumping and swimming, throwing the spear, archery, wrestling and various forms of armed combat. The equipment used included wooden staves, a wooden effigy of the enemy, the *palus,* and effigies of horses, for cavalry training. Hunting was also an aspect of military training.[14]

The formation of a professional army meant that ever larger groups of the male population were excluded from physical training. About the same time, however, the Greek idea of physical culture began to influence Rome, finding expression, for instance, in the improved hygiene demanded by wealthy Romans. From the middle of the third century B.C. they began

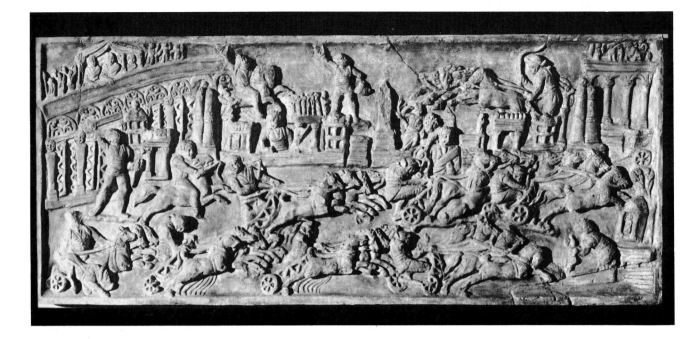

installing bathrooms in their houses, and this eventually became the general fashion. They were called *balnea* or *balneae,* from the Greek *balaneion.* *Thermae,* from the Greek *thermos,* were public baths supplied with hot water, and the first were built in Rome in the first century B.C., financed by private funds.[15] The equipment of these baths reflected the influence of the Hellenistic gymnasiums, particularly in the attention paid to body-care. *Palaestrae,* devoted to physical training only, were unusual, according to Vitruvius.[16]

Systematic physical training, which came to the fore in the Greek Hellenistic conception of physical culture, met with an unfavourable reaction, or even outright opposition, from the Romans. This was the natural result of a tradition of training, which served purely military ends. In military terms, the human body had no particular value *per se,* and therefore its cultivation was pointless. The Romans saw no sense in Greek athletics; they found them not only useless but harmful, as they considered them a "softening" influence. The nakedness of Greek athletes was also unacceptable in Rome, as it offended traditional morals. Cicero, who was otherwise a great admirer of Greek civilization, objected to naked athletes because stripping in public was widely proclaimed the source of all evil. The Romans also found it difficult to take an active part in physical training because they felt a sense of superiority, which prevented them from subjecting their bodies to training under the supervision of professional trainers, all of whom were slaves or freedmen. Seneca, Pliny the Younger and the Elder, Tacitus, Juvenal and many other writers all spoke out against athletics.[17]

The nature of Roman society was clearly reflected in its public festivals, in which many ancient rites survived, to ensure the fertility of the land — a relic of the rural character of the old Latin settlements. These rites included sacred processions, bloody and bloodless sacrifices, various forms of ritual purification, races which were influenced by magic and ecstatic dances.

In the new economic and social conditions of Rome as an urban centre, the rites acquired a new dimension and were enriched with Etruscan and, later, Greek and Oriental influences: the effect of the military Roman society was, however, the most marked.[18]

Four-in-hand races in the Circus Maximus. On the left a stand with noble spectators. Relief on a Roman sarcophagus.

A professional charioteer of the stable of Whites (factio albata) with his horse. Roman mosaic.

A professional charioteer dressed in the colours of his stable. In his right hand he is holding the palm of victory, in his left a part of the reins. Roman marble statue.

At first all the festivals were organized in honour of the gods, the most important of whom were Mars and Jupiter. March was the month for Mars, the god of war, as it was the start of the war season and, in the Etruscan calendar, the beginning of the New Year. In the course of this month, military trumpets and sacred shields were consecrated to Mars, processions were held and young boys underwent their initiation rites, putting on man's dress to show that they were ready for military service. Wearing the garb of Roman warriors, the priests of Mars, *Salii,* danced ancient war dances and sang in praise of the god. The young élite of Roman society probably held chariot races on the Campus Martius in honour of the god.[19]

Jupiter was the supreme Roman god, the protector of the state, also known as Stator, "the stayer of rout", and Victor, "he who brings victory". Ceremonial processions were held in May to honour Jupiter, and ended in the hurling of effigies from a bridge into the river — perhaps as a symbolic re-enactment of the sacrifice of human prisoners to the god. In October, when the military season ended, two-in-hand chariot races took place; one of the two victorious horses was killed with a spear-thrust, and his head, the sacred trophy, was fought over by the inhabitants of two of the quarters of Rome. Chariot races were also held at the festival devoted to the god Consus, the Consualia, which was held in August.[20]

Under the guidance of the Roman magistrates, the religious rites gradually became stereotyped as the state religion. Festivals were established as state holidays, *feriae,* days spent in devotion to the gods. Some of them were annual festivals, other marked special occasions, particularly a military victory. Throughout the duration of the festival all other activities ceased, while the priests carried out the requisite rites. Roman citizens, however, were under no obligation to take part, if they did not wish to.[21]

Public games, *ludi,* were performed at some of the festivals. They were based on military religious ritual. Before the army went into battle, the general in command made a ceremonial sacrifice to Jupiter, in the temple on the Capitol, and gave thanks there after his return. The most impressive of all Roman ceremonies took place in celebration of a victory — *triumphus,* and involved a procession along the Sacred Way, from the Campus Martius, through the Forum, to the Capitol. At its head were the Roman officials and members of the Senate, followed by trumpeters; behind them came the war booty and standards, bearing the names of the conquered cities and peoples. Exotic animals and important prisoners were also led in the procession, for later execution. In the course of his triumph the victorious general was raised to divine status; he rode in Jupiter's chariot, drawn by four horses, and wore Jupiter's robes, his face painted to resemble the statue of the god, in the shrine on the Capitol. He was surrounded by all the ancient Etruscan divine attributes, and represented the personification of the power of Rome.[22]

The general was followed in the procession by his commanders, his adult sons and other relatives, and the victorious army drew up the rear. The Roman soldiers, wreathed in the laurels of victory, shouted *"Io triumphe!"* as they marched, and also enjoyed the special privilege of singing and reciting improper verses about their leader — the *licentia triumphi.*

The triumphs allowed numerous secular elements to creep into the traditional Roman festivals; although they retained the nature of a religious rite, a man, the victorius warrior was the centre of attention. On that particular day his military prowess raised him to the level of the gods, of Jupiter himself, and yet he remained human. A slave, walking in front of his chariot, was charged with reminding him: "Do not forget that you are mortal!"

The triumph ended with public games, which were set in motion by a procession *(pompa)* from the Capitol to the place where the games were to

be held. Gradually these games differed from the war celebration, the triumph, and became purely popular entertainment. The games were called *ludi,* and this became the common term for free time and entertainment as well.

From 366 B.C., at the latest, these games became a separate institution and were held regularly every September. They were the Roman or Great Games – *Ludi Romani* or *Ludi Magni* – and were unique for almost 150 years. After the end of the third century B.C. five more games came into being, the Plebeian Games *(ludi plebei)* from 220 to 173, followed by the *ludi Apollinares,* the *ludi Megalenses,* the *ludi Ceriales* and the *Floralia.* Two of them were dedicated to Greek gods, Apollo and Ceres, and one to the Great Mother of Asia Minor, whose cult was influencing Rome to an ever increasing degree, alongside other Oriental cults.

At first the games lasted one day only, but this increased in the course of time to several days, and under the late republic seventeen days in the year were devoted to public games. There were three types of performance: games in the circus, *ludi circenses,* games with animals, *venationes,* and theatrical performances, *ludi scaenici.*[23]

The circus games were of Etruscan origin; according to Livy, the Roman historian, the first performance was in Rome, when the Etruscan victory over the Latins was celebrated. They consisted of chariot races and boxing matches, and Etruscan competitors were imported for the occasion. The first Etruscan king, Tarquinius Priscus, had a sports ground prepared for the occasion, in the centre of the new town; it occupied a valley 650 metres long and 100 metres wide. It is said that tribunes were erected for upper-class spectators and were rebuilt by the last Etruscan king, Tarquinius Superbus. This laid the foundations for the Circus Maximus, where the Roman Games were held.[24] The Circus Flaminius, established on the Campus Martius, was added in 221 B.C.

Chariot racing was the principal item on the programme of games in the circus. In the ancient world chariots were no longer used for military purposes. In Roman culture a chariot was the attribute of the supreme god,

Top right: Two men with shields (bestiarii) attack a lion in the amphitheatre. Fresco from Ostia.

Right: Hunting animals with a net for the games in the amphitheatre. Mosaic from Piazza Armerina, Sicily, 3rd or 4th century A.D.

Jupiter, and chariot races were part of the religious rites. In the circus the races lost their ritual significance, but seem at first to have remained a socially exclusive activity, as the charioteers were young *equites.* Chariot driving was part of their training and, unless military occasions intervened, could only be demonstrated during such festivals.

Besides chariot races, the circus included artistic equestrianism, acrobatic leaps from one horse to another, known as the *ars desultoria.* The performers in this case also seem to have been young Romans, superseded later, perhaps, by Numidians accepted into the Roman army. Horse racing was never added to the list of events.[24]

In the early second century B.C. Greek athletics, wrestling, boxing and foot races found their way into the circus games. 186 B.C. was the date of the first performance by Greek athletes in the Circus Maximus, and in the eighties so many competitors arrived in Rome that the success of the Olympic Games was threatened. Greek athletes appeared before the Roman public several times in the first century B.C., but both, these so-called Greek Games − *certamina Graeca* − and the idea of Greek athletics, remained unwelcome in Rome. In 44 B.C. Cicero wrote to his friend Atticus that the Greek Games had not aroused the interest of the Roman spectators, nor did he mind in the least, as his own views on Greek Games were well known.

At the same time as the appearance of Greek athletics, the use of exotic animals was introduced in the circus games. Roman military expansion, moreover, ensured that this became an increasingly frequent occurrence. Games using animals, *venationes,* were based on the hunt or on the confrontation of different animals. From the outset this form of entertainment was extremely popular.

Under Greek influence, theatrical performances, *ludi scaenici,* also became an accepted form of entertainment from the second century B.C. onwards. They never reached great heights of popularity, however, and almost to the end of the republican era plays were produced in improvised wooden buildings, which were torn down after the performance.[25]

From the middle of the third century B.C. theatrical performances in the Roman Forum took place more frequntly. These were arranged and financed by private individuals, by politicians and military leaders trying to gain political and popular support. The principal source of entertainment was a fight for life between two gladiators. This form of contest originated in Campania and was used by victorious military leaders in honour of their ancestors. In the beginning the actors in these performances were prisoners

A fight with wild animals in the amphitheatre. On the left two dead contestants − bestiarii. Roman mosaic.

The bestiarii fighting with wild animals in the amphitheatre. On the left the spectators' stands. Roman relief.

of war, in particular captives of high status. Their place was later taken by athletes who were specially trained in private gladiator schools. Candidates from conquered peoples were trained alongside members of the lower social classes of Rome. The proprietors of these schools, *lanistae,* would rent out their trained gladiators, at a price, to those who wished to arrange a festival.[26]

The number of gladiator contests grew rapidly. In 264 B.C. a duel between three pairs was presented for the first time, in 216 there were twenty-two pairs, in 200 twenty-five pairs, in 183 sixty pairs, and in 174 B.C. several performances of this kind could be arranged. In the first century B.C. combat between a hundred couples was common, and in 65 B.C. Caesar arranged a contest between 320 pairs of gladiators in silver armour. The gladiator games were not part of the public games, *ludi,* but were called *munera,* spectacles. They steadily became extremely popular.[27]

In the course of the first century B.C., the Roman Republic became involved in a deepening crisis which was reflected in the disintegration of society as a whole. Inner tension culminated in slave rebellions, the greatest of which was led by Spartacus, from the gladiator school of Capua. Oriental cults, with their ecstatic mysterious rituals, acquired ever greater influence over Roman society, and were a disintegrating force. Private games, initiated by military leaders, became more and more ostentatious, until the distinction between them and the official ones was barely noticeable. This characterized the growing influence of individual military leaders, some of whom, Sulla and Caesar, usurped dictatorial powers. Military leaders became the owners of gladiator schools — Caesar owned a school of five thousand gladiators in Capua — and could, therefore, depend not only on their mercenary army, but a private guard of gladiators. This profound social crisis led to the downfall of the republican regime in Rome, during the first century B.C.

*Ruins of the amphitheatre in the
south Italian town of Puteoli (now
Pozzuoli). A.D. 440–495.*

Entertainments of Imperial Rome

Augustus, Emperor from 27 B.C. to A.D. 14, initiated a new era of Roman history. The power of the Empire was now in the hands of one man, endowed with divine omnipotence, and Rome, a metropolis with a million inhabitants by this time, was its representative. Rome was the seat of noble families with inconceivable wealth, and merchants brought grain and goods from all over the world into its harbours. Men and women thronged the streets — not only Romans, but Negroes, Egyptians, Asians, blonde-haired Germans, painted Britons, Jews, Greeks and many others, contributed to the medley of costume and language. There were large numbers of proletarians, too, making a living as best they could, but increasingly subsidized by the state.

The city prided itself on its monumental public buildings, temples, palaces, parks and gardens; thousands of shops offered goods from the most exotic places. There were innumerable restaurants, inns and bars, many of which stayed open all night. Wandering minstrels performed there, acrobats, dancers, and astrologists, and the visitors gambled with dice and knucklebones. Bets could also be laid on fights between cocks, quails and partridges. Repeated attempts to close these drinking houses, or at least to put restrictions on the drinking hours, were ineffectual; so, too, were attempts to fine gambling or limit it to the Saturnalia. The concentration of the population in a large urban centre brought with it increased prostitution and criminal activity, and secret societies of the oriental type, with orgiastic features, proliferated.[28]

The Roman emperors sought to provide the inhabitants of this heterogeneous agglomeration with entertainment which would occupy their spare time, as well as strengthening imperial authority and popularity. Public entertainments, therefore, became an important part of imperial policy and a characteristic feature of life in the capital. The festivals, like state subsidy, however, were soon considered the people's right — *panem et circenses*, bread and games, as the poet Juvenal put it. Each of the emperors tried to outdo his predecessor, using all the republican forms of entertainment, as

173

A gladiators' school in Pompeii. The training ground and houses for the gladiators.

well as new ideas of increasing grandeur. As many as a thousand birds were set free among the spectators and lottery tickets were thrown into the air. The fortunate man who caught one stood to win prizes ranging from vessels, grain tickets, garments, gold, pearls, and animals, to boats, houses and even land.

New ritual occasions were added to the old, to celebrate a variety of gods, but most of all the emperors and their victorious campaigns and anniversaries. The cult of the emperors was instrumental in consolidating the widely differing parts of the Empire, and was affected by Near Eastern influences, as well as new ideas all contributing to the state religion. The number of regular official celebrations grew; in the first century A.D. they accounted for 88 days, in the second century 135, and in the fourth 176. There were also specially ostentatious games on *ad hoc* occasions, for example when the Emperor Titus organized games in A.D. 80, which lasted 100 days, and the celebration of Trajan's victory over the Dacians in 107, which lasted 123 days. Festivities of this kind included games in the circus and amphitheatre, scenic games and Greek plays.[29]

Games in the circus, *ludi circenses,* retained their traditional form and even some aspects of their former exclusivism. The chariot drivers wore the colours of their stables, as in the days of the late republic and up to the fourth century A.D. the stables, *factiones,* were private enterprises, run mainly by members of the equestrian order. Of the Red, White, Green and Blue, the last two gradually became prime favourites.

The opening ceremony was derived from the triumphs; the magnificent procession − *pompa* − was headed by the organizer of the races, dressed as a triumphal general with the old divine attributes. The ancient privilege of soldiers in the triumphal processions to ridicule and criticize was preserved in the right to express to the ruling emperor requests, reasons for discontent,

174

A gladiators' fight. The man armed with a sword (secutor) is about to deliver a fatal blow. Roman relief from the Via Appia. 3rd century A.D.

and complaints about unpopular officials. At a time when political activity among citizens was virtually non-existent, this was one of their few opportunities for free expression, and it gave a political slant to the circus games. The emperors accepted the demands made upon them on these occasions, and those who acted accordingly, increased their popularity considerably.[30]

The races themselves became more varied, and more dramatic. The signal to start was given when a white scarf, or *mappa,* was thrown onto the track. In addition to the traditional two- and four-in-hand races, there were events with six or even ten-in-hand. As a rule, each of the stables was represented by one chariot, but there were sometimes two, or even three, wearing the colours of the stable. There were seven rounds, and in the course of one day ten, or later even twenty-four races took place. The trickiest places were the turning posts, where collisions frequently occurred, and a race would often end with a bloody pile of human bodies, horses and vehicles lying on the course. The charioteers carried knives to free themselves from the reins in emergencies, but disastrous endings were common, as shown by epitaphs recording the death of many charioteers, between the age of eighteen and twenty-two.[31]

Under the Emperor Augustus, young men from noble families performed the traditional *lusus Troiae* in the circus. The old custom was revived in order to preserve the ancient traditions, and is described by Virgil in his *Aeneid.* "They galloped apart in equal ranks, and the three companies, parting their bands, broke up the columns; then recalled, they wheeled about and charged with levelled lances. Next they enter on other marches and other countermarches in opposing groups, interweaving circle with alternate circle, and making and armed mimicry of battle. And now they bare their backs in flight, now turn their spears in charge, now make peace and ride on side by side."[32]

The tradition of equestrian skills, *ars desultoria,* continued to play a part in the circus games, at least in the early years of the Empire. The performers were probably members of the equestrian order. The charioteers were by

A gladiators' duel with spears. The boys keep the fighters supplied with weapons. Relief on a Roman sarcophagus.

now mainly professionals, drawn from the lower social orders, freedmen and slaves, and other nationals beside Romans. They were organized according to their stables, and the successful ones were idolized by the crowd. The victors acquired the wreath of glory, together with garments, large sums of money, and an improved social status. Their names were sometimes recorded in the lists of victors, and those who could claim a thousand wins were particularly honoured. The originally exclusive character of the races was reflected not only in the relatively high social standing of the charioteers, but also in the fact that from time to time members of the highest social class would take part. Official decrees were passed, in an attempt to control this but, in the early third century A.D. the Emperor Caracalla himself did not hesitate to enter, sporting the Blue colours.[33]

In addition to the old Circus Maximus and Circus Flaminius, two new buildings were erected. The Circus Maximus was also extended to comprise a magnificent temple with a capacity of 200,000. It was one of the places where the imperial cult was born and where it grew; the emperor regularly took part in these festivities. For their own entertainment, however, the Roman emperors constructed a large hippodrome inside the palace, on the Palatine, where exclusive races were staged for the members of the court, as early as the end of the first century A.D.

Public games in the circus were popular among all social groups. The system of distinguishing the competitors according to colours created a simple and effective means by which the spectators could identify with the performers. It was not based on clan, locality, nationality or social groups, and each spectator could choose at will the team he wished to support. Collective loyalty to the colour in question enhanced every moment of excitement, anger or despair, and frantic applause, shouting and cheering would fill the air. Fanaticism inevitably flourished. Pliny the Elder tells of a fan who took swallows with him to the games, their feet dyed the colour of his winning team, to bring rapid news of victory to his home. Another fan, despairing over the defeat of his colour, flung himself on the funeral pyre and was consumed in the flames with the dead charioteer. The emperors had their favourite colours, too, and the gifts they bestowed on their champions ran into hundreds of thousands of *sestertii*. Caracalla, who supported the Blues, had some of the fans of other colours murdered in the circus. Rivalry between stables also led to bribery, to attract drivers from the other side, and attempts were made to poison the horses of opposing clubs.[34]

A gladiator with a helmet, sword and small round shield. Statue from Pompeii, 1st century A.D.

Scene from an amphitheatre showing duels between gladiators armed with various weapons. Roman mosaic, 4th century A.D.

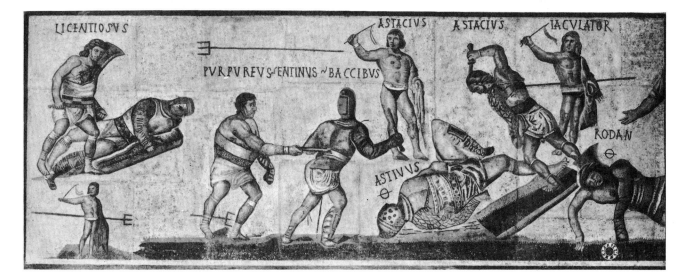

Bronze statue of a gladiator with a sword, his head protected by a special helmet that covered his face.

Ammianus Marcellinus described the significance of the games to the Roman masses, in the fourth century A.D.: "Now let me describe for you this mass of people, unemployed and therefore with too much time on their hands. For them the Circus Maximus is temple, home, social club and centre of all their hopes. You can see them beyond the city, arguing about the races ... and declaring that the country will come to ruin unless their favourite wins in the next races. And on the day they all rush to the circus even before daybreak, to secure a place."[35]

On one occasion the Emperor Caligula was so irritated by the noise of the crowd that he had the whole auditorium cleared. The chaos that ensued resulted in a battle, in which many people were killed. There were frequent disturbances, leading to outbreaks of violence between the fans and the soldiers, sometimes of a political nature. The supporters established their own organizations, bearing the colours of the two most favoured stables, the Blues and Greens.[36]

Another growing attraction in the Roman Empire was the games held in the amphitheatre, an oval construction completely surrounded with many-tiered stands, like a modern sports stadium. Five amphitheatres were erected in Rome, the largest being the Colosseum, in which three tiers of seats accommodated 50,000 spectators. Beneath the arena a complex system of passages, rooms, stables and changing-rooms housed the animals and the performers, with special equipment which enabled the scenery of the arena to be changed.

The amphitheatre served for the performance of wild animal fights, *venationes,* gladiatorial shows, and mock naval battles, *naumachiae.* The performers were professionals recruited from the ranks of prisoners of war, criminals, slaves, freedmen and citizens of the lowest social order. Their social status was low, although successful gladiators could acquire tremendous popularity, especially with the women of upper-class Roman society. From the late second century onwards, there is evidence of associations of gladiators, distinguished according to the weapons used.[37]

In the course of the first century the training schools for gladiators came under state control. The danger of the schools becoming training grounds for personal armies, employed against the Emperor and the Roman state, was thereby removed. At the end of the first century A.D., four schools were set up which were affiliated to the Colosseum, and were able to provide 10,000 gladiators on demand. The basic training was a military one, but this was later divided into at least sixteen special forms of combat. As well as the trainers, these institutions employed doctors, masseurs, armourers, bandage specialists and tailors. The *bestiarii,* who fought wild beasts, and those engaged in the water games, were also specially trained.

Games in the amphitheatre were also organized in honour of the Emperor, and gladiatorial combats gradually assumed this role, but, in the early years of the Empire, they maintained their traditional function at celebrations of the dead. The games were organized by state officials, and in the provinces, this task fell to the priests of the cult of the Emperor.

The morning of the games was originally devoted to fights with wild beasts, and the midday period taken up with executions of criminals and those considered enemies of the state and the Emperor, among whom Christians were included. In the afternoon there were gladiatorial combats. As the games developed, however, this order, which reflected the historical genesis of the games, was abandoned and each event acquired an individual significance.[38]

In the course of the *venationes,* various wild animals were hunted, including bears, lions, panthers, rhinoceri and elephants. During Nero's reign, 400 bears and 300 lions were killed on a single occasion. The hunters

Above: Gallery in the Colosseum. The recesses contained shops with refreshments for the spectators. They were also favourite stands for the Roman prostitutes.

Left: The space under the arena of the Colosseum. The remains of rooms for animals, gladiators and technical equipment for scene changes in the arena.

179

were armed with bows and arrows, but it was not unusual for a cavalry unit to be engaged. Combat between animals was also popular — a rhinocerus against an elephant, an elephant against a bull or bear and so forth. The animals were sometimes linked by long ropes, and were goaded or stabbed into fury, or straw dummies were thrown into the arena to enrage them. In Nero's time the floor of the arena, on one occasion, opened up to reveal a magic forest, with bushes of gold and perfumed fountains. The exotic beasts in the forest then proceeded to devour each other. Once, under Septimius Severus, the arena was given the appearance of a ship, which broke open to reveal a host of wild beasts. Trained animals were also produced in the arena, like the lions at Domitian's games that would catch hares, carry them carefully in their mouths, let them go and then recapture them; or the elephants that knelt before the Emperor, and then with boys and women dancing on their backs, executed a little dance themselves. Four elephants would even be taught to carry a fifth, and seals learned to wave to the audience and answer to their names.

A duel between two women gladiators, armed with swords and shields.

Combats between armed *bestiarii* and wild animals were allotted an important place in the programme. Bull fights were introduced from Thessaly, where they had featured in religious ceremonies as *taurokathapsiai*. The bulls were roused to fury with red rags, and fought by Thessalonians on foot or on horseback; they leapt on to the bull's back, caught it by the horns and brought the animal to the ground, before killing it.

The performances were sometimes enlivened by the use of wild beasts to carry out the execution of criminals; the beasts were let loose in the arena to tear the victims to pieces. When the death of these victims was incorporated into mime, the actors involved actually experienced the suffering and eventual death of the characters they represented. The story of Orpheus was sometimes enacted. Enchanting Nature with his lyre, the trees and cliffs bent down to him, and birds and beasts gathered round. Tragedy struck, however, when a wild bear was let into the arena, and tore him to pieces. Another favourite was the story of Laureolus, chief of the brigands, who was eventually caught, nailed to a cross and savaged by wild beasts. On other occasions the "actors" were dressed in priceless tunics of gold thread, and purple cloaks, wreathed with gold. As the ceremony reached its climax, specially prepared cloth was set on fire, and the "actor" died in the flames. The costume was named the *tunica molesta* — "troublesome tunic".

The technical equipment of the arena made it possible to create a lake, filled with large fish and incredible water creatures. Its principal purpose, however, was for the performance of naval battles, in which hundreds, or even thousands, of sailors, oarsmen and fighters took part.

Gladiatorial contests were among the biggest mass attractions of the amphitheatre. They began with a ceremonial procession, in which the gladiators addressed the Emperor with the words: *Morituri te salutant* — "those who go to their death, greet thee". After their weapons had been checked, they embarked on mock-duels until military fanfares signalled the start of the real fights. The gladiators fought with their national weapons, Thracians with round shields and a straight sword or dagger, Samnites with a large shield and straight sword, Britons in war chariots; some were equipped with lassoes and curved staves, others with long spears. The *retiarii* were particularly favoured, wearing only a light tunic and carrying a net, in which to catch the enemy, and then kill him with a trident or dagger.

Inspectors were on hand to urge on the fearful whips, staves and red-hot irons, while the spectators added their shouts of "Kill! Hit! Strike!" The contests usually ended in the death of one of the gladiators. A wounded man could ask for mercy by laying down his arms and raising his right index finger, and the noisy crowd would vote for life or death by signalling thumbs up or

Scenes from the amphitheatre:
1) Three musicians blow their trumpets, a woman plays the organ; a supervisor raises the winning gladiator's hand while the defeated rival lies on the ground.
2) Pairs of gladiators fight with various weapons. Some of them are bleeding, one admits defeat by raising his forefinger.
3) A man condemned to death is tied to a post and torn by a leopard. Another is borne on a chariot towards an attacking leopard. A bestiarius hunts a stag and an antelope. A comic dwarf shows off a performing bear.
4) A wounded wild donkey. A bear and a bull, tied together with a rope, fighting each other. A bestiarius with a whip driving a condemned man by the hair towards a lion. Mosaic, Leptis Magna, North Africa, 2nd century A.D.

thumbs down. A doomed gladiator then received the *coup de grâce* from the winner. Figures dressed up as the god of the underworld made certain of his death with red-hot irons, and representatives of Etruscan Phersu, or his Greek counterpart, Charon, carried the body off by the "Gate of the Goddess of Death". The dust on the arena floor was swept smooth again, traces of blood covered with sand, and the next fight would proceed.[39] Combats between armed women, and between midgets, were later additions to the games, along with acrobats that jumped through circles of flames or danced on tight-ropes, and fights between weakened animals, including toothless lions.

The reality of death, and the content of the performances in the amphitheatre aroused distaste among the more educated elements of Roman society. Some writers deplored the games as the "senseless amusement of the fanatical crowd", but others valued them as an education in cold-blooded courage. The games were, however, never subjected to harsh criticism, as their popularity was rooted in the militant traditions of Roman culture. In Roman eyes, it was natural for some classes to have no rights, and their lives no value. Humane ideas were foreign to the Roman culture of the time.[40]

Under the rule of the emperors, theatrical plays also flourished but the popularity of the circus and the games in the amphitheatre far exceeded them. Three stone-built theatres, each seating six to ten thousand spectators were available in the city but it was only on great ceremonial occasions that all three were in use. Theatrical performances, of Greek tragedies and comedies, were popular with the educated social classes, but the wider public preferred less taxing entertainment − *attelana, mimus, pantomimus,* or extravagantly produced ballets.

In imperial times, Greek sports − *certamina Graeca* − were included in the public games. Towards the end of the first century A.D., a large stadium was built especially for the presentation of this form of entertainment, and the ground-plan of the stadium has been preserved in one of the squares of Rome − the Piazza Navona. Running races were held, but the principal events were the heavy athletic disciplines of wrestling, the *pankration*, and above all, boxing. The latter was made even more exciting by the use of the *caestus*, a fist bandage with metal spikes, so that in Roman times boxing was truly a life-and-death matter.[41]

The Roman emperors tried to revive the glory of the Olympic Games, and their patronage helped to overcome the decay brought about by the Roman conquest of Greece; in the first to third centuries A.D. the Games were revitalized, ancient buildings were restored and modernized, new buildings erected, and the race tracks extended. The cult of the emperors was reflected in the marble statues erected in their honour. The growing number of spectators from throughout the Empire brought Olympia its greatest era of popularity. Once more, as in the days of Pindar in the fifth century B.C., poets sang the glory of the victors.

There were also chariot races, whose traditionally exclusive nature was revealed in the fact that members of the imperial family and rulers of the Roman provinces entered their own competitors. The glory of victory was enjoyed by the owner, rather than the driver, of the winning chariot. Nero was the only emperor to compete in the games; in the ten-in-hand race, in A.D. 67, he fell from the chariot, and failed to complete the course, but he was, nevertheless, rewarded with the victor's wreath. In view of this and similar occurrences the organizers of the Olympic Games refused to accept the results as official. Nero also entered the Isthmic Games.[42]

The Roman emperors organized official games in Italy, which were modelled on the Panhellenic Games. Augustus instituted the Actian Games to celebrate his victory at the Battle of Actium, and these comprised many

A gladiator fully armed. His head, face and throat are covered by a special helmet, his left hand and leg are protected by shields, his right hand holds the sword. Stele from Ephesus in Asia Minor.

Scene from the amphitheatre: A duel between gladiators, one of whom is dressed only in a loincloth and fights with a trident, while the other is heavily armed and fights with a sword and shield. A terra-cotta plaque, 2nd or 3rd century A.D.

A professional boxer with protective bandages reaching to his elbows and a caestus round each fist. Roman mosaic from Pompeii, 1st century A.D.

athletic events. They were held every fourth year, as the fifth in the cycle of Panhellenic Games and became very popular, continuing until the fall of the Roman Empire. Official chronology also took these games into account, at least during the reign of Augustus. Augustus also established a special stadium on the Campus Martius in Rome, for Greek athletes; after numerous adaptations, it held 15,000 spectators, and the programme consisted of heavy athletics. The boxing matches were most popular with the crowd and were the favourite of the emperor himself. Athletic events were included in the celebration of the Augustalia too. The ceremony instituted by Nero, the Neronia, only occurred twice, in A.D. 60 and 65, but the Capitol Games, instituted by Domitian in A.D. 86 were of greater importance. The diversity of the programme ensured its popularity, and the Games ranked alongside the Panhellenic Games, for the duration of the Empire.

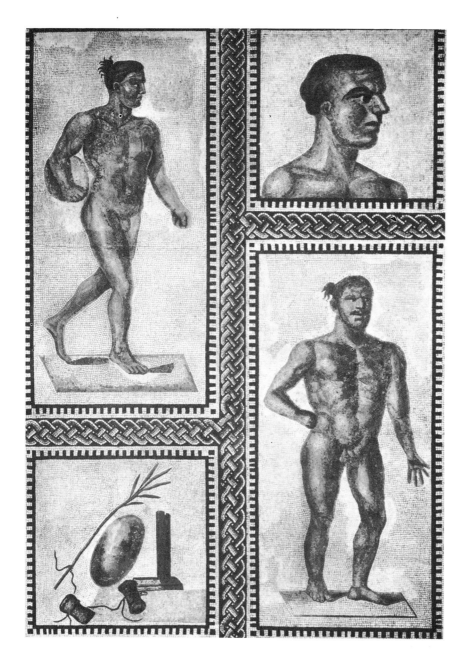

Professional athletes. Mosaic from the Caracalla Baths in Rome.

The hundreds of athletes who took part in the wrestling matches were professionals, originating at first in the Hellenized eastern regions of the Empire. They were free men, who were accorded the respect due to them in the Hellenistic world. By this time the athletes had their own centres in Rome, and a special meeting place, the *curia athletarum*, adorned with statues of successful colleagues. Statues of famous athletes were also set up in their native towns, and the floor of a room in Caracalla's baths was covered with their portraits. Greek inscriptions have survived, recording the honour paid to atheltic organizations by the emperors[43] and these acts of approval were instrumental in the break-down of Roman opposition. As a result, Greek athletics were incorporated into the Roman festivities.

The public games, organized under the Roman emperors, had no equal before or afterwards. They provided entertainment for hundreds of thousands of spectators. They created the maximum of excitement through the shedding of blood, through the agonal principle, through the new means

Top and above: A Roman circus token made of bone and found in Egypt, decorated on one side with the head of Hercules. The letters on the reverse may indicate the location of the seat.

of identification with the performers, and through the magnificence and variety of the spectacle. By the presence of the Emperor, in whose honour the games were held, the old religious rituals acquired a new function as a secular ceremony. The monumental buildings provided a clearly defined and enclosed space for the spectacle, and the employment of professional performers meant that the people were not actively engaged. The frequent performances gave the people sufficient opportunity for relaxation in the passive role of spectators, and their organization ensured the state official control of their leisure activity.

An important aspect of physical culture in imperial Roman times was increased hygiene and greater passive care of the body. The emperors themselves contributed to the establishment of public baths, *thermae*, which were equipped with central heating and every convenience. The largest of the eleven baths built were by Titus, Trajan, Caracalla and Diocletian, each covering about five hectares; their monumental ruins can still be seen in Rome today. Besides these public conveniences, all wealthy Romans had baths in their own homes.

The public baths offered tubs, steam baths, warm and cold swimming pools, and massage rooms. A Greek-style *palaestra* was one of the facilities, but instead of the physical training, which should have taken place there, it was mostly used for ball games.

The coloured balls were either stuffed − *pila*, or made of leather, filled with air − *follis* or *folliculus*. It is clear from the fragmentary sources that there were various games for a single player, or two players, but group games predominated, called *sphaeromachiae* (from the Greek words *sphaira*, meaning "ball" and *mache*, "battle"), which were noisy contests to get hold of the ball. The most popular was the *harpaston* − *harpastos* meaning "grasped" or "robbed". All the ball games, which were extremely popular, retained their original Greek names. They were considered part of Greek physical training and were played before bathing.[44] Like the Greek gymnasiums, Roman *thermae* were equipped with corners for resting, libraries, and colonnades, where companions could wander and hold discussions. The baths became social and cultural, as well as callisthenic centres, and were an integral part of Roman imperial life.

Through the medium of Greek medical literature, the importance of exercise for general health was established in Roman thought. The Greek physician Galen did most to further this attitude. He was active in the second century A.D., first as medical adviser in the gladiators' school in his native Pergamon, and later in Rome, where he became personal physician to the Emperor Marcus Aurelius. In his writings he poured scorn on professional athletics, and following traditional Greek medicine, especially that of Hippocrates, he supported remedial gymnastics. In contrast to the artificial training of professional athletes, he stressed the value of natural movement, rowing, running, jumping, fencing, carrying weights, throwing the javelin, and riding on horseback. He particularly recommended ball games, which exercised the whole body in a natural way.[45]

In the third century A.D., the Greek writer Philostratus gave a detailed account of the traditional disciplines in Greek athletics, outlining their history and assessing their importance.[46]

Although Roman civilization continued to reject Greek physical culture, it seems clear that its influence was felt, at least in the belief that physical and mental health were connected.[47] Juvenal's *mens sana in corpore sano,* "a healthy mind in a healthy body", is a distant echo of the Greek ideal of *kalokagathia.*

There were certain innovations, too, in the Roman system of education. In keeping with the Greek conception of education, learning of all kinds was

The head of a professional athlete with the characteristic lock of longer hair on the top of his head. Roman mosaic.

kept strictly free of utilitarian aspects, and regarded purely as a way of spending free time. *Ludus*, the name for a school, reflected this attitude. When the Emperor Hadrian established an institution of higher learning on the Capitol in Rome, in the second century B.C., it was called the Schola Romana, or Athenaeum, derived from Aristotle's word, *schole*, used for free time. The content of the teaching was also the same as the Greek system, except for one fundamental difference — the exclusion of gymnastics.

The strict military regime of Roman schools, and the use of corporal punishment, were both attacked, in the first century A.D., by the writer Quintilian, who emphasized the importance of games for the young. He stressed their creative and educational significance, and believed that a child who did not play would in later life be unable to learn to work.[48]

Very important in higher education were the schools of rhetoric, where special attention was paid to all-round cultivation of bodily movement in the curriculum. There were rules for every gesture, every gathering of the toga, every modulation of the voice. Once again it was Quintilian who elaborated the rules, which caused a contemporary to complain. "What Quintilian teaches us is not oratory, but the pantomime of oratory."

It was also Quintilian's belief that a degree of physical training was necessary for young people.[49] Travel became a regular feature in the life of wealthy young men, keeping them in good condition and broadening their mental horizons. Although physical culture had no place in the Roman state schools, it was included in the education of the sons of wealthy families,

An amphitheatre with fighting gladiators. A palaestra is partly visible on the right. Fresco from Pompeii, 1st century A.D.

The Caracalla Baths in Rome. Public baths of monumental size with pools, baths, steam rooms, massage rooms, palaestrae, libraries and social rooms. Beginning of the 3rd century A. D.

Women with boxing dumb-bells and a discus or a ball. They are probably not athletes but actresses or dancers Mosaic from Piazza Armerina, Sicily, 3rd or 4th century A.D.

a socially exclusive, private means of preparing them for the career of army officer. It was from these families that the leading men in military, as well as public life were drawn. The schooling was based on the traditional training of the *equites* and took place within the organizations set up for these young men, *collegia iuvenum*. Some of them were named after the gods, like the society dedicated to Venus, in Pompeii, but most of them bore the names of emperors, like the Traianenses and Antoniniani. The exclusive character of the society's membership was occasionally stressed in its name, as in that of the Nongenti, the Nine Hundred.

Each society had its own board of administration, headed by a *magister*, usually an influential official and former member of the institution. The *praefectus* was responsible for training, and the *procurator* was in charge of the society's property. Sons or grandsons of the emperors were appointed as youth leaders.

Revenue was derived from state subsidies, collections and, above all, gifts from wealthy patrons. The equipment of the premises and surrounding land reflected the club's resources. One club building of this kind, excavated at Pompeii, was amply decorated with its own insignia. Nearby there was an open swimming pool and a *palaestra*. Greek gymnastics seem to have had some influence, and Nero himself was in favour of it.[50] Nevertheless, the traditional and fundamental element was equestrianism, the socially exclusive physical activity of the Roman *equites*.

From fragmentary evidence it is clear that the members of these societies performed for the public in chariot races, equestrian exhibitions and mock-battles — the *lusus Troiae*. It is probable that, apart from infrequent performances in the circus, these were private occasions, possibly held in the emperor's personal hippodrome.

The forms of physical culture in imperial Rome reflected the standards, the nature and the needs of the state and its society at that time. The active participants were specialized professionals on the one hand, or members of the aristocratic families on the other. Spectators' curiosity was appeased by games in the circus and amphitheatre.

The amphitheatre in the town of Thysdrus in North Africa (now El Djem in Tunisia). It had a capacity of 50,000 spectators. A.D. 190-240.

EPILOGUE

Towards the end of the third century A.D. the Roman Empire was in a state of profound crisis. The power of the emperors had been extended beyond all bounds of limitation and, at the same time, the territorial integrity of the Empire began to fall apart. Rome was no longer the capital, and power was transferred to various provincial centres, like Nicomedia in Asia Minor, Mediolanum (Milan) and Ravenna in northern Italy, Sirmium in Pannonia, and Augusta Treverorum (Trier) in Germany. In 395 the Empire was officially divided into two parts, the western and the eastern Roman Empires respectively. Constantinople became the capital of the latter, a city founded on the site of the ancient Greek colony of Byzantion, on the European side of the Straits of Bosporus (now Istanbul). This Byzantine Empire, as it came to be called, adopted the Roman system of administration and power, but in language and culture it was Greek.

The territory of the Empire was ever more rapidly broken up by attacking barbarians – the Alemanni, Franks, Sarmatians, Visigoths, Vandals, Huns, Ostrogoths, and in the East, by attacks from the New Persian Empire. The disintegration was accompanied by profound social change and the beginning of a new official ideology. During the fourth century A.D. oriental cults were permanently barred from the Roman Empire, which now accepted Christianity as the state religion, and in the Byzantine Empire the emperor himself became head of the church. All these changes had a profound effect on physical culture.

In the course of the first three centuries A.D. the Roman *thermae* had spread throughout the Empire, and wherever Romans settled extensive baths were installed. They were centres for the passive care of the body, but also centres of social life – a manifestation of the Roman way of life and the sign of Romanization. There were organizations of Roman youths, *collegia iuvenum*, in many cities, and Roman public games also followed imperial power into all parts of the ancient world, in the first three centuries. Games in the amphitheatre became the most popular; like the baths, the amphitheatre

The text within the mosaic reads (partial/illustrated lettering):

PERCVRIONEM
DICTVM·DOMI
NIMEIVT
TELEGENI
PROLEOPARDO
MERITVMHA
BEANTVESTRI
FAVORISDONA
TEFISDENARIOS
QVINGENTOS

ADCLAMATVMEST
EXEMPLOIVOM
NVSSICDISCANP
FVTVRIAVDIANT
PRAETERITI·VNDE
TALEOVANDOTALE·
EXEMPLOQVAESIO
RVMMVNVSEDES
DERETVAMV·
NVSEDES
STADIES·
MAGERIVSDO
NATHOCISTHABE
REHOCESTPOSSE
HOCESTIA·NOXEST
IAMVNERETVO
SACCISMISSOS

MAGERI

SPITTARA   VICTOR   BVLL

A bestiarius fighting a leopard.
Above him a man with sacks of
money for victorious fighters. Detail
from a Roman mosaic from North
Africa, 3rd century A.D.

Statue of a fully armed gladiator. His
head, face and throat are protected
by a helmet, his body and legs with
shields.

was a landmark in every Roman city. Besides Italian towns, North Africa, Spain and Gaul built extensive amphitheatres, while many smaller ones were scattered throughout the Empire, from Seville to Jerusalem, from the borders of the Sahara to Scotland. In the eastern parts of the Empire, games in the amphitheatre superseded the traditional Greek athletics, which were popular in Hellenistic times and, in Greece itself, ancient Greek theatres were adapted for this purpose.

During the fourth century A.D., however, primarily under the influence of Christianity, limitations were gradually put on these games. Apart from purely humanitarian concerns, the reminder of the thousand of Christians martyred in the arena, hardened the Christian attitude. Among large sections of the population, however, the restrictions met with strong opposition, as illustrated in an incident, which apparently occurred in Rome in 404 when a monk, Telemachus, tried to put a stop to games in the arena by rushing between the gladiators and pulling them apart. Although he succeeded in interrupting the games, it enraged the spectators to such an extent that they tore him to pieces on the spot.

One by one, the games were banned, the first being the gladiatorial contests. In 399 the imperial gladiator schools were closed down, and the games ceased at the end of the fourth century in the eastern part of the Empire, and in the fifth century in the West. In both regions, however, combats with animals seem to have continued into the sixth century A.D.[1]

At first, Greek athletics roused no opposition from the Christians; this may have been partly due to the influence of Greek philosophy on Christian thought, but was also because Christianity evolved in the context of

190

A Byzantine emperor with his court watches chariot races in a hippodrome. A relief on the pedestal of an Egyptian obelisk built in Constantinople (now Istanbul) by the Emperor Theodosius I, around A.D. 390.

Rider with a four-in-hand and with the wreath of victory in his right hand. Byzantine mosaic.

Hellenistic culture, of which physical culture was a part. Christians, moreover, used the parable of the disciplined life of an athlete in their persuasions. The need for strict ascetic discipline and harsh preparation, the concept of the good life as a constant struggle against the sinful world, in which victory would bring the victor's laurels and happiness after death, were all ideas drawn from the imagery of athletics. Athletic contests were parables of the moral struggle led by Christians, and God himself appeared in early Christian writings as the umpire judging the struggle, the Divine Gymnasiarch.[2] Eventually, however, Christianity rejected athletic games as a form of pagan culture.

During the Roman domination of the Hellenistic world the Greek gymnasiums were in steady decline and in the course of the fourth century A.D. Christianity helped to complete their downfall. Public athletics also disappeared, including the Olympic Games, which were forbidden by the eastern emperors from A.D. 394 to 426 at the time of the destruction of the pagan temples. Olympia was devastated by barbarian attacks, and earthquakes and floods finally buried this ancient cultural centre under several metres of sand.[3]

The only sporting event to survive the destruction of the ancient world was chariot racing, which continued for another thousand years. Games in the circus never became as popular, in the western part of the Empire, as games in the amphitheatre, but the situation was very different in the East. The situation varied from place to place; in Asia Minor chariot racing was practically unknown in the first to third centuries A.D. whereas races were held in Egypt, in continuity of the Greek tradition. In Syria and Palestine the provincial rulers erected many new hippodromes, which in Antioch, Laodicea, Berytus, Tyre and Caesarea, for instance, held as many as 100,000 spectators. The popularity of chariot racing here seems to have derived from local tradition, strengthened by Hellenistic influences. Races of the Greek type were probably held between individual chariots and charioteers, and not, as in Rome, between different stables with their "colours".[4]

From the fourth century A.D., however, there was a significant change in the organization of the races, both in the East and West. The charioteers' organizations were replaced by a society financed and directed by the state, and the stables were also taken out of private ownership. The chariot races

Professional African boxer. He has a caestus on his hand and protects his head from the blows of his opponent by raising his arms. Terracotta statuette, 1st century A.D.

Left: Scene from a circus: A charioteer driving a four-in-hand with the reins tied round his waist. Roman mosaic from Barcino (now Barcelona), 3rd or 4th century A.D.

Right: A pankratiast about to kick his opponent. Bronze statuette, Gallo-Roman work.

Pankration. Roman mosaic from North Africa (now Tunisia), end of the 2nd century A.D.

came under the direct patronage of the emperor and hippodromes were added to all the imperial palaces where he took up temporary residence. In both parts of the Empire, the emperors supported the races held in their honour and strengthened their authority. These races were organized along Roman lines.[5]

When the western Roman Empire disappeared under the flood of barbarian invasions at the end of the fifth century A.D., the practice of chariot racing was lost with it. It enjoyed a new lease of life in the eastern empire, however, in the sixth and seventh centuries A.D. A large and magnificently decorated hippodrome, seating 100,000 spectators, was erected in Constantinople, the capital. Open riots, however, often developed, reflecting the economic, social, political and religious problems of the Byzantine Empire. In 532, a conflict of this kind escalated into a confrontation with the imperial power, known as the Nika revolt, which flared up in the capital and was suppressed at the cost of 30,000 lives. The Byzantine emperors, therefore, attempted to restrain the traditional function of the hippodrome as the forum for complaints against authority, and refused to accept pleas and proposals presented to them on the occasion of the races.

At the same time, the races became part of the court ceremonial and, therefore, an attribute of imperial power. This fundamentally changed the purpose of the clubs of partisans, who lost their independence and became part of the imperial clique. The partisans were allotted special seats in the hippodrome, dressed in the blue or green of their favourites, and applauded loudly to welcome and honour the emperor. They performed the same function at other court occasions, on diplomatic visits, imperial weddings, and, of course, coronations.[6]

The direct link between chariot racing and the majesty of the emperor, who was also head of the Byzantine church, put an end to Christian attacks on the sport. In the early years the Christian church held the same attitude to racing as Greek athletics, and important dignitaries took pleasure in competing. Gradually, however, Christian opposition grew, and Tertullian, at the turn of the second to the third century, saw them as the Devil's device, personified in the white cloth, or *mappa*, used to start the race. In the sixth century, Cassiodorus called the races the work of the Devil and the charioteers, followers of black magic. In the Byzantine Empire, however, the resistance not only weakened, but in view of the new social function of the races, directly linking them with the emperor and the church, the Christian liturgy itself was affected. In art this was seen in representations of the emperor as a charioteer, welcomed by God himself; Elijah was depicted as a holy charioteer, and, very frequently, Christ himself was shown ascending to Heaven in a racing chariot.[7]

Chariot racing continued in the Byzantine Empire throughout the Middle Ages in Europe. It was the temporary rule of the Crusaders in Constantinople, on their way from Europe to Jerusalem, that brought about the gradual decline of the sport from the twelfth century onwards. The Byzantine Empire itself declined, and was finally defeated by the Turkish conquest of Constantinople in 1453.[8]

Chariot racing, a sport which was taking shape for several millennia in the Near East, Egypt, the Aegean, the Greek world and the Roman Empire, disappeared with the birth of the New Age, symbolically, perhaps, at the point where the sea links Asia with Europe. There, too, ends the history of sport and games in the ancient world.

Scene from the amphitheatre: Two bestiarii fighting with wild animals. Mosaic from the palace in Constantinople, 5th or 6th century A.D.

Notes

PROLOGUE

1 Groos, Menschen; Groos, Tiere; Lorenz, Böse; Lorenz, Verhalten
2 Bernatzik, Völkerkunde, p. 692 ff
3 Frobenius, Kulturgeschichte, p. 33 ff, 82 ff; Jensen, Beschneidung; Eliade, Rites, p. 24 ff
4 Kerényi, Wesen; Huizinga, Homo; Damm, Spiele; Culin, Games; Bogeng, Geschichte, I; Diem, Weltgeschichte, I
5 Bandi-Maringer, Eiszeit; Burkert, Homo; Dashler, Cattle Keeping; Eliade, Rites; Frazer, Bough; Frobenius, Menschenjagden; Jensen, Myth; Levy, Gate; Meuli, Opferbräuche; Sethe, Urgeschichte
6 Gaster, Drama; Gaster, Thespis; Sethe, Denkmal
7 Frobenius, Kulturgeschichte; Caillois, Man, p. 88 ff; Levy, Gate, p. 23 ff
8 Lorenz, Böse, p. 373 ff; Wiemann, Phylogenese, p. 55 ff
9 Damm, Spiele; Ulf, Sport
10 Jensen, Myth, p. 151 ff; Jensen, Wettkampf-Parteien; Janssen, Mikronesien, p. 161 ff; Hofstätter, Gruppendynamik
11 Frobenius, Kulturgeschichte; Caillois, Man, p. 88 ff; Otto Stierkulte; Olivová, Sobre
12 CAH I,2, p. 249 ff
13 Mellaart, Çatal Hüyük, XIII, p. 170 ff, ill. 61–63
14 CAH, I,2

THE OLDEST CIVILIZATIONS

The Near East

1 Bonnet, Reallexikon; Ebeling, Geschichte; Kramer, Tablets; Kramer, Sumerians; Schmöckel, Geschichte; Schmöckel, Ur; Riemschneider, Welt; Matthiae, Ebla
2 CAH, I,2, p. 162 ff, 736, 755
3 Zimmerli, Menschenbild; Garbini, Cività; Herodotus, I,10
4 Kramer, Mythologies
5 CAH, I,2; Ueberhorst, Geschichte, I, p. 180; Falkenstein – Soden, Hymnen
6 CAH, I,2, p. 121, 123, 269, 342; Strommenger – Hirmer, Mesopotamien, No. 18; Hančar, Pferd, p. 472 ff, 486 ff; Wiesner, Fahren, p. 76–90
7 CAH, I,1, p. 138 ff, 144; Goetze, Kleinasien, p. 63, 128; Hančar, Pferd, p. 472 ff; Wiesner, Fahren, p. 76–81; Salonen A., Hippologica; Salonen E., Waffen; Potratz, Pferd
8 Ebeling, Bruchstücke; Kammenhuber, Hippologica, p. 298 ff, 314 ff
9 Wiesner, Fahren, p. 80, 87 ff; CAH, I,2, p. 589; Bible, I,9, 19; II,10,26; Greenhalgh, Warfare, p. 44
10 Hančar, Pferd, p. 406 f, 414 ff, 551 f; Knauth – Nadjmabadi, Fürstenideal, p. 73
11 Schmöckel, Kulturgeschichte, p. 103, 377
12 Strommenger – Hirmer, Mesopotamien
13 Knauth – Nadjmabadi, Fürstenideal, p. 95; Kramer, Tablets, p. 120
14 Moortgat, Bildende Kunst, p. 50–55; Moortgat, Bildwerk, p. 31 f; Akurgal, Hethiten, No. 84–87, 105, 133, 146 f
15 Strommenger – Hirmer, Mesopotamien, No. 18, 187–203, 246–256, 260, p. 117; Parrot, Assur, No. 65; Xenophon, Cyropaedia, I, 4
16 Haupt, Cuneiform Terms, p. 127–132
17 Lesky, Literatur, p. 617 ff; Xenophon, Cyropaedia, VIII,3
18 Schmöckel, Sumer, p. 153; Zimmern, Neujahrsfest, p. 1–14; Olivová, Sport
19 Ehelolf, Wettlauf, p. 267–272; Lesky, Scheinkampf, p. 73–82; Gaster, Thespis, p. 267
20 Zimmern, Neujahrsfest, p. 18 f, 22; Zimmern, Zum Neujahrsfest, I, p. 126 f; Schmöckel, Sumer, p. 153
21 Strommenger – Hirmer, Mesopotamien, No. 45, 46, 48; Ueberhorst, Geschichte, I, p. 103, 183
22 Ehelolf, Wettlauf, p. 267 ff; Zimmern, Zum Neujahrsfest, II, p. 18, 19; Assyrian Dictionary

Egypt

23 Breasted, History; Buck, Coffin Texts
24 Žába, Ptahhotep; Kees, Ägypten, p. 66
25 Lexa, Život, I, p. 73, 209
26 Davies – Gardiner, Paintings; Erman, Welt, p. 65; Erman, Ägypten, p. 334
27 Lexa, Život, I, p. 204–208; Lexová, Dances; Brunner – Traut, Tanz; Ueberhorst, Geschichte, I, p. 196 f
28 Wilsdorf, Ringkampf; Touny – Wenig, Sport
29 Erman, Ägypten, p. 695; Hayes, Scepter
30 Driot – Vardier, L'Égypte
31 Touny – Wenig, Sport; Decker, Quellentexte, p. 49 ff; CAH, I,2, p. 355 f, 709 f
32 Greenhalgh, Warfare, p. 20
33 Touny – Wenig, Sport, p. 41, 102 f; Decker, Quellentexte, p. 51
34 Wolf, Welt, p. 89; Scharff – Moortgat, Ägypten, p. 135 f; Decker, Pharao
35 Brunner, Erziehung
36 Touny – Wenig, Sport, p. 24, 28
37 Kees, Ägypten, p. 251 f; Kees, Götterglaube; Bonnet, Reallexikon; Erman, Ägypten, p. 378 ff; Schott, Fest

38 Otto − Hirmer, Art, p.24; Schäfer, Mysterien; Sethe, Denkmal; Sethe, Ramesseumpapyrus

39 Decker, Bibliographie, No. 148−175; Decker, Pharao, p.60 f

40 Lexa, Život, I, p.205; Lexová, Dances; Kees, Opfertanz; Sethe, Ramesseumpapyrus, p.123

41 Erman, Ägypten, p.378 f; CAH, I,2, p.1; Herodotus, II, 63

42 Sethe, Ramesseumpapyrus, p.98 f, 168 f

43 Touny − Wenig, Sport, No. 6; Decker, Quellentexte, p.82−84

44 Herodotus, II, 91; Badawy, Min, p.163 ff

45 Davies − Gardiner, Paintings, No. XL; Herodotus, II, 48

The Aegean

46 Prehistory, p.22 ff

47 Marinatos, Thera; Marinatos, Atlantis

48 Prehistory, p.217, 268, 302 ff

49 Nilsson, Minoan Religion; Willetts, Ancient Crete; Faure, La vie

50 Schachermeyr, Kultur, p.131 ff, 179 ff; Matz, Kreta, p.93; ff; Prehistory, p.224 ff

51 Evans, Palace, III, Tab. 25; Marinatos − Hirmer, Crete, ill.109; Schachermeyr, Kultur, p.133

52 Hood, Minoans, p.130; Matz, Kreta, p.90; Prehistory, p.230 ff; Nilsson, Minoan Religion, p.241 ff, 370 f

53 Schachermeyr, Kultur, p. 136 f, 140 ff, 158; Hood, Minoans, p.138; Higgins, Minoan

54 Evans, Palace, I, p.689 ff; IV, p.594 f; Prehistory, p.245

55 Nilsson, Minoan Religion, p.287; Hood, Minoans, No. 98; Buchholz − Karageorghis, Altägäis; Chadwick, World

56 Marinatos − Hirmer, Crete, No. 14, 96, 97, 107, 117, 180; Prehistory, p.206 ff, 235 f

57 Nilsson, Minoan Religion, p.72 ff

58 Nilsson, Minoan Religion, p.146 ff; Burkert, Religion, p.77

THE GREEK WORLD

The Mycenaean Warriors

1 Prehistory, p.242 ff; Marinatos − Hirmer, Kreta

2 Greenhalgh, Warfare, p.30 f; Lejeune, Civilization, p.49

3 Boardman, Overseas, p.61 ff; Segert, Schrift; Naveh, Consideration

Homer's Sports Reporting

4 Homer, Iliad, XXIII

5 Lesky, Homeros; Ridington, Background; West, Greek, p.205 f; Strömberg, Bellerophontes

6 Homer, Iliad, IV, 388 ff; XI, 699; XXIII, 680; Homer, Odyssey, IV, 625; VIII, 186 f; XIII, 260; XVII, 167

7 Homer, Odyssey, VIII, 145 f, 160

8 Homer, Odyssey, XVIII, 13 ff

9 Andronikos, Totenkult, p.122 ff; Schweitzer, Kunst, No. 56 ff

10 Homer, Iliad, XI, 699; XXIII, 679; Homer, Odyssey, VIII, 100 ff; Pope, Gymnastik

11 Greenhalgh, Warfare; Anderson, Horsemanship; Wiesner, Fahren; Snodgrass, Armour

12 Greenhalgh, Warfare, p.44

The Ideal of Harmonious Personality

13 Pape, Handwörterbuch, p.6, 349, 353; Menge − Güthling, Hand- und Schulwörterbuch, I, p.104

14 Jaeger, Paideia, I, p.26 ff; Delmore, Gymnasion; Forbes, Education

15 Lesky, Literatur, p.107 ff; Murray, Greece, p.192 ff

16 De Ste. Croix, War, p.355 ff, esp. 371−6; Lobel − Page, Fragmenta, Sappho, fr.50, Olivová, Kalokagathia

17 Pausanias, 3, 14, 8−10

18 Plutarch, Lycurgus, XVI, 6

19 Nilsson, Feste, p.190 ff

20 Oliva, Sparta, p.45 ff

21 Busolt − Swoboda, Staatskunde, II, p.701

22 Willetts, Crete, p.113

23 Oliva, Sparta, p.130 f

24 Oliva, Sólon, p.42 ff

25 Ruschenbusch, Solonos nomoi, F 74 a,b,c,e

26 Zschietzschmann, Wettkampf, II, p.17, 31

27 Diehl, Anthologia, Solon, fr.13

The Panhellenic Games

28 Burkert, Religion; Burkert, Homo Necans; Meuli, Opferbräuche

29 Schoemann − Lipsius, Alterthümer, p.509, 530, 533; Jüthner, Leibesübungen, p.63; Nilsson, Feste, p.140 f; Meuli, Agon, p.58; Ringwood, Features; Roller, Games

30 Herrmann, Olympia, p.49 ff

31 Bengtson, Spiele, p.29 f; Drees, Ursprung

32 Andronikos, Totenkult, p.122 ff

33 Archaic Period, p.89

34 Ziehen, Olympia, col. 1 ff; Deubner, Kult; Drees, Olympia; Mezö, Geschichte, p. 59 ff, 221 ff; Schoemann − Lipsius, Alterthümer, II, p.53 ff; Bengtson, Spiele, p.57 ff; Finley-Pleket, Games; Biliński, Agoni; Biliński, L'agonistica; Buhmann, Sieg; Krause,

35 Schoemann — Lipsius, Alterthümer, II, p.69—71; Krause,
   Pythien, p.1—53

Olympia; Krause, Gymnastik

36 Krause, Pythien, p.71 f,
   107—146
37 Krause, Pythien, p.72—74,
   165—209
38 Ziehen, Olympia; Bengtson,
   Spiele; Finley — Pleket,
   Games
39 Gardiner, Athletics, p.53 ff;
   Garduber, Sports; Hyde,
   Victor

Classical Beauty

40 Schachermeyr, Perikles, p.64,
   118
41 Hermann — Blümner, Lehrbuch, p.312 ff; Delorme,
   Gymnasion
42 Herodotus, VIII, 89; Plato,
   Laws, 2, 689 D; Mehl,
   Schwimmkunst
43 Hermann — Blümner, Lehrbuch, p.309, 339
44 Pausanias, 6, XX, 10—14
45 Bengtson, Spiele, p.69 ff
46 Schoemann — Lipsius, Alterthümer, II, p.173
47 Plutarch, Aristides, XXI, 1
48 Pausanias, 9, II, 6
49 Schoemann — Lipsius, Alterthümer, II, p.458 ff
50 Deubner, Feste, p.22 ff
51 Thucydides, II, 37—41

Scientific and Professional
Gymnastics

52 Phillips, Medicine, p.28 ff;
   Jüthner, Leibesübungen,
   p.109 ff; Popplow,
   Leibesübungen, p.132 ff
53 Plato, Republic, 376E—403C
54 Aristotle, Politics, VIII,
   1338b—1339a
55 Ibid., VIII, 1337b
56 Jaeger, Paideia, I, p.379,
   392 f
57 Jüthner, Leibesübungen,
   p.195
58 Pausanias, 8, XXXIX, 3;

Rudolph, Kampfsport, p.13

59 Jüthner, Turngeräte, p.65 f
60 Rudolph, Kampfsport, p.63 ff
61 Bengtson, Spiele, p.80 ff
62 Ziehen, Olympia, col.150
63 Jüthner, Leibesübungen,
   p.94 ff

The Greek Tradition

64 Walbank, World, p.72 f
65 Ibid., p.208 ff
66 Grimal, Hellenismus, p.184 ff
67 Oehler, Gymnasium,
   col.2004—2026; Walbank,
   World, p.60 ff
68 Popplow, Leibesübungen,
   p.147 f
69 Oehler, Gymnasium
70 Grimal, Hellenismus, p.251;
   Walbank, World, p.64, 117 f
71 Oehler, Gymnasium,
   col.2005 f
72 Grimal, Hellenismus, p.251 f
73 Ibid., p.252
74 Oehler, Gymnasium,
   col.2005; Grimal, Hellenismus, p.216 ff; Walbank,
   World, p.117 f
75 Grimal, Hellenismus, p.285 ff
76 Bible, II, 4, 7; Grimal, Hellenismus, p.256; Kranz,
   Probleme
77 Harris, Jews, p.54—69, 93 f
78 Klee, Geschichte, p.20—42;
   Harris, Athletes, p.226
79 Walbank, World, p.71 f
80 Pleket, Soziologie, p.70 ff;
   Finley — Pleket, Games,
   p.77 ff
81 Bengtson, Spiele, p.83 ff
82 Pleket, Soziologie, p.73; Finley — Pleket, Games, p.79 f
83 Herrmann, Olympia, p.182

THE ROMAN EMPIRE

Etruscan Games

1 Scullard, Cities, p.21—57;
   Pallottino, Etruscans
2 Herodotus, I, 94
3 Heurgon, Daily Life,
   p.186—205

4 Ducati, Storia, II; Haufmann,
   Plastik; Lerici, Nuove tes-
   timonianze; Mansuelli, Et-
   ruria; Camporeale, Vet-
   ulonia; Bianchi Bandinelli
   — Torelli, Etruria; Sprenger
   — Bartoloni, Etrusker;
   Christofani, L'arte; Poulsen,
   Tomb Paintings;
   Schmidtchen — Howell,
   Leibesübungen
5 Bronson, Chariot, p.104 f;
   Snodgrass, Arms, p.162
6 Heurgon, Life, p.210 f;
   Herodotus, I, 167
7 Heurgon, Life, p.212 ff
8 Gardiner, Athletics, p.120;
   Poulsen, Tomb Paintings,
   p.24 ff
9 Vitruvius, De architectura, 5,
   I, 1
10 Herodotus, I, 94, 167

Roman Festivals

11 Gabba, Rome, p.10 ff
12 Pfister, Iuventus, p.250 ff,
   270, note 36
13 Scullard, Festivals, p.165, 185
14 Delbrück, Kriegskunst, I,
   p.442—460; Vegetius, Epitoma, McIntosh, Education,
   p.52 ff
15 Backhaus, Spiele, p.240 ff,
   218
16 Balsdon, Life, p.168
17 Harris, Sport, p.53 ff
18 Bailey, Phases, p.144
19 Fowler, Festivals, p.40—65,
   208
20 Fowler, Festivals, p.17; Scullard, Festivals, p.193 f, 166
21 Fowler, Festivals, p.38 ff
22 Bailey, Phases, p.170 ff
23 Fowler, Festivals, p.40 f
24 Livy, I, 35; Rawson, Chariot-
   racing
25 Friedlaender, Sittengeschichte, p.446, 487, 516 f;
   Scullard, Festivals, p.185
26 Livy, I, 28, 21; Balsdon, Life,
   p.292 f
27 Friedlaender, Sittengeschichte, p.466

Entertainments of Imperial Rome

28 Balsdon, Life, p.152 ff; Morgan, Sports, p.120 f; Hopfner, Mysterien; Carcopino, Life
29 Friedlaender, Sittengeschichte, p.435 f
30 Cameron, Circus, p.162
31 Friedlaender, Sittengeschichte, p.461 ff
32 Vergil, Aeneid, V, 580–587
33 Friedlaender, Sittengeschichte, p.447 ff
34 Harris, Sport, p.213 f; Friedlaender, Sittengeschichte, p.455
35 Ammianus Marcellinus, XXVIII, IV, 28
36 Cameron, Circus, p.13 ff
37 Friedlaender, Sittengeschichte, p.468 f; Liebenam, Geschichte, p.121–3
38 Balsdon, Life, p.293 ff
39 Friedlaender, Sittengeschichte, p.487 ff; Balsdon, Life, p.293 f; Toynbee, Animals; Pearson, Arena; Raven, Rome; Grant, Gladiators
40 Lintott, Violence, p.6, 22–34, 41–51; Auguet, Games, p.198
41 Friedlaender, Sittengeschichte, p.516 ff, 446 ff
42 Herrmann, Olympia, p.183 ff
43 Friedlaender, Sittengeschichte, p.543 f; Finley – Pleket, Games, p.80 f
44 RE, IV, col.2831–34; Wegner, Ballspiel
45 Galen, De sanitate tuenda, 41; Galen, De parva pila, 2–3
46 Jüthner, Philostratos
47 Langenfeld, Quellen
48 Bonner, Education; Väterlein, Roma, p.23 f
49 Quintilianus, Institutio, 9, 4, 56; McIntosh, Education, p.43
50 Friedlaender, Sittengeschichte, p.553 ff, Pfister, Iuventus, p.254 ff

EPILOGUE

1 Friedlaender, Sittengeschichte, p.507 ff; Robert, Gladiateurs
2 Harris, Jews, p.66 ff
3 Herrmann, Olympia, p.196 ff
4 Cameron, Circus, p.208 ff; Boutros, Sport
5 Cameron, Circus, p.217 ff
6 Ibid., p.214 ff, 230 ff
7 Harris, Jews; Harris, Sport, p.229 f; MacCormack, Art, Pl.30–33, p.122–127
8 Cameron, Circus, p.308

Bibliography

Akurgal E., *Die Kunst der Hethiten*, Munich 1961

Ammianus Marcellinus, *Res gestae*

Anderson J. A., *Ancient Greek Horsemanship*, Berkeley – Los Angeles 1961

Andronikos M., *Totenkult*, in: Archaeologica Homerica, Vol. III, W. Göttingen 1968

The Archaic Period. History of the Hellenic World, Athens – London 1975

Aristotle, *Politics* (Trans. by H. Rackham, The Loeb Classical Library), London 1959

Assyrian Dictionary of the Oriental Institute of the University of Cologne, 1956

Auguet R., *Cruelty and Civilization: The Roman Games*, London 1972

Backhaus W., *Öffentliche Spiele, Sport und Gesellschaft in der römischen Antike*, in: Ueberhorst, Geschichte der Leibesübungen, 2, Berlin – Munich – Frankfurt-am-Main 1978, p. 200–249

Badawy A., *Min, the Cosmic Fertility God of Egypt*, in: Mitteilungen des Instituts für Orientforschung, 1959

Bailey C., *Phases in the Religion of Ancient Rome*, London 1932

Balsdon J. P. V. D., *Life and Leisure in Ancient Rome*, London 1969

Bandi H. G. – Maringer J., *Kunst der Eiszeit. Levantenkunst. Arktische Kunst*, Basel 1955

Bengtson H., *Die Olympischen Spiele in der Antike*, Zurich – Stuttgart 1972

Bernatzik H. A., *Die neue grosse Völkerkunde*, Vienna 1962

Bianchi Bandinelli R. – Torelli M., *Etruria – Roma*, Torino, 1976

Bible I, II

Biliński B., *Agoni ginnici. Componenti artistiche ed intellettuali nell' antica agonistica greca*, Warsaw 1979

Biliński B., *L'agonistica sportiva nella Grecia antica. Aspetti sociali e ispirazioni letterarie*, Rome 1959

Blümel C., *Der Diskosträger Polyktets*, Berlin – Leipzig 1930

Blümel C., *Sport und Spiel bei den Griechen und Römern*, Berlin 1934

Boardman J., *The Greeks Overseas*, Harmondsworth 1973

Bogeng G. A. E., *Geschichte des Sports aller Völker und Zeiten*, I, II, Leipzig 1926

Bonner S. F., *Education in Ancient Rome. From the elder Cato to the younger Pliny*, Cambridge 1977

Bonnet H., *Reallexikon der ägyptischen Religionsgeschichte*, Berlin 1952

Bossert H. Th., *Altanatolien*, Berlin 1942

Bossert H. Th., *Altsyrien*, Tübingen 1951

Boutros L., *Phoenician Sport. Its Influence on the Origin of the Olympic Games*, Amsterdam 1981

Breasted J. H., *A History of Egypt from the Earliest Times to the Persian Conquest*, London 1925

Bronson R.C., *Chariot Racing in Etruria*, in: Studi in onore di Luisa Banti, Rome 1964, p. 89–106

Brunner H., *Altägyptische Erziehung*, Wiesbaden 1957

Brunner H. – Traut E., *Der Tanz im alten Aegypten*, Glückstadt – Hamburg – New York 1938

Buchholz H. G. – Karageorghis V., *Altägäis und Altkypros*, Tübingen 1971

Buck A. de, *The Egyptian Coffin Texts*, I–VII, Chicago 1935–1961

Buhmann H., *Der Sieg in Olympia und in den anderen panhellenischen Spielen* (Diss.), Munich 1975

Burkert W., *Griechische Religion*, Stuttgart 1977

Burkert W., *Homo Necans. Interpretation altgriechischer Opferriten und Mythen*, Berlin – New York 1972

Busolt G. – Swoboda H., *Griechische Staatskunde*, II, Leipzig 1926

Caillois R., *Man, Play and Games*, New York 1961

Cambridge Ancient History, I, 1, *Prolegomena and Prehistory*, Cambridge 1970, I, 2, *Early History of the Middle East*, Cambridge 1971

Cameron A., *Circus Factions: Blues and Greens at Rome and Byzantium*, Oxford 1976

Camporeale G., *I commerci di Vetulonia in età orientalizzante*, Firenze 1969

Carcopino J., *Daily Life in Ancient Rome*, London 1941

Cassiodorus, *Variae*

Chadwick J., *The Mycenaean World*, Cambridge 1966

Charbonneaux J. – Martin R. – Villard F., *Archaic Greek Art 620–480 B.C.*, London 1971

Charbonneaux J. – Martin R. – Villard F.,

Classical Greek Art 480—330 B.C., London 1972

Cristofani M., *L'arte degli Etruschi: Produzione e consumo*, Torino 1978

Culin S., *Games of the North American Indians*, Washington 1907

Damm H., *Die gymnastischen Spiele der Indonesier und Südseevölker*, Leipzig 1922

Dashler W. W., *Native Cattle Keeping in Eastern Africa*, in: Man, Culture and Animals. The Role of Animals in Human Ecological Adjustments, Washington 1965, p. 153—168

Davies N. M. — Gardiner A., *Ancient Egyptian Paintings*, Vol. I-III, Chicago 1936

Decker W., *Annotierte Bibliographie zum Sport im alten Ägypten*, Cologne 1978

Decker W., *Bibliographie zum Sport im alten Ägypten für die Jahre 1978 und 1979 nebst Nachträgen aus früheren Jahren*, in: Stadion V, 2, 1979, p. 11—192

Decker W., *Quellentexte zu Sport und Körperkultur im alten Ägypten*, Cologne 1975

Decker W., *Die physische Leistung Pharaos*, Cologne 1971

Delbrück H., *Geschichte der Kriegskunst im Rahmen der politischen Geschichte*, I, Berlin 1900

Delorme J., *Gymnasion. Etude sur les monuments consacrés à l'éducation en Grèce, des origines à l'Empire romain*, Paris 1960

Deubner L., *Attische Feste*, Berlin 1966

Deubner L., *Kult und Spiel im alten Olympia*, Berlin 1936

Diehl E., *Anthologia lyrica Graeca*, Leipzig 1961

Diem C., *Weltgeschichte des Sports*, I, Stuttgart 1967

Diogenes Laertios, *History of the Philosophers*

Drees L., *Olympia. Götter, Künstler und Athleten*, Stuttgart 1967

Drees L., *Der Ursprung der Olympischen Spiele*, Stuttgart 1962

Drioton E. — Vardier J., *L'Egypte*, Paris 1962

Ducati P., *Storia dell'arte Etrusca*, Vol. II, Florence 1927

Ebeling E., *Bruchstücke einer mittelassyrischen Vorschriftensammlung für die Akklimatisierung und Trainierung von Wagenpferden*, Berlin 1951

Ebeling E., *Geschichte des alten Morgenlandes*, I, II, Berlin 1929, 1939

Ehelolf H., *Wettlauf und szenisches Spiel im hethitischen Ritual*, in: Sitzungsberichte der preussischen Akademie der Wissenschaften, XXI, Berlin 1925, p. 267—272

Eliade M., *Rites and Symbols of Initiation. The Mysteries of Birth and Rebirth*, New York 1965

Erman A., *Ägypten und ägyptisches Leben im Altertum*, I, II, Tübingen 1885

Erman A., *Die Welt am Nil*, Leipzig 1936

Evans A. J., *The Palace of Minos at Knossos*, I—IV, London 1921—1936

Falkenstein A. — Soden W., *Sumerische und akkadische Hymnen und Gebete*, Zurich — Stuttgart 1953

Faure P., *La vie quotidienne en Crète au temps de Minos (1500 avant Jesus Christ)*, Paris 1973

Finley M. J., *Early Greece: The Bronze and Archaic Ages*, London 1970

Finley M. J. — Pleket H. W., *The Olympic Games: The First Thousand Years*, London 1976

Forbes C. A., *Physical Education in Greece*, New York — London 1929

Forrest W. G., *The Emergence of Greek Democracy, the Character of Greek Politics 800—400 B. C.*, London 1978

Fowler W. W., *The Roman Festivals of the Period of the Republic*, [1]1899, New York [2]1969

Frazer J. G., *The Golden Bough, A Study in Magic and Religion*, Vol. I—XII, London 1925—1930

Friedlaender L., *Sittengeschichte Roms*, Vienna 1934

Friedlaender L. — Wissowa G., *Darstellungen aus der Sittengeschichte Roms*, I—IV, Leipzig 1919—1921

Frobenius L., *Kulturgeschichte Afrikas*, Cologne 1954

Frobenius L., *Menschenjagden und Zweikämpfe. Weltgeschichte des Krieges* I, Hanover 1903

Gabba E., *Republican Rome, the Army and the Allies*, Oxford 1976

Galen, *De parva pila*

Galen, *De sanitate tuenda*

Garbini G., *The Ancient World*, London 1966

Gardiner E. N., *Athletics of the Ancient World*, Oxford 1930

Gardiner E. N., *Greek Athletic Sports and Festivals*, London 1910

Gaster Th. H., *Canaanite Ritual Drama*, New York 1946

Gaster Th. H., *Thespis. Ritual, Myth and Drama in the Ancient Near East*, New York 1961

Goetze A., *Kleinasien*, Munich 1957

Grant M., *Gladiators*, London 1967

Greenhalgh P. A. L., *Early Greek Warfare. Horsemen and Chariots in the Homeric and Archaic Ages*, Cambridge 1973

Grimal P., *Der Hellenismus und der Aufstieg Roms*, in: Fischer Weltgeschichte, Vol. 6, Frankfurt-am-Main 1965

Groos K., *Spiele der Menschen*, Jena 1899

Groos K., *Spiele der Tiere*, Jena 1896

Hančar F., *Das Pferd in prähistorischer und frühhistorischer Zeit*, Vienna — Munich 1956

Harper P. O. *The Royal Hunter. Art of the Sasanian Empire*, Leyden 1978

Harris H. A., *Greek Athletes and Athletics*, London 1964

Harris H. A., *Greek Athletics and the Jews*, Cardiff 1976

Harris H. A., *Sport in Greece and Rome*, London 1972

Haufmann G.M., *Etruskische Plastik*, Stuttgart 1956

Haupt P., *The Cuneiform Terms for Sport*, in: Beiträge zur Assyriologie und semitischen Sprachwissenschaft, Leipzig 1927, Vol. 10, Book 2, p. 127—132

Hayes W. C., *The Scepter of Egypt. A Background for the Study of the Egyptian Antiquities in the Metropolitan Museum of Art*, Part II. *The Hyksos Period and the New Kingdom (1675—1080 B.C.)*, Harvard 1959

Herodotus, *History* (Trans. by A. D. Godley, The Loeb Classical Library), London 1975

Hermann F. — Blümner H., *Lehrbuch der griechischen Privatalterthümer*, Tübingen 1882

Herrmann H. V., *Olympia, Heiligtum und Wettkampfstätte*, Munich 1972

Heubeck A., *Die homerische Frage. Ein Bericht über die Forschung der letzten Jahrzehnte*, Darmstadt 1974

Heurgon J., *Daily Life of the Etruscans*, London 1964

Higgins R., *Minoan and Mycenaean Art*, London 1967

History of the Hellenic World. Prehistory and Protohistory, Athens 1974. *The Archaic Period*, Athens — London 1975

The History of the Revolution and Diffusion of Sports and Games in Different Cultures. Proceedings of the 4th International HISPA Seminar, Leuven, Belgium, April 1—5, 1975, Brussels 1976

Hofstätter P. R., *Gruppendynamik. Die Kritik der Massenpsychologie*, Hamburg 1957

Hood S., *The Minoans*, London 1971

Homer, *Iliad* (Trans. by A.T. Murray, The Loeb Classical Library), London 1971

Homer, *Odyssey* (Trans. by A.T. Murray, The Loeb Classical Library), London 1974

Hopfner Th., *Die griechisch-orientalischen Mysterien*, Leipzig 1924

Hrozný B., *Hethitische Keilschrifttexte aus Boghazköy*, Leipzig 1919

Hyde W. W., *Olympic Victor Monuments and Greek Athletic Art*, Washington 1921

Huizinga J., *Homo ludens*, Hamburg 1958

Jaeger W., *Paideia. Die Formung des griechischen Menschen*, Berlin — Leipzig 1934

Janssen R., *Spiele in Mikronesien*, Bonn 1971

Jensen A. E., *Beschneidung und Reifezeremonien bei Naturvölkern*, in: Studien zur Kulturkunde, Vol. I, Stuttgart 1932

Jensen A. E., *Myth and Cult among Primitive People*, Chicago — London 1963

Jensen A. E., *Wettkampf — Parteien. Zweiklassen — System und geographische Orientierung*, in: Studium Generale,

Vol. I, Heidelberg 1947

Jüthner J., *Die antiken Turngeräthe,* Vienna 1896

Jüthner J., *Die athletischen Leibesübungen der Griechen,* Vienna 1965

Jüthner J., *Philostratos über Gymnastik,* Leipzig 1909

Kammenhuber A., *Hippologia Hethitica,* Wiesbaden 1961

Kees H., *Ägypten. Kulturgeschichte des Alten Orients,* Munich 1933

Kees H., *Der Götterglaube im alten Ägypten,* Berlin 1956

Kees H., *Opfertanz des ägyptischen Königs,* Leipzig 1912

Keller O., *Die antike Tierwelt,* Leipzig 1909

Kerényi K., *Vom Wesen des Festes,* in: Paideuma. Mitteilungen zur Kulturkunde, I, 2, 1938

Kirk G. S., *War and the Warrior in the Homeric Poems,* in: Vernant J. P. (ed.), Problèmes de la guerre en Grèce ancienne, Paris 1968

Klee Th., *Zur Geschichte der gymnischen Agone in griechischen Festen,* Berlin 1918

Knauth W. – Nadgmabadi S., *Das altiranische Fürstenideal. Von Xenophon bis Ferdousi. Nach den antiken und einheimischen Quellen dargestellt,* Wiesbaden 1975

Kornexl E., *Begriff und Einschätzung der Gesundheit des Körpers in der griechischen Literatur von ihren Anfängen bis zum Hellenismus,* Innsbruck – Munich 1970

Kraay C. M. – Hirmer M., *Greek Coins,* London 1966

Kramer K., *Studien zur griechischen Agonistik nach den Epinikien Pindars* (Diss. Inaugural), Cologne 1970

Kramer S. N., *From the Tablets of Sumer,* Indian Hills, Colorado 1956

Kramer S. N., *Lamentation over the Destruction of Ur,* in: Assyriological Studies, 12, Chicago 1940

Kramer S. N., *Mythologies of the Ancient World,* New York 1961

Kramer S. N., *The Sumerians; their History, Culture and Character,* Chicago 1963

Kranz M., *Probleme der Leiblichkeit im biblischen Judentum,* Cologne 1965

Krause J. H., *Die Gymnastik und Agonistik der Hellenen aus den Schrift- und Bildwerken des Alterthums,* 1, 2, Leipzig 1841

Krause J. H., *Olympia oder Darstellung der grossen Olympischen Spiele,* Vienna 1838

Krause J. H., *Die Pythien, Nemeen und Isthmien,* Leipzig 1841

Lange K. – Hirmer M., *Egypt. Architecture, Sculpture, Painting,* London 1956

Langenfeld H., *Quellen zur Sportgeschichte, I Antike,* Münster 1980

Lejeune M., *La civilisation mycénienne et la guerre,* in: Vernant J. P. (ed.), Problèmes de la guerre en Grèce ancienne, Paris 1968, p. 31–51

Lerici C.M., *Nuove testimonianze dell'arte e della civiltà Etrusca,* Milan 1960

Lesky A., *A History of Greek Literature,* London 1966

Lesky A., *Homeros,* Stuttgart 1967

Lesky A., *Ein ritueller Scheinkampf bei den Hethiten,* in: Archiv für Religionswissenschaft, Vol. 24, Berlin 1926, p. 73–82

Levi M. A., *Il senso della storia greca,* Milan 1979

Levick B., *The cenatus consultum from Larium,* in: The Journal of Roman Studies, LXXIII, 1983, p. 97–115

Levy G. R., *The Gate of Horn. A Study of the Religious Conceptions of the Stone Age and their Influence upon European Thought,* London 1948

Lexa F., *Veřejný život ve starověkém Egyptě* (Public Life in Ancient Egypt), I,II, Prague 1955, 1956

Lexová I., *Ancient Egyptian Dances,* Prague 1935

Liebenam W., *Zur Geschichte und Organisation des römischen Vereinswesens,* Leipzig 1890, Aalen 1964

Lintott A. W., *Violence in Republican Rome,* Oxford 1968

Livy, *History*

Lobel L. – Page D., *Poetarum Lesbiorum fragmenta,* Oxford 1955

Lorenz K., *Das sogenannte Böse. Zur Naturgeschichte der Agression,* Vienna 1963

Lorenz K., *Über tierisches und menschliches Verhalten. Aus dem Werdegang der Verhaltenslehre,* I,II, Munich 1965

Lorimer H. L., *Homer and the Monuments,* London 1950

MacCormack S. G., *Art and Ceremony in Late Antiquity,* Berkeley – Los Angeles – London 1981

Maier F. G., *Die Verwandlung der Mittelmeerwelt,* in: Fischer Welgeschichte, Vol. 9, Frankfurt-am-Main 1968

Mallwitz A., *Olympia und seine Bauten,* Munich 1972

Mansuelli G. A., *Etruria and Early Rome,* London 1966

Marinatos S. N., *Some Words about the Legend of Atlantis,* Athens 1969

Marinatos S., *Thera,* I–V, Athens 1967–1972

Marinatos S. – Hirmer M., *Crete and Mycenae,* London 1960

Marinatos S. – Hirmer M., *Kreta, Thera und das mykenische Hellas,* Munich 1976

Maróti E., *Bibliographie zum antiken Sport und Agonistik,* in: Acta Universitatis de Attila József nominatae. Acta Antiqua et Archaeologica 22, Szeged 1980

Matthiae P., *Ebla: an Empire Rediscovered,* London 1980

Matz F., *Kreta, Mykene, Troja. Die minoische und homerische Welt,* Stuttgart 1957

McIntosh P. C., *Physical Education in Rome,* in: McIntosh P. C. – Dixon J.G. – Munrow A.D. – Willetts R.F., Landmarks in the History of Physical Education, London 1981, p. 37–62

Medner S., *Das Ballspiel im Leben der Völker,* Münster 1956

Mehl E., *Antike Schwimmkunst,* Munich 1927

Mellaart J., *Çatal Hüyük. A Neolithic Town in Anatolia,* London 1967

Meuli K., *Der griechische Agon. Kampf und Kampfspiel in Totenbrauch, Totentanz, Totenklage und Totenlob,* Cologne 1968

Meuli K., *Griechische Opferbräuche,* in: Phyllobolia für Peter von der Mühl, Basel 1945

Mezö F., *Geschichte der Olympischen Spiele,* Munich 1930

Miller S.G., *Arete. Ancient Writers, Papyri and Inscriptions on the History and Ideals of Greek Athletics and Games,* Chicago 1979

Moortgat A., *Die bildende Kunst des alten Orients und die Bergvölker,* Berlin 1932

Moortgat A., *Bildwerk und Volkstum Vorderasiens zur Hethiterzeit,* Leipzig 1931

Moortgat A., *Die Kunst des Alten Mesopotamien. Die Klassische Kunst Vorderasiens,* Cologne 1967

Morgan M. G., *Three non-Roman Blood Sports,* in: Classical Quarterly, 1975, p. 117–122

Moscati S., *Le antiche civiltà semitiche,* Milan 1961

Murray O., *Early Greece,* Glasgow 1980

Naveh J., *Some Semitic Epigraphical Considerations on the Antiquity of the Greek Alphabet,* in: American Journal of Archaeology, 77, 1973

Nilsson M. P., *Griechische Feste von religiöser Bedeutung mit Ausschluss der attischen,* Leipzig 1906

Nilsson M. P., *A History of Greek Religion,* Oxford 1925

Nilsson M. P., *The Minoan – Mycenaean Religion and its Survival in Greek Religion,* Lund – London – Oxford – Paris – Leipzig 1927

Oberhuber K., *Die Kultur des alten Orients,* Frankfurt-am-Main 1972

Oehler J., *Gymnasion,* in: Pauly-Wissowa Realencyklopädie, VII, 2, 1912, col. 2004–26

Oliva P., *The Birth of Greek Civilization,* London 1981

Oliva P., *Solón,* Prague 1971

Oliva P., *Sparta and her Social Problems,* Prague, Amsterdam, 1971

Oliva P. – Olivová V., *Spartakus,* Prague 1960

Olivová V., *Chariot Racing in the Ancient World,* in: History of Physical Education and Sport, 1985 (in print)

Olivová V., *Games and Sports Elements in Ancient Mesopotamia,* in: History of Physical Education and Sport, 2, Tokyo 1974, p. 47–70

Olivová V., *Kalokagathia − The Greek Ideal of the Harmonious Personality,* in: Canadian Journal of History of Sport, Vol. XIV, 2, 1983, p. 1−15

Olivová V., *Lidé a hry. Historická geneze sportu* (Men and Games. The Historical Genesis of Sport), Prague 1979

Olivová V., *Sobre el orígen de los juegos taurinos,* in: Iberoamericana Pragensia, XI, Prague 1977, p. 149−169

Otto E., *Beiträge zur Geschichte der Stierkulte in Ägypten,* Leipzig 1938

Otto E. − Hirmer M., *Egyptian Art and the Cult of Osiris and Amon,* London 1968

Pallottino M., *The Etruscans,* London 1975

Pape W., *Griechisch-deutsches Handwörterbuch,* Brunswick 1906

Parrot A., *Assur,* London 1961

Parrot A., *Sumer,* London 1960

Pausanias, *Desceription of Greece* (Trans. by W. S. Jones and H. A. Ormerod, The Loeb Classical Library), London 1926

Pearson J., *Arena. The Story of the Colosseum,* New York − St. Louis − San Francisco − Toronto 1973

Pfister G., *Die römische iuventus,* in: Ueberhorst, Geschichte, 2, p. 250−279

Phillips E. D., *Greek Medicine,* London 1973

Plato, *Laws*

Plato, *Republic*

Pleket H.W., *Zur Soziologie des antiken Sports,* in: Mededelingen van het Nederlands Instituut te Rome, XXXVI, Rome 1974, p.57−87

Plutarch, *Aristides* (Trans. by B. Perrin, The Loeb Classical Library), London 1968

Plutarch, *Lycurgus* (Trans. by B. Perrin, The Loeb Classical Library), London 1967

Poliakoff M., *Studies in the Terminology of the Greek Combat Sports,* in: Beiträge zur klassischen Philologie, 146, Königstein / Ts. 1982

Pope A., *Die Gymnastik bei Homer und ihre grundlegende Bedeutung für die Gestaltung der späteren Gymnastic* (Diss. Inaugural), Universität Rostock, Rostock 1936

Popplow U., *Leibesübungen und Leibeserziehung in der griechischen Antike,* Stuttgart 1967

Potratz J. A., *Das Pferd in der Frühzeit,* Leipzig 1938

Poulsen F., *Etruscan Tomb Paintings,* Oxford 1922

Prehistory and Protohistory. History of the Hellenic World, Athens 1974

Quintilianus, *Institutio oratoria*

Raven S., *Rome in Africa,* London 1969

Rawson E., *Chariot-racing in the Roman Republic,* in: Papers of the British School at Rome, Vol. XLIX, 1981, p.1−16

Reallexikon der Assyrologie, E. Ebeling − B. Meissner (ed.), Berlin − Leipzig 1932−1938

Ridington W. R., *The Minoan-Mycenaean Background of Greek Athletics* (Diss.), Philadelphia 1935

Riemschneider M., *Die Welt der Hethiter,* Stuttgart 1955

Ringwood I.C., *Agonistic Features of Local Greek Festivals. Chiefly from Inscriptional Evidence* (Diss. Inaugural), Columbia Univ., Poughkeepsie 1927

Robert L., *Les Gladiateurs dans l'Orient Grec,* Amsterdam 1971

Robinson R.S., *Sources for the History of Greek Athletics,* Cincinnati ²1955

Roller L. E., *Funeral Games* (Thesis), Pennsylvania 1977

Rudolph W., *Olympischer Kampfsport in der Antike, Faustkampf, Ringkampf und Pankration in den griechischen Nationalfestspielen,* Berlin 1965

Ruschenbusch E., *Solonos nomoi,* in: Historia, Einzelschriften, 9, Wiesbaden 1966

Salonen A., *Hippologica accadica,* Helsinki 1955

Salonen E., *Die Waffen der alten Mesopotamier. Eine lexikalische und kulturgeschichtliche Untersuchung,* Helsingfors 1965

Salvianus, *De gubernatione Dei*

Schachermeyr F., *Ägäis und Orient,* in: Österreichische Akademie der Wissenschaften phil-hist., Klassische Denkschriften 93, Vienna 1967

Schachermeyr F., *Griechische Geschichte. Mit besonderer Berücksichtigung der geistesgeschichtlichen und kulturmorphologischen Zusammenhängen,* Stuttgart 1960

Schachermeyr F., *Die minoische Kultur des alten Kreta,* Stuttgart 1964

Schachermeyr F., *Perikles,* Stuttgart 1969

Schäfer H., *Die Mysterien des Osiris in Abydos unter König Sesostris III,* Leipzig 1904

Scharff A., − Moortgat A., *Ägypten und Vorderasien im Altertum,* Munich 1950

Schmidtchen V. − Howell M., *Leibesübungen bei den Etruskern,* in: Ueberhorst, Geschichte der Leibesübungen, 2, p. 168−199

Schmökel H., *Geschichte des alten Vorderasien,* Leiden 1957

Schmökel H., *Kulturgeschichte des alten Orient,* Stuttgart 1961

Schmökel H., *Das Land Sumer,* Stuttgart 1956

Schmökel H., *Ur, Assur und Babylon. Drei Jahrtausende in Zweistromland,* Stuttgart 1955

Schneider G., *Kulturgeschichte des Hellenismus,* 1, 2, Munich 1969

Schöbel H., *The Ancient Olympic Games,* London 1966

Schoemann G. F. − Lipsius J.H., *Griechische Alterthümer,* I, II, Berlin 1902

Schott S., *Das schöne Fest vom Wüstentale. Festbräuche einer Totenstadt,* Wiesbaden 1952

Schweitzer B., *Die geometrische Kunst Griechenlands,* Cologne 1969

Scullard H. H., *The Etruscan Cities and Rome,* London 1967

Scullard H. H., *Festivals and Ceremonies of the Roman Republic,* London 1981

Segert S., *Altaramäische Schrift und Anfänge des griechischen Alphabets,* in: Klio 1963, Vol. 41, p.38−57

Sethe K., *Das Denkmal memphitischer Theologie der Schabakostein des Britischen Museums,* in: Sethe K., Dramatische Texte zu altaegyptischen Mysterienspielen, I, Leipzig 1928

Sethe K., *Der dramatische Rameseumpapyrus. Ein Spiel zur Thronbesteigung des Königs,* in: Sethe K., Dramatische Texte zu altaegyptischen Mysterienspielen, II, Leipzig 1928

Sethe K., *Urgeschichte und älteste Religion der Ägypter,* Leipzig 1930

Smith W. S., *The Art and Architecture of Ancient Egypt,* London 1958

Snodgrass A., *Arms and Armour of the Greeks,* Ithaca − New York 1976

Snodgrass A., *Early Greek Armour and Weapons from the End of the Bronze Age to 600 B. C.,* Edinburgh 1964

Sprenger M. − Bartolini G., *Die Etrusker: Kunst und Geschichte,* Munich 1977

Staehelin E., *Zur Bedeutung der Jagd im alten Ägypten,* in: Decker W., Annotierte Bibliographie zum Sport im alten Ägypten, Cologne 1978, p.23−35

Ste. Croix De G. E. M., *The Origins of the Peloponnesian War,* London 1972

Strömberg R., *Die Bellerophontes − Erzählung in der Ilias,* in: Classica et Mediaevalia, XXI, 1960, p. 1−15

Strommenger E., *Der Garten in Eden. 7 Jahrtausende Kunst und Kultur in Euphrat und Tigris,* Munich 1978

Strommenger E. − Hirmer M., *Fünf Jahrtausende Mesopotamiens,* Munich 1962

Tertullian, *De spectaculis*

Thuillier J. P., *Les sports dans la civilisation Etrusque,* in: Stadion VII, 2,. 173−202

Thucydides, *History*

Touny A. D. − Wenig S., *Der Sport im alten Ägypten,* Leipzig 1969

Toynbee J. M., *Animals in Roman Life and Art,* London 1973

Tutto su Roma antica, Florence 1963

Ueberhorst H., *Geschichte der Leibesübungen,* I, II, Berlin − Munich − Frankfurt-am-Main 1972, 1978

Ulf Ch., *Sport bei den Naturvölkern,* in: I. Weiler, Der Sport bei den Völkern der alten Welt, Darmstadt 1981, p.14−52

Väterlein J., *Roma ludens. Kinder und Erwachsene beim Spiel in antiken Rom,* Amsterdam 1976

Vegetius, *Epitoma rei militaris*

Vergil, *Aeneid* (Trans. by H. R. Fairclough, The Loeb Classical Library), London 1974

Vermeule E. T., *Götterkult,* Göttingen 1974

Vitruvius, *De architectura libri decem*

Walbank F. W., *The Hellenistic World,* Brighton 1981

Weege F., *Der Tanz in der Antike,* Halle/S. 1926

Wegner E., *Das Ballspiel der Römer,* Würzburg 1938

Weigall A., *Ancient Egyptian Works of Art,* London 1925

Weiler I., *Der Sport bei den Völkern der alten Welt. Eine Einführung. Mit dem Beitrag: Sport bei den Naturvölkern von Ch. Ulf,* Darmstadt 1981

West M. L., *Early Greek Philosophy and the Orient,* Oxford 1971

Wiemann H., *Die Phylogenese des menschlichen Verhaltens im Hinblick auf die Entwicklung sportlicher Betätigung,* in: Ueberhorst, Geschichte, I, p. 48−61

Wiesner J., *Fahren und Reiten,* in: Archaeologia Homerica, Vol. I, F. Göttingen 1968

Willetts R. F., *Ancient Crete. A Social History,* London − Toronto 1965

Willetts R. F., *Everyday Life in Ancient Crete,* London 1969

Willetts R. F., *Social Aspects of Greek Physical Education,* in: McIntosh P. C. − Dixon J. G. − Munrow A. D. − Willetts R. F., Landmarks in the History of Physical Education, London 1981, p.6−36

Willimczik K., *Leibesübungen bei Homer,* Stuttgart 1969

Wilsdorf H., *Ringkampf im Alten Ägypten,* Würzburg 1939

Wolf W., *Die Welt der Ägypter,* Stuttgart 1954

Wood R. − Wheeler M., *Roman Africa in Colour,* London 1966

Xenophon, *Cyropaedia*

Žába Z., *Les Maximes de Ptahhotep,* Prague 1956

Ziehen L., *Olympia,* in: Pauly-Wissowa Realenzyklopädie der klassischen Altertumswissenschaft, XVII, 2, 1937; XVIII, 1, 1939

Zimmerli W., *Das Menschenbild des Alten Orients,* Munich 1949

Zimmern H., *Zum babylonischen Neujahrsfest,* I,II, in: Berichte über die Verhandlungen der königlichen sächsischen Gesellschaft der Wissenschaften zu Leipzig. Philologisch-historische Klasse, Vol. 58, 1906, p.126− 156; Vol. 70, 5, 1918

Zimmern H., *Das babylonische Neujahrsfest,* in: Der Alte Orient. Gemeinverständliche Darstellungen herausgegeben von der Vorderasiatisch-ägyptischen Gesellschaft, Vol. 25, Leipzig 1926

Zschietzschmann W., *Wettkampf − Übungsstätte im Griechenland,* I, Stadion, II, Palästra − Gymnasion, Stuttgart 1961

Index

Numbers in italics refer to illustrations

207

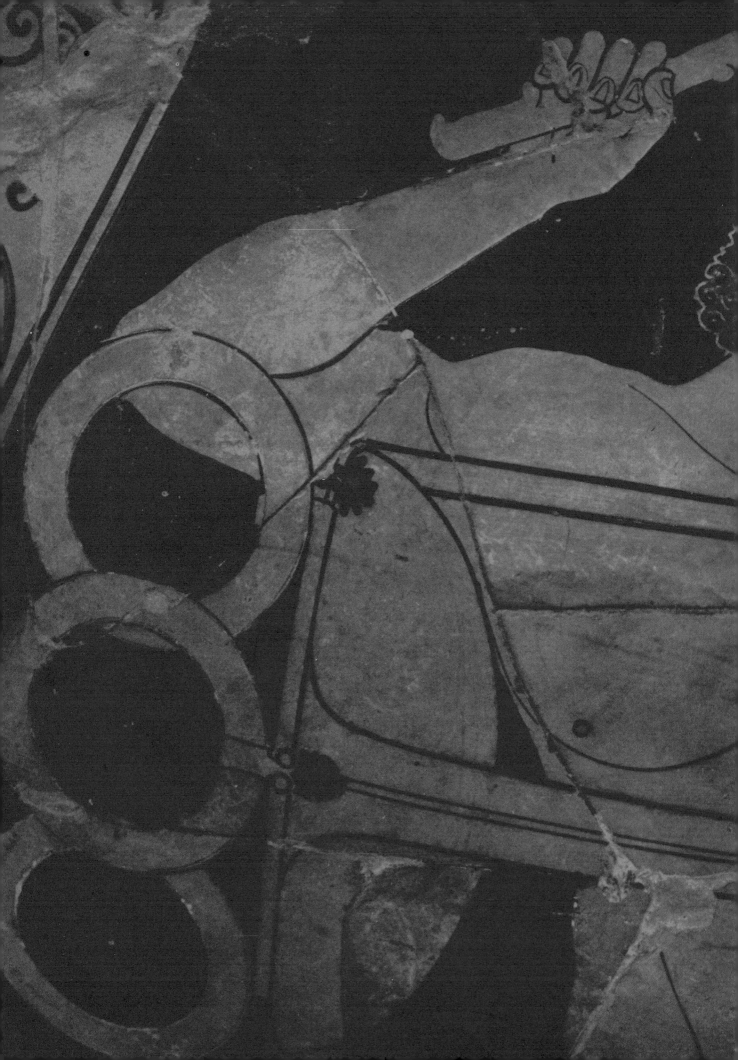